ALL THE LIVES
WE EVER LIVED

ALL THE LIVES
WE EVER LIVED

Seeking Solace in Virginia Woolf

KATHARINE SMYTH

Atlantic Books
London

This edition published by arrangement with Crown, an imprint of the Crown Publishing Group, a division of Penguin Random House LLC, New York.

First published in hardback in Great Britain in 2019 by Atlantic Books, an imprint of Atlantic Books Ltd.

1 2 3 4 5 6 7 8 9

A CIP catalogue record for this book is available from the British Library.

Image of *To the Lighthouse*, holograph notes: Henry W. and Albert A. Berg Collection of English and American Literature, The New York Public Library, Astor, Lenox, and Tilden Foundations. Pages 305–8 constitute an extension of the copyright page.

Hardback: 978-1-78649-285-2
E-book: 978-1-78649-287-6
Paperback: 978-1-78649-286-9

Printed and bound in Great Britain by TJ International Ltd, Padstow, Cornwall

Atlantic Books
An Imprint of Atlantic Books Ltd
Ormond House
26–27 Boswell Street
London
WC1N 3JZ

www.atlantic-books.co.uk

For my mother

"It was strange how clearly she saw her, stepping with her usual quickness across fields among whose folds, purplish and soft, among whose flowers, hyacinths or lilies, she vanished."

—VIRGINIA WOOLF, *To the Lighthouse*

ALL THE LIVES
WE EVER LIVED

Perhaps there is one book for every life.

One book with the power to reflect and illuminate that life; one book that will forever inform how we navigate the little strip of time we are given, while also helping us to clarify and catch hold of its most vital moments. For me, that book is *To the Lighthouse*, Virginia Woolf's novel about her parents, Julia and Leslie Stephen, who died when Virginia was thirteen and twenty-two, respectively. First published in 1927, it tells the story of the Ramsays, a family of ten who, along with an assorted group of friends, spends the summer on a remote island in the Hebrides. Tells the story of the Ramsays? I should rephrase: *To the Lighthouse* tells the story of *everything*.

I first read it as a junior in college, a literature student studying abroad at Oxford University. It was Christmas 2001, and my parents and I were visiting my father's family on the south coast of England. After dinner, I joined my father and Robert, his older brother, in the sitting room. My father was listening to Handel and reading, and I was listening to my uncle talk about books. An eccentric, shuffling bachelor, he asked about Oxford and told idealized stories of his own time there; he scoffed at the novels I had been assigned and wrote me a syllabus of his own. As he left the room to find me a copy of his magnum opus, a history of one of England's ancient woodlands, my father looked up from his sailing magazine and smiled. "He's sweet," he said.

"He makes me nervous," I said. "I think he thinks I'm an idiot."

"No," my father said. "He thinks you're twenty."

Robert returned. I expressed admiration for *Forest People and Places* and then we each settled down into our respective worlds—mine, the sitting room in which Mrs. Ramsay joins her husband late at night, a room much like the one in which our minds now roamed, and feels herself swinging from branch to branch, flower to flower, climbing, climbing, as she murmurs the words of poetry her husband had recited at dinner. My father and uncle drank brandy; my father smoked cigarettes and my uncle cigars. The logs on the fireplace cracked and blackened. Earlier my father had latched the wooden shutters and drawn the heavy velvet drapes; now, in the softened space he had created, the music seemed to strengthen and the stillness of the night to grow. So too on that far-flung Scottish island, where Mr. Ramsay sets down his book and looks up at his wife, who, still climbing, nevertheless begins to sense the pressure of his mind.

Did I already suspect the revelatory role these words would play for me? I don't think so: *To the Lighthouse* is a work that rewards—that demands—reading and rereading; it was not until at least my second time through it that I had the impression of actually swimming round beneath its surface. But already, as I curled up with that book by the fire, it was beginning to reciprocate and even alter my experience, while also giving me a vocabulary by which to fathom that experience, so that I would always understand that Christmas night, a night on which I relished my father's vices rather than cursing them, as a version of that final sitting room scene, and its tacit, book-tinged intimacy a version of Mrs. Ramsay's final triumph.

A FEW WEEKS later, my parents called me from Boston. After eight years of failed cancer treatments, they said, my father's oncologists had decided to remove his bladder altogether. My father assured me he was pleased. He hadn't been feeling well for some time, he said, and I remembered that over the holidays I had occasionally turned to see him grimacing. There was one more thing, my mother said. The surgery would mean that he could no longer drink. No longer drink! How marvelous that would be, and yet, how impossible to imagine.

At the time of the twelve-hour operation, I was visiting Amsterdam with a group of college friends. My mother called almost hourly with updates. Dim sum, a trip to the Van Gogh museum, and a walk through the red-light district were all interrupted with medical reports: "Well, they've removed the bladder completely, and they're about to build a new one from the intestine." We were watching an impeccably choreographed and oddly sterile orgy scene at a midnight live sex show when my mother called one last time to say that the surgery was over and couldn't have gone better. For weeks I had been having nightmares, but with this news I immediately lost a bit of interest. Of course it had been a success, I thought.

It was this same winter that Virginia Woolf, escaping the prim ranks of Women Writers to which my high school teachers had consigned her, became instead the nexus of my reading life. My tutor, Shane, was a sharp, wry Beckett scholar who had taught me James Joyce earlier in the year; his comprehension of British modernism was so effortless and unsentimental that my own hard work and enthusiasm embarrassed us both. Miffed by Woolf's snarky dismissal of Joyce—a "queasy undergraduate scratching his pimples," she famously called him—Shane never missed an opportunity to ridicule her snobbishness and eccentricity. On the day we were to discuss *Orlando*, he brought in a particularly unflattering photograph of Vita Sackville-West, her friend and paramour. "How anyone could write a love letter to *that* is beyond me," he chortled. I enjoyed his irreverence; certainly I needed reminding that one mustn't take literature so seriously all the time. But as I read my way through every one of Woolf's novels, my own admiration for her only intensified. It wasn't long before I began to answer Shane's questions with uncharacteristic certainty, and though I couldn't always locate the corresponding textual evidence, I never failed—as I had constantly during our Joyce tutorial—to produce the exact response for which he had been angling. He soon grew frustrated by this instinctive, unscholarly version of literary criticism, but when he told me, not at all complimentarily, that I seemed to have "an intuitive sense of Woolf," I was overjoyed.

One week after my father's operation—I was for-aging for *Mrs. Dalloway* criticism in the depths of the Bodleian Library, a pleasure that, as Woolf acerbically recalls in *A Room of One's Own*, had been denied her as a woman some seventy years earlier—my mother called again. My father was fine, she said, but he had reacted badly when they tried to switch him from a feeding tube to solid food. When she called the following day, it was to say that he was actually suffering from delirium tremens, or alcohol withdrawal. The previous evening, he had started to complain of a terrible smell, then to frantically wave away the hundreds of tiny gnats he saw swarming the hospital room. (Neither my mother nor the doctors smelled or saw anything unusual.) Within hours he had become incoherent, hostile, and violent. He shouted at doctors, nurses, and my mother; he tried to tear out his many tubes; he had several near-fatal seizures; and he was moved to intensive care and re-strained. My mother related all this only after the worst was over.

I wanted to go home. The next available flight to Boston left in two days' time, and I spent those days trying to ignore the morbid scenarios being staged in my mind. On the plane, I grew increasingly frightened, convincing myself that he had died during the flight, and that my mother would greet me at the airport with the news. But she didn't. She drove me to the hospital instead. Due to a bed shortage, my father had been placed in the ICU burn ward, where the other patients were contained in giant temperature- and moisture-controlled clear plastic bubbles. Asleep when we walked in, he was lying in what seemed, from its multiple fold-ing parts, like a very uncomfortable bed. His body was shrunken and corpse-like, but for his right arm, which was badly swollen where the doctors had pinched a nerve during the operation. Tubes ran in and out of his veins, and his face was yellow. His lips were two contiguous pieces of flaking skin. My mother introduced me to his nurse, a friendly, talkative woman who said, "Don't worry, he won't remember any of this."

"I'll remember all of this" came a pitiful and totally unfamiliar voice from the bed. I went to him, uneasily patted his head, and said hello. Sedated and only half-awake, he could barely open his eyes, and when he did, he gave me a clouded, heavy-lidded, tortoise look. He asked us to help him sit up; we failed at sliding his body farther up the bed, and he began to swear viciously under his breath. It was only then I noticed the thick leather bands that restrained all four of his limbs. He was very weak, but whenever he wanted to move he would bang his arms as hard as he could, up and down against the bonds. In a few days, both wrists would bruise deep violet. Finally the flailing exhausted him, and he slumped over to one side. We continued to sit there, talking to his cheerful nurse, and I watched him as he slept. He shook violently, and coughed and wheezed with each breath.

We visited every morning and evening. Sometimes he slept for our entire visit, and sometimes he was talkative, but—paranoid, hallucinatory, malevolent—he was almost never himself. Unsure of his whereabouts, he initially thought himself in my mother's native Australia, then in Madras—a city to which he had no connection—and finally at our summerhouse in Rhode Island. One particularly persistent hallucination was his belief, which he explained again and again, that he was lying next to an Arab. He would look to his left, as though someone were there, and repeatedly apologize: "Look, I'm terribly sorry, but I can't move over any further . . ." Occasionally he was kind. He would smile at me; the nurses said he often looked for me when I was not there. But his most consistent preoccupation was wanting to leave. He kept asking me in a whisper to get a "short, sharp knife" and cut his restraints. When I said no, he grew furious. "Dad, I can't," I said. "Rubbish," he said. "Of course you can." Even in his stupor, he could upbraid me for being too bound by convention.

It was eight days before he was finally deemed well enough to move to a regular hospital room. He was free of cancer for the first time in a decade—a diagnosis of kidney cancer and the removal of his right kidney had plagued him before the bladder—and he did not recall any of the days he'd spent in the ICU. Now, no longer angry, he was desperately sad. He cried often, from embarrassment, and when he learned he still could not go home. Mostly, though, he cried because he'd never drink again—if he did, his doctor said, he'd drink himself to death. Still, his surgeon assured me he would live to see my children. It was a hope I had never thought to have.

On the morning of the day I returned to England, my mother and I drove him straight from the hospital to an inpatient drug and alcohol rehabilitation facility called Faulkner. The rooms of the clinic were cold and spare, and the halls slick, the color of old chewing gum. Patients loitered by the exit. I could not connect them to my father, to what I knew of his sophistication; how uncivilized, how demeaning, to admit him to such a lonely, ugly place. While he attended an AA meeting, my mother and I went to a support group for families. I took a dislike to the woman who ran it, and to her platitudes about a higher power, and saw at once that these kinds of mantras were something my father would never embrace.

We met in his room to say good-bye. I threw my arms around him and sobbed into his shirt. "Hey," he said. "Hey. Don't worry—I'll be fine here." Distressing as it was to leave him, I was gratified that he was acting like a father again. And as it turned out, he enjoyed his weeklong stay at Faulkner (the longest his insurance would allow). He loathed the mandatory meetings each morning and evening, but he was a big hit with the other patients, who loved his English accent and thought him hilarious. He in turn was moved and horrified by their stories. "God, people have tough lives," he told me later. "Their problems make mine look like a piece of cake."

Less than ten days after my father left rehab, he had a glass of wine. He confessed it with shame to my mother and poured the rest of the bottle down the sink. Within six months, he was back to drinking the equivalent of three bottles daily.

MY PARENTS RETURNED to England three months after the operation. I was surprised by how well my father looked—apparently his uncanny ability to appear fit and healthy had endured. I was also surprised by his mood, which, unlike the curt, distracted voice to which I'd grown accustomed on the phone, was gentle and subdued. But he was thin, and he walked with a hunch. His right hand was temporarily paralyzed where the nerve had been pinched during surgery. He was in extreme and constant pain. My parents picked me up in Oxford, and we embarked on a short, Virginia Woolf–inspired road trip that finished at my grandmother's house. At every stop, my father wandered away from the car and lit a cigarette. We went first to Knole, the historic family estate of Vita Sackville-West that was the model for Orlando's own ancestral residence, and next to Charleston, the country home of Duncan Grant and Vanessa Bell, Virginia's older sister. We visited Berwick Church, where Grant and Bell had painted every inch of wall as they had their home, and finally Monk's House, Leonard and Virginia's own country home in nearby Rodmell. I do not much remember the interior, except that it was dark and shabby, with spindly, inhospitable chairs, well-worn upholstery, paintings dull with time.

It is the garden I recall, with its path of weathered stone weaving through flower beds and opening onto a larger lawn. There was a shaded pool in front, slithering with silver fish, and, in back, a bare and sunlit room where she wrote—including, in less than a fortnight, the first twenty-two pages of *To the Lighthouse*. ("Never never have I written so easily, imagined so profusely," she wrote in her diary of its creation, and later, in a letter to Vita, "close on 40,000 words in 2 months—my record.") The present caretakers had placed on her desk an empty teacup and a few scattered pages of her diary, and I imagined her setting off, only a moment before, across the yellow pastures that lay beyond the garden gate. Her ashes had once been buried beneath an elm, but the tree had subsequently died, and in its place— off to one side and ensconced in purple columbine— was a bronze bust in her likeness, with an epitaph taken from *The Waves*: "Against you I will fling myself, unvanquished and unyielding, O Death!" It was a warm, brilliant day—a *good* day—but coupled with my recollection of those places is the image of my father, his body bent as though he were walking into the wind, lighting a cigarette and drifting away from the houses toward the deep green of the woods or fields in the distance.

PART ONE

1

"The house was all lit up, and the lights after the darkness made his eyes feel full, and he said to himself, childishly, as he walked up the drive, Lights, lights, lights, and repeated in a dazed way, Lights, lights, lights, as they came into the house."

When I was five, my parents bought a summerhouse. For years we had spent our weekends sailing, driving between our home in Boston and the Rhode Island marina where we kept the boat, and for years my parents had admired the row of waterfront cottages they could see from the highway bridge. One weekend, leaving me with friends, they stopped at a local real estate agency. "The houses on the water almost never come up," the agent said, not quite truthfully, "but one came on the market this morning." She took them to see it, a wooden house built in 1890 and in a state of price-deflating disrepair. Sheets of plastic were stapled across its windows; to one side was a garage, to the other a desiccated lawn and concrete steps leading to the water. The small adjoining lot was full of rubble, all that remained of a shack annihilated by a hurricane fifty years before. A night nurse was the house's current occupant, and my parents had to wait until midnight before they were shown inside. They found rooms cramped and badly lit. Dampness seeped from the basement's earth floor.

A bare wooden deck faced the water, but it, too, was wrapped in thick plastic. We'll take it, my parents said, and in the morning signed the papers.

Both architects, they spent the coming months drawing up plans. They tore down walls and put up new ones; winterized the basement and made it their bedroom. A new deck ousted the living room, and the old deck became the dining room. The garage was transformed into a studio, the empty lot to the south a garden, and every wall that faced the water became a wall of windows. We devoted our weekends that winter to supervising the renovation. A beastly wind leapt off the basin, slipping through cracks and ripping at the plastic sheets that now stood in for windows altogether. The house then was a skeleton; from the water, it looked like an architectural cross section. We wore winter coats indoors. I spent my time collecting the sawdust that drifted like snow into the corners of rooms—I liked how light and downy and dry it was—and when, come spring, the house was finally finished, I mixed this sawdust with glue, molded it in the shape of a heart, and baked it in the oven.

That summer my parents planted an olive tree, a dogwood, a Japanese maple, and star magnolias. They put in rose bushes, honeysuckle, and a porcelain vine to soften the deck. They hoped a wisteria plant would gently envelop the trellis over the sunken yard; instead the vine grew freakishly, its weighty boughs promising to fell the structure altogether. My father vowed each summer to rip the wisteria out at its roots, and each summer my mother protested, citing the two glorious May weeks in which it shot forth its cloud of amethyst flowers. There were rolls of sod that steamed in the sunlight—my father carried them from the car, set them down on the soil, and gave them a push, unfurling each one like a long green carpet. For a few weeks they showed at the seams, but then the roots plaited together, and I could no longer tell where one piece stopped and the next began. Something similar happened inside, where the rooms at first were neat and spare: one day I looked around me and realized our expanding lives had filled the gaps. We learned quickly how bleached things become in a house on the water, how exhaustively salt and light leach color, leaving behind pale blues and yellows. The spines of books, the cork-tiled floors, the rugs and prints and bed linens—each became a cheerfully bloodless version of itself. Before my parents were finished they built a dock and then they put down a mooring of their own. There is a photograph of the three of us posing beside this hunk of chain and metal; it was the last time we would see it before sending it down to the bottom of the sea, to settle in the mud and provide a stay against the tides to come.

The next summer—I must have been about seven—my father and I built a doll's house. It was a pretty Victorian home with two bay windows, a wraparound verandah, and scalloped trim along the eaves, and it demanded many months of work; I can still recall the care with which we affixed each individual baluster and shingle, the tackiness of the glue we used to wallpaper the rooms. We painted the woodwork in colors reminiscent of our Boston home: dark green, slate blue, taupe, and russet red. In another photograph from that time, the half-finished doll's house sits at the end of the dining table; through curtainless windows, you can see the lights on the far shore double in the water's surface. My father is consumed by the application of some fixture or other, and I, wearing a flannel, rose-print nightgown, hair matted, am standing on a chair and supervising. I loved playing with that house when it was finally finished; and yet the greatest pleasure of all was in its construction, in the evenings that my father and I passed together in nearly wordless concentration.

The divide between week and weekend was extreme then, and when I considered the difference, I thought of something he had told me when we were sailing, as our boat, *Mistral*, was heeling and the wind filling our throats. In Boston our lungs were black and horrible, he said, but in Rhode Island they were lovely and shiny and pink. It was an image I held on to as I went about my days—days that I filled with pointed yet purpose-less tasks (paddling to nearby sand dunes; watering the rock wall moss), much as a cat will suddenly decide that *now* is the moment she must leap from the window and dash to the couch.

The specter of boredom gave rise to ingenuity, I think, which is how I came to clomp down the beach in my roller skates, and make the acquaintance of a horse-shaped boulder I named Star, and build a nest beneath the billiard table, and run barefoot up and down the street; by mid-July, I could stick sewing needles deep into my heels without sensation. I loved beachcombing best, though—every day I spent hours wandering the rocky strand at the foot of the seawall, collecting sea glass, broken bits of blue-and-white china, lady's slip-pers, conch shells, the forsaken skeletons of horseshoe crabs, and, once, a rusty key chain from the Stone Bridge Inn, a hotel a mile down the road that had shuttered twenty-five years earlier. When I'd gathered enough shells, my father took me to the hardware store to buy a diamond drill bit—the only tool strong enough, he said, to bore into the lady's slippers and make a necklace for my mother. It was years before I noticed the peculiar quality of light the days here possessed, how on afternoons and evenings the house would flood with lemon heat, or how the reflection of the water outside, at once blue and gold and glittering, would throw itself against the ceiling, transforming the rooms into a string of tide pools. But from the very beginning, I felt that light within my lungs.

"IF LIFE HAS a base that it stands upon," Virginia Woolf wrote in "A Sketch of the Past," her longest and most abundant memoir, "if it is a bowl that one fills and fills and fills—then my bowl without a doubt stands upon this memory. It is of lying half asleep, half awake, in bed in the nursery at St Ives. It is of hearing the waves breaking, one, two, one, two, and sending a splash of water over the beach; and then breaking, one, two, one, two, behind a yellow blind. . . . It is of lying and hearing this splash and seeing this light, and feeling, it is almost impossible that I should be here; of feeling the purest ecstasy I can conceive." This brilliant, sea-filled nursery belonged to Talland House, the nineteenth-century home in Cornwall where Virginia, her parents, and her seven siblings spent every summer until she was thirteen. She called this recollection "the most important of all my memories," and, much like the schism between my own childhood weeks and weekends, its radiance was in sharp contrast to her impressions of her family's London home, a dim, narrow six-story townhouse in

Kensington where "busts shrined in crimson velvet, enriched the gloom of a room naturally dark and thickly shaded," and where, in the words of her sister Vanessa, "faces loomed out of the surrounding shade like Rembrandt portraits."

Talland House—its light, its cresting water—would be consecrated in Virginia's imagination, saturating not only *To the Lighthouse* but also *Jacob's Room* and *The Waves*. "To go sailing in a fishing boat," she waxed in her late fifties, "to scrabble over the rocks and see the red and yellow anemones flourishing their antennae; or stuck like blobs of jelly to the rock; to find a small fish flapping in a pool; to pick up cowries; to look over the grammar in the dining room and see the lights changing on the bay. . . . All together made the summer at St Ives the best beginning to life conceivable." The tumbling passage conveys the lasting vigor of these memories; as Hermione Lee notes in her terrific biography of Woolf, Talland House "is where she sites, for the whole of her life, the idea of happiness. . . . Happiness is always measured for her against the memory of being a child in that house."

When Virginia's mother died of rheumatic fever in 1895, the Stephens' visits to Talland House abruptly ceased. "Father instantly decided that he wished never to see St Ives again," she recalled. "And perhaps a month later Gerald [Duckworth, Virginia's half brother] went down alone; settled the sale of our lease to some people called Millie Dow, and St Ives vanished for ever." Some thirty years later, this sudden, devastating break—the actual and figurative end to Virginia's childhood—would spark the plot of *To the Lighthouse*, in which she transposed Cornwall's Talland House, seemingly in its entirety, to the Hebrides, a cluster of islands off the coast of Scotland to which she had never been. ("An old creature writes to say that all my fauna and flora of the Hebrides is totally inaccurate," she wrote to Vita, and to Vanessa: "there are no rooks, elms, or dahlias in the Hebrides; my sparrows are wrong; so are my carnations.") This house and its story are, quite literally, at the novel's center, as vital to it as the Ramsays and their friends; which is why, during a trip to England to celebrate my grandmother's ninety-ninth birthday, I made a St Ives pilgrimage: I wanted to see what the Cornish landscape might teach me, not just about *To the Lighthouse* and its author but also about those homes by which we measure happiness.

It was a clear afternoon in June when I boarded the train in my grandmother's village; sipping wine, passing through Tiverton—the namesake of our Rhode Island town—I was feeling as dreamy as Virginia about the coming journey. "This time tomorrow," she wrote in 1921, "we shall be stepping onto the platform at Penzance, sniffing the air, looking for our trap, & then— Good God!—driving off across the moors to Zennor— Why am I so incredibly & incurably romantic about Cornwall?" My train pulled in at half past eight, but the sun was still high above the houses, and I thought I could see through the gaps in the buildings the white stripe of Godrevy Lighthouse. Then, suddenly, I turned a bend and St Ives Bay unveiled itself, the same view, more or less, that causes Mrs. Ramsay to stop short, exclaiming aloud at its beauty. "For the great plateful of blue water was before her," we first hear of the novel's beacon, "the hoary Lighthouse, distant, austere, in the midst; and on the right, as far as the eye could see, fading and falling, in soft low pleats, the green sand dunes with the wild flowing grasses on them." I had read those words a hundred times, and the image they had always conjured was of a seascape much nearer and brighter than this one; for here the lighthouse stood no taller than a matchstick upon its little pile of black rock, and I had to squint to see the thin green lines of land.

But I liked this readjustment of my vision; in fact it was an enlargement, the gentle pop of a jigsaw puzzle fitting together; and then again when I took a wrong turn after dinner and the cobblestone path curved round and up to reveal a vast sandy beach, with regular waves coiling and crashing in rows of four. The last bit of light shone through between the clouds, and the water beat against the sand—I would hear it all night through my bedroom window—and I knew then what Virginia meant when she wrote, addressing Cornwall's pull for her, of "old waves that have been breaking precisely so these thousand years," and when she wrote, in her original notes for *To the Lighthouse*, that "the sea is to be heard all through it." As much as anywhere I've ever been, the sea is the lifeblood of St Ives.

The following morning, I made my way to Talland House. I didn't have a house number, so I relied on Woolf to help me find it. "A square house," she said, "like a child's drawing of a house; remarkable only for its flat roof, and the crisscrossed railing." When, at the end of a cul-de-sac, it finally materialized, I felt a stab of disappointment. Its ivory walls were streaked with rust, and a tangle of exterior metal staircases, providing access to second- and third-floor flats, crept up the rear. A Ford Focus was parked in the driveway. I was still debating my approach when a beefy young man in blue sweatpants walked out with a Rottweiler—the epitome of a Virginia Woolf fan, in other words. "Yeah?" he asked, suspicious.

"I'm just looking at the house," I said. "You know Virginia Woolf lived here?"

"Yeah?"

"Is it okay if I look around?"

"Yeah," he said again, gesturing toward a snarl of vegetation. "There's a lawn round back if you like."

I thanked him, wondering how many seekers had appeared at his door, then plunged into the upper garden. I knew the grounds were greatly changed; much of the land had been sold off, and a parking lot replaced the orchard. But I could still see what Leslie Stephen had meant by "a garden of an acre or two all up and down hill, with quaint little terraces divided by hedges of escallonia." A stepping-stone path led off to the left and I followed it down into a clearing with a tiny pond, hidden from the house above. My heart beat faster with the thrill of trespassing, and perhaps because this was itself a childhood feeling, I had a strong sense of how much *fun* it would have been to be a child in this garden, with its climbing trees and secret hollows; I thought of Cam, the Ramsays' youngest daughter, picking flowers and tearing villain-like across the bank.

Then, throwing off the cloak of greenery, stepping onto the main lawn, I finally met the Talland House I knew from pictures. The ivy had been stripped from its façade, and its railing replaced by an addition, but I recognized the two sets of French doors that opened onto steps leading down to the grass—there's a photograph of Henry James perched here, reading—and, above them, the wrought iron verandahs that feature in one

of Virginia's earliest memories: her mother emerging
"onto her balcony in a white dressing gown" as passion
flowers spilled from the walls. All morning the scraps of
text had been surfacing, all morning they had blended
and echoed; the landscape had been pulling phrases
out from deep within my mind, and my head was all
a jumble, so that it was Mrs. Ramsay standing on the
balcony in a white dressing grown, and Leslie Stephen
striding back and forth along the terrace, and even my
own mother, stopping, growing grayer-eyed, and saying as she looked across the basin, This is the view my
husband loves. And meanwhile I had grown bolder and
was peering through the French doors into the drawing
room where over a century before the Stephens had sat
reading while ten-year-old Virginia looked on, chin in
hand, her gaze startlingly curious; and that was when
I heard the gardener, crossing the lawn with a stack of
severed branches in his arms.

I apologized, explaining that I was interested in
Woolf and her house, adding that I'd come all the way
from America. He was in his early forties, friendly,
weathered, with strawberry blond hair. "I could show
you some pictures if you're interested," he said.

"Oh, yes!" I said, and he raised his bundle of branches:
"Let me just put these down and I'll get them for you."

I looked through windows in his absence. One revealed a generous foyer, another a bedroom with a collection of dead-eyed, antique teddy bears. The door to
the upstairs apartments was open, and I climbed the
narrow stairs toward the attics, which in *To the Lighthouse* "the sun poured into," drawing from "the long
frilled strips of seaweed pinned to the wall a smell
of salt and weeds, which was in the towels too, gritty

with sand from bathing." I had always loved that image—it reminded me of the light and sea smells of Rhode Island—and in fact all descriptions of the Ramsays' home suggest a space as bleached and weathered as a rowboat, a space that even at the book's beginning maintains only the flimsiest barrier between the family and the elements. Doors and windows are flung open; the rose-patterned wallpaper is faded and flapping. Ruined by wet, the "crazy ghosts of chairs" drag their entrails all over the floor. This encroachment by nature prefigures "Time Passes," the novel's middle section in which the chaos that Mrs. Ramsay has up until then succeeded at keeping at bay begins to penetrate the home. But the attics on the day of my visit were dark and dry, with clean blue carpets and bolted doors that precluded further exploration; and even the rooms facing the bay seemed unusually hermetic, as if they hailed from an altogether different book.

The gardener came back covered in blood. "I cut myself looking for the pictures," he said apologetically, holding up three large black-and-white photographs, or rather, photocopies of photographs, encased in rickety frames, ribboned with cobwebs, and now, slightly smeared with red. He assured me he was all right and turned the frames around to reveal their written descriptions. "Family by front door c. 1892," read one, and another, "Adrian, Thoby, Vanessa, Virginia with dog." I was struck by Virginia's fidgety hands, the girls' heavy skirts, the obvious intimacy between sisters; Virginia leans complacently against Vanessa, who looks as if she'd take a knife to anyone who crossed her strange and visionary younger sister. "You're welcome to them," he said, "if you can get them back to America." Looking closer, I saw that spiders had attached their egg sacs to the glass, but I accepted the photos gratefully and held out my hand to say good-bye. The gardener hesitated: "I'm a bit bloody, I'm afraid." We shook with his left instead.

Before leaving, I paused at the bottom of the lawn and looked one last time at the house. Time passes, I thought, yes, but what does that *mean?* To the shock and despair of all who have read *To the Lighthouse*, Mrs. Ramsay dies unexpectedly midway through the novel; with her gone, the Scottish property is abandoned, its light extinguished. Swallows nest in the drawing room, plaster falls from the rafters, and then, finally, there comes a tipping point, a moment at which the weight of one feather would result in the house's total ruin. Mrs. McNab, the housekeeper, eventually intervenes to protect against collapse, but not before Woolf can offer an alternate rendition of its fate:

> In the ruined room, picnickers would have lit their kettles; lovers sought shelter there, lying on the bare boards; and the shepherd stored his dinner on the bricks, and the tramp slept with his coat round him to ward off the cold. Then the roof would have fallen; briars and hemlocks would have blotted out path, step, and window; would have grown, unequally but lustily over the mound, until some trespasser, losing his way, could have told only by a red-hot poker among the nettles, or a scrap of china in the hemlock that here once some one had lived; there had been a house.

Woolf's pastoral vision of the future could just as easily be a vision of the past; the prickly, poisonous foliage restores the land to wilderness, while the figures she chooses to populate the scene—lovers, tramps, and shepherds—are eternal. But as I gazed up at Talland House, at its labyrinthine staircases and additions, at the nearby flats and cranes (for a rising apartment block will soon obstruct Talland's lighthouse view), I felt a twinge of nostalgia for that more elemental prophecy. The reabsorption of the Stephens' home into the earth, so that it lived on in language for trespassers like me and not as some grotesque distortion of itself, seemed infinitely preferable to this current portrait of time's passage.

I was halfway down the drive when the gardener ran toward me with a garbage bag—"To carry the pictures," he explained. We slid them in together and he handed me a folded piece of paper. "My CV," he said, "in case you ever need a gardener in the States." He admitted that after twelve years he was being let go—apparently the landlord had decided that Talland House no longer needed full-time upkeep. I thought of Mrs. Ramsay as she joins her husband on the lawn, lamenting the fifty pounds that it will cost to mend the greenhouse. Even so, she says, the gardener's beauty is so great that she couldn't possibly dismiss him.

We said good-bye again, and as I walked down the hill to the beach, it occurred to me, for the first time in all my years of reading and rereading *To the Lighthouse*, that Mrs. Ramsay's refusal to fire the gardener is in fact another iteration of her power to protect against entropy; and that, conversely, the dismissal of Andrew

Shaw—for that was the name on the CV—may well have been the first step toward Woolf's vision of a timeless, sylvan future. Perhaps the garden will grow wild after all.

TWENTY YEARS AFTER my parents bought and renovated the Rhode Island house, I found my father on the hammock, looking out over the water and smoking a cigarette. We had driven that morning from the hospital, where he had spent the past month in intensive care following complications from chemotherapy and radiation. He seemed calm, and though his face and frame were thin, he held himself easily beneath his navy-blue sweater, always able, even on that night, to command the space around him. I was sorry to have caught him smoking, but I still admonished him gently. "It might not matter," he said. "I'm still waiting to hear my prognosis."

He patted the ropy spot beside him, and I sat down. The ghost of a hurricane was passing through; the sky over the basin was soft and heavy with black fog. Ropes strummed against the metal masts of sailboats, and the lights of the faraway houses sent shocks of white across the water. The grass, neglected these few weeks, had already grown calf-high. When I commented on how pretty it was, he said, "Yes, but not too pretty."

By morning, the hurricane had scoured the sky and left in its place a beautiful fall weekend. I was sitting on the front porch beneath a rising sun, drinking tea and nestled in one of the white Adirondack chairs. Things were ending, a faint melancholy drifting. But that was true of all Septembers.

Later, the sun swung round to the west, I stood at the
end of the dock, wearing an old bathing suit and staring
down into water made bottle green by my shadow. The
house was drenched in light, the dock too, light thinner
than that of midsummer, it was like wheat, and the air
was laced with cold. ("The sun seems to give less heat,"
says Lily Briscoe, a young, unmarried painter and the
Ramsays' houseguest, of September in the Hebrides,
looking round her at the grass and flowers.) My father
was returning *Solent*, our new sailboat, to the mooring; I could see him from where I stood, a slight figure
across the water, now reaching for the mooring wand,
now disappearing down below. There had been a mix-
up with the engine, and though he was supposed to rest,
he had spent his day flushing diesel from the bilges. I
wouldn't wait for him to swim—he hadn't been swimming all summer. ("I'm hopeless, Petal.") So I dove.

I followed the sun across the water, and back again,
and then, pausing breathless at the ladder, thought how
this year the basin seemed to hold more life than usual.
I could feel the bump bump of comb jellies against me,
could see starfish heaped in messy piles on the bottom. Could see, too, schools of flashing minnows—they
steered clear of my moving body, but when I held still,
they pressed my arms and legs with their mouths. Before going inside I took the last outdoor shower of the
season. It was here, lamenting the end of summer a few
years earlier, that I had consoled myself with fancy,
with the idea that I could return to this place and this
peace for as long as I lived. Even if my parents are gone,
I thought, even if I have a family of my own, even if
the roof leaks and the weeds grow rampant, even if I
must learn how to prune the roses and pressure-wash

the deck, even then this house and its happiness will remain. This ever-shifting view, I thought, this water, this feeling: These are steadfast. These are constant.

Upstairs my mother was dooming three restless lobsters to a pot of boiling water, and my father sitting along the deck rail, listening to Haydn. One hand grasped the edge of the roof and the other held a cigarette. A glass of red wine sat on the table beside him. When I think of him on that evening, and on other evenings like it, he is wearing his sea-colored down vest, and with large eyes that are also the color of the sea, he is studying the water. "Communing with nature," he called it facetiously, but then again, I've never known anyone to sit for so many hours at a time with just a cigarette, a drink, and a view that is always different and always the same.

I like the look of a lobster dinner: white flesh, yellow butter, reddened shells collecting in a black pot. When we had finished eating, I carried the remains to the end of the dock. The night air was bracing, the water polished onyx; the silence of the basin was enormous, and the sky was sharp with stars. I overturned the pot, and the scarlet skins, their undersides a pallid white, sank. In the morning they would make a dash of color on the silty brown sea floor, but at night they simply disappeared and the surface resealed.

I didn't go back immediately. I could see the white lights of the yacht club dock, and beyond it, the shadowy bulk of the old railway bridge. The raised oval of the island to the south, and the silhouette of land across the way. I could see, too, through the bare windows of our own home, my parents moving from room to room like dolls—my father returning to the deck, my mother retiring downstairs. (Oh, the curiosity that arises, Woolf writes, when "we linger in front of a house where the lights are lit and the blinds not yet drawn, and each floor of the house shows us a different section of human life in being." Who are these people, she asks, what are they, and what are their thoughts and adventures?)

I drew a breath.

2

From the basin to the river to the bay to the sea: At
the edge of the Atlantic, we lost sight of land, so that
the world seemed naught but sky and water, and we the
center, always the center. The waves then were large
and swollen, as if the ocean were a giant eiderdown
someone was plumping—our friends Frank and Carol
became seasick, and my mother fell about the galley as
she cooked. My father stood astride the tiller, squinting
at the bluish void, and I whispered kind things to my
pet caterpillars, foraged that morning from the garden,
lest they too were ailing and unhappy. But then the sea
began to settle, the sun to set, and—this was my first
overnight passage—we were still alone on the ocean as
I fell asleep in my bow cabin, lulled by the slip-slop of
lesser waves against the hull and the bravery of my father, who had taken the night watch.

It was still dark when I heard him whispering my
name. He put his finger to his lips and beckoned me
to follow; he was animated, but I could see on his face
that he would not yet tell me why. I tiptoed through the

cabin after him. The sea and sky were flat and leaden, though there was a spray of light on the horizon; I was chilly in my nightgown, and he wrapped me in foul weather gear that came almost to my knees. I demanded answers. He bid me to be patient. Then, suddenly, he pointed east toward the light: "There!" I turned to see a sleek, inky thing slide through the water; it disappeared and then rose the unmistakable V of a tail—a whale! She was a massive, noble creature, so close that we could see the scars and notches on her hide; every so often she exhaled magnificently, sending up a watery plume. There were others, too, farther away, their bodies solid and glistening as they threaded the water's surface like yarn on a loom. My father squeezed my hand. "Aren't they fantastic," he breathed. For at least fifteen minutes, the herd followed us north; beneath us lay the others in their bunks, so distant that they may as well have lain on the ocean floor.

I once asked my grandmother if she was closer to her mother or her father growing up. "You know how sometimes in childhood one has these sorts of daydreams," she said, "asking oneself, If I had to choose between my parents, which one would I choose?" I nodded. "Well, I never could make a decision, so I suppose that I was fond of them both equally." I nodded again. I could see how such a thing was possible. But not for me: I was the daughter of a god.

3

"That was the source of her everlasting attraction for
him, perhaps; she was a person to whom one could say
what came into one's head."

"Yes, of course, if it's fine to-morrow," says Mrs. Ramsay
to James, her six-year-old son, in the opening lines of
To the Lighthouse. "But you'll have to be up with the
lark." Her promise—a voyage to the lighthouse!—fills
the boy with overwhelming happiness; his world grows
radiant and colorful, and even the refrigerator he is cutting from the pages of an Army and Navy catalogue
takes on a glow. We might think of this as the Mrs.
Ramsay filter—the special scrim with which she over-
lays experience, so that in her presence all is rimmed
with gold as if it were the magic hour. But when Mr.
Ramsay pauses at the drawing-room window to tri-
umphantly announce that it will rain, the child's joy
curdles into fury: "Had there been an axe handy, or a
poker, any weapon that would have gashed a hole in his
father's breast and killed him, there and then, James
would have seized it." Mr. Ramsay's interruption is in-
tolerable to his son, as is the satisfaction he takes in dis-
abusing his wife and child of their illusions. Compared

to his father, James thinks, his mother is "ten thousand times better in every way."

Virginia felt a similar reverence for her own mother, the presence of whom "obsessed" her until she sought to describe Julia and her effect in *To the Lighthouse* some thirty years after her death. When she imagines her, it is always as being at the heart of life—Julia was "the whole thing," she was "in the very centre of that great Cathedral space which was childhood." (She was also diffuse, wafting through the family places: "Talland House was full of her; Hyde Park Gate was full of her.") But her mother's centrality made her hard to see. Virginia's first memory was "of red and purple flowers on a black ground—my mother's dress; and she was sitting either in a train or in an omnibus, and I was on her lap. I therefore saw the flowers she was wearing very close." It's a fitting metaphor for her mother's outsized presence: the figure of Julia Stephen, extending nearly to the edge of Virginia's peripheral vision, becomes her world's defining landscape. Yet the memory also anticipates the difficulty that she will later face in seeking to describe a parent who filled so much of her domain. "I suspect the word 'central,'" she writes, "gets closest to the general feeling I had of living so completely in her atmosphere that one never got far enough away from her to see her as a person."

Such moments of intimacy between mother and daughter seem to have been scarce—that may be why the memory embedded itself so deeply. Virginia's recollections of Julia are usually of her in company, of her conducting whatever muddled, vibrant orchestra it was that held the room. In the rare instances her mother is unburdened, able to turn her attention to her youngest daughter, whispering to her to remove a crumb from her father's beard or laughing at one of her stories, the daughter flushes with pleasure.

AS AN ONLY child, I read *To the Lighthouse* with a sense of envy—what I would give, I thought, for the hustle and bustle of the Ramsay household, for the gift of Mrs. Ramsay's matriarchy and the happy chaos of having seven siblings. I thought of my parents' wide, elegant townhouse in Boston, of its sparse rooms and drifting dust motes, of its dusky silence like that of an empty church. I remember being struck by its stillness as early as seven or eight, when family friends had blown in from England like a wind and then departed, leaving nothing. For all my father's extroversion, my parents were private people. And I was private too, entertaining myself with books and paints and garden pets (caterpillars, yes, but also salamanders, baby birds, and ladybugs), forming alliances with rhododendron bushes and nicely shaped stones, making of that house a wonderland, and yet feeling—as perhaps we all do; I'm not sure—an intermittent nostalgia for a different kind of life, one in which my parents threw Christmas parties and I had to shout to be heard.

But there was always play. In England, my father and I gathered fallen conker chestnuts, attached them to pieces of string, and staged battles in my grandmother's garden. At other times he morphed into a plodding monster: "Fee-fi-fo-fum, I smell the blood of an Englishman!" he intoned as I ran shrieking through the halls. Later he told me always to be on the lookout for good Y-shaped branches, and when I finally found one, he cut it down, smoothed off the bark, and nailed to it a thick rubber band. I stood with him in the boiler room as he sanded, the hot, dry smell of sawdust blending with the lingering paint and epoxy. "Every girl should have her own slingshot," he said.

Despite these games, though, it had never occurred to me that my father at seven or eight was as complete a person as I was at that age—that he had vast tracts of experience, only a fraction of which had anything to do with me. I stumbled into this realization one evening when, consoling me for some unfairness that befalls the very young, he welcomed me into his own childhood, offering up its muddy creeks and makeshift forts. It was a formative moment from which I drew the least formative of lessons, for as he continued to reminisce—about cycling to the village hardware store to buy the pieces for his model airplanes; about gray kneesocks and family picnics by the river Thames—my main response was regret that this particular child, my father, would never know of my existence. What I didn't consider, and what seems even more striking now that I understand what half a lifetime of experience actually feels like, were the limitations of knowledge his past necessarily implied. The boy he was would never know me, certainly, but more to the point, I would never know him.

HERE'S WHAT I did know: My father was taut and self-contained, neither short nor tall, a dark-haired man of forty or so with hooded blue eyes, my eyes, who was remarkably at ease in his own skin. He seemed to vibrate; I see him beavering away, at what? Sanding the hull of the boat in winter, fine flecks of crimson antifouling carpeting the asphalt, or varnishing the teak of the cockpit—my *devoirs*, he called these endless tasks. His weekend clothes were spattered with paint, the kitchen sink always full of brushes. I never knew anyone to sweat so much; he mopped his brow with a white cotton handkerchief he carried in his pocket. But he always smelled clean, faintly of shaving cream, and in fact I think of him as neat and dry, and of his clothes as soft; one was always wanting to burrow into his shoulder. When my mother was driving, and he in the passenger seat and I behind him in the back, he would slip his hand around the seat for me to hold, wordlessly and for just a few minutes, until I felt a light squeeze and he pulled back his arm. I never felt safer than when he smoothed my hair when I was upset or falling asleep. His palm was firm against my head; he would repeat the same motion, over and over, and say the same thing, over and over: "There, there. There, there."

So he was physically affectionate, and capable and vigorous; what else? Very, very funny—I couldn't stop giggling when I was with him. He liked tall tales and silly games, like the threat of draconian hiccup cures or the sudden disappearance of my dessert; his was a theatrical, good-natured kind of humor, and I loved showing him off to my friends, for he made them laugh as well. He had a sense of solemnity, too; he understood, for instance, the gentleness with which one should be woken. And he could be stern; he disliked childishness. He raised his voice less often than my mother, but when he did it was more frightening.

He taught me how to build a fire, how to tie knots, how to play tennis, darts, and snooker; he found me a child-sized cue; he called the red balls "pinks." I see him crouching on the floor, his face level with the billiard table, and telling me to aim for his nose—"Just kiss it," he would say. He taught me how to sail; I remember the first time we left the basin in the Laser; the wind was strong, we hiked out over the water, and suddenly the boat shot forward, its bow lifting clear of the waves. "We're planing, Katharine!" he cried. "We're planing!" and I couldn't stop laughing because he was so happy. We built snowmen; we danced, my feet on his, to the *American Graffiti* soundtrack; we skated on a pond in the woods, the same pond into which we released my tadpoles when they sprouted little legs, and he told stories about what they were getting up to beneath the ice.

We shared the creamy layer atop the yogurt, the jelly on pâté, the wishbone when my mother pulled apart a chicken. I wished for a swimming pool; I don't know what he wished for, nor would he have told me, not just because wishes were secrets but because he was private in that way. On special occasions, he poured red wine into my water: "It's what all the little French children drink," he said.

He seemed to me impossibly wise—he knew all about the Etruscans, and how to lay a carpet, and the lyrics to *The Pirates of Penzance*. He read books on the Industrial Revolution and British canals; he read the Russians, trying to keep the characters straight upon a napkin. Fiercely liberal, adamantly irreligious, a devout consumer of the newspaper, an amenable tourist: I see him strolling about the sites my mother found (the Vimy Memorial appears, with its tunnels and its sea of graves), reading plaques with his arms folded behind his back and exclaiming, "Isn't that interesting!"

or "Isn't that sad!" And he was full of sayings and bits and pieces of poetry, puffing up his chest for delivery of Wilde or Shakespeare or Shaw. But he was not an intellectual, and I see now that there was a superficiality to his wealth of knowledge, as if it were a lake both infinitely wide and finger-deep.

I feel I could go on forever; the memories spill forth like silver mesh, linked above all by the deference he showed me and my vision, his willingness to absorb that vision and make it his own. It's a talent shared by Mrs. Ramsay, who, shortly after her husband dashes James's hopes, tries to soothe her child by finding in the Army and Navy catalogue the most complicated of shapes to extract, one that "would need the greatest skill and care in cutting out." Her response suggests an implicit understanding of James and his perspective; far from condescending, she knows that the successful removal of a rake or mowing-machine at six is just as important as penning a masterpiece at fifty.

And yet there lurks among the Ramsay children a certain anxiety about their mother, a longing for the kind of relentless care that a woman in her place could never give them. Prue Ramsay, already a young woman, vows that she will never grow up and leave her mother; James knows that her attention will waver the instant his father demands it. Jasper, in possession of her focus for the first time all evening, feels it slip away again at a clatter in the hall. Is it any wonder that these children are the creation of a writer who couldn't remember being alone with her mother for more than a few minutes without someone interrupting—a writer who, at the age of thirteen, relinquished her to the greatest interruption of all? For all my envy of the Ramsays and the fluster of their circus home, I'm grateful not just that my father was a parent in the mold of Mrs. Ramsay but also that I had him largely to myself.

Long after his mother's death, James—now sixteen—remembers following her through the house, watching from afar as she asks a servant about a certain blue platter. "She alone spoke the truth," he thinks, "to her alone could he speak it." Was my father's appeal for me as a child as simple as that—feeling seen by him, feeling understood and respected? Or was it rather a gift more ephemeral? For it's telling that what James calls "the truth" is no more than an exchange about table settings; his mother's power is such that the most banal of utterances becomes sacred, the most ordinary of paths divine. So, too, with my father, so too with all great parents, I think, who need only to exist in the world, asking a question of a shopkeeper or frowning as they turn the page, to overpower us with love.

4

"She knew from the effort, the rise in his voice to
surmount a difficult word that it was the first time he
had said 'we.'"

"How did father ask you to marry him?" Virginia Woolf
once asked her mother, their arms linked as they de-
scended the stairs to the dining room. Julia was startled:
"She gave her little laugh, half surprised, half shocked.
She did not answer." Somehow Virginia learned the
story: "He asked her in a letter; and she refused him.
Then one night when he had given up all thought of it,
and had been dining with her, and asking her advice
about a governess for Laura, she followed him to the
door and said 'I will try to be a good wife to you.'"

I recognize this tale—its simplicity and its sugges-
tiveness; the sparseness of its detail and the omissions
it contains. I have asked the same question of my own
mother, and of my father too, and I have been met, if
not by shock, by a mix of bashfulness, stubborn privacy,
and forgetfulness; so that the narrative I have pieced together of my parents' courtship also hangs upon phrases
that probably count for too much and unfolds in rooms
like stage sets, shadowy and unfinished. The story is
true and yet not true; we must fill in the blanks as best

we can. "Perhaps there was pity in her love," Virginia
ventures of her mother's motives. "Certainly there was
devout admiration for his mind."

My father, Geoffrey Smyth, was twenty-five when
he first met my mother in 1972. An architect who ran
his own firm out of the spare room of his flat on New
Cavendish Street, he had lived in the West End of London for years, ever since studying at the Architectural
Association in nearby Bedford Square. (These were Virginia's stomping grounds as well; Gordon and Fitzroy
Squares, where she lived with her siblings after their
father's death, were a few blocks away, as was Tavistock Square, her home with Leonard and the birthplace
of *To the Lighthouse*.) My father then was extroverted
and handsome, with dark hair and long sideburns; he
was energetic and lean, one of those people who is so
comfortable in his body that he seems to forget that he
has one. There was also something raw about his looks
(strangers on the street used to ask if he was Malcolm
McDowell, of *A Clockwork Orange*). He drove a cherry-
red BMW.

Several years earlier, the *Evening Standard* had
named him one of London's most eligible bachelors, but
he'd since started dating an Australian architect named
Vivien—she was talented, aloof, and very beautiful,
with big brown eyes, a wardrobe full of Marimekko,
and white-blond hair she wore in a long braid down her
back. Most evenings my father and his friends would
stop in one of the neighborhood pubs for a pint before
heading to Schmidt's for *knödel* or the Agra for a curry.
On one such night, Vivien introduced him to a couple
she had known in Sydney. My mother, Minty, was
twenty-six, another Australian architect who lived in a

nearby studio apartment. She and her boyfriend, John, who was older, had recently moved to London by way of Indonesia. My mother was skinny, with short, curly hair that she dyed red with henna. She was shy and easily impressed—a very different kind of woman from Vivien. My father bought them a round of drinks, his loud voice cutting through the crowd. "God, he's overwhelming," said John as they were walking home. "I think he's nice," my mother said.

They met him again a few months later, when they followed a big group from the pub back to his flat—he was always inviting people over, and he never wanted anyone to leave. The flat had been completely empty when he first moved in; he installed a shower and a cooker, bright yellow kitchen cabinets and a window box for red geraniums. An Egg chair hung from the living room ceiling, and the bedroom he painted dark brown. My mother remembers Vivien standing in the kitchen in a towel that night, upset because she had wanted a shower and a quiet evening in.

Months passed. My mother and John broke up, reconciled, broke up again; they had the kind of relationship in which someone was always storming out at midnight. One day she bumped into Vivien on the street; she mentioned she was looking to work for a smaller firm, and Vivien, who had left my father for another man, mentioned he was looking for a new employee. That's how my mother found herself at an Italian restaurant on my father's twenty-sixth birthday, interviewing for a position to design a new branch of the Bank of Cyprus. By the end of lunch he had offered her a job. He asked her to suggest a salary, and she named an amount. "Is that too much?" she asked. "Nothing's too much if you earn it," he said—which can only mean she asked for not nearly enough.

The following weekend he invited her to the house he shared with his mother on Hayling Island, off the south coast. It was a warm spring day and they drove with the windows down, listening to Motown; that night, they cooked a roast and slept in separate beds. Another evening he took her to a private casino in Belgravia with his most charming and dissolute friends— his hand brushed hers during a game of blackjack, and it felt to her like an electric shock. She had worked with him for just over a fortnight when he invited her on an office outing to Venice, where he'd rented an apartment overlooking the Grand Canal. She accepted, wondering all the while what he was thinking. They were leaving for Italy in less than a week when he finally kissed her at a party. "Can I come up?" he asked as they were driving home. She said no. They went to his place instead.

It rained every day in Venice, as it did for Leonard and Virginia when they stopped there on their honeymoon in 1912. (Virginia thought Venice a "detestable" place.) My parents went out to dinner and discussed Le Corbusier, trying to impress each other with their vast reserves of architectural knowledge; they never spoke like that again. My mother visited the fish market, which she had read that one must do in Venice, and she came home with a gigantic squid she didn't know how to butcher; it squirmed from her arms and crawled across the kitchen floor. They spent, I believe, a great deal of time in bed. Their last stop was Siena, its medieval streets rain-slick and deserted. The hotel proprietor offered them a room without a bathroom. "I've got to have a bathroom," my father said, and my mother felt incredibly irritated with him, a mood that lasted several weeks. (My father, for his part, thought the Venice trip a smashing holiday—that was his phrase, "a smashing holiday"—so much so that when we returned to Italy as a family some years later, he refused to visit Venice for fear of corrupting his memories.)

My mother quit her new job within the month, but their relationship continued. They took two weeks at Christmas to ski and two weeks in summer to sail; on Fridays they had a curry dinner in the West End and then, on empty roads free of speed limits, raced down through darkness to the house on Hayling Island. Weekends were spent sailing with friends; on returning to London at midnight, they stopped in Chinatown for roast duck and Singapore noodles. My mother's early irritation was soon replaced by insecurity—she couldn't stop comparing herself to Vivien, whose departure, my father's friends said, had shattered him. She worried she had won him on the rebound; she couldn't believe he really wanted her, even after they were married. But this disquiet was most often made up for by the excitement of his world, she swept up in his slipstream.

I once asked my father to describe my mother as she was during those years. Very petite, he said, and very pretty, and bright-eyed and competent and conscientious and hardworking and just fine. Above all, game for things: he pictured her thrashing around on the foredeck in thirty knots of wind in the waters of the Solent, changing headsails on a twenty-nine-footer. A woman so eagerly subsumed might have been a relief after Vivien and her resistance.

When John proposed to my mother on her return from Venice, she refused him. My father's life was more interesting, and it was already becoming her own.

TOWARD THE END of "The Window," the first section of *To the Lighthouse*, Paul Rayley, another Ramsay house-guest, fulfills Mrs. Ramsay's intentions for him by proposing to Minta Doyle on the beach. Soon afterward, Minta realizes she has lost her grandmother's brooch, and the party climbs down the cliff to look for it. Paul throws himself into the hunt, assuring Minta that he excels at finding things; when the tide rises too high, he vows to wake at sunrise to continue his search in secret. As they walk back to the house, the lights of the town appear below "like things that were going to happen to him—his marriage, his children, his house," and he thinks how he and Minta "would retreat into solitude together, and walk on and on," and "what an appalling experience he had been through," and how "it took his breath away to think what he had been and done." Indeed: "It had been far and away the worst moment of his life when he asked Minta to marry him." As for Minta, Nancy Ramsay has the feeling as she watches her weep that "it might be true that she minded losing her brooch, but she wasn't crying only for that. She was crying for something else."

When I describe my parents' early relationship, I have to fight the urge to sentimentalize, to highlight all that was sweet between them while smoothing out all that was discordant. Not because I'm invested in the narrative of some spotless union, I don't think, because they are my parents, but because one likes to believe that courtship *is* sweet—wasn't an expectation of sweetness at least in part behind Virginia's wish to know the story of her father's proposal? But *To the Lighthouse*—its marrow the tender, thorny, and ultimately triumphant marriage of the Ramsays—reveals the terrors that surround such sweetness, reminds us that to bind oneself to another human being is to take a leap of faith not just sublime but monstrous, and that anyone who does so without some sliver of terror shot through the joy is not thinking hard enough. Mrs. Ramsay shares what Leslie Stephen called his wife's "exalted views of love and marriage"; her insistence upon matrimony and children for all is so central to her character that when Lily thinks of her later, she appears "at the end of the corridor of years saying, of all incongruous things, 'Marry, marry!' " Yet even Mrs. Ramsay is aware of a tension at work in her impulse to celebrate Paul and Minta's engagement. "What could be more serious than the love of man for woman," she thinks, "what more commanding, more impressive, bearing in its bosom the seeds of death; at the same time these lovers, these people entering into illusion glittering eyed, must be danced round with mockery, decorated with garlands."

Love bears in its bosom the seeds of death—is that what Paul senses as he sees the events of his life marching before him, fixed now without further surprise? Or as he envisions walking on with Minta, their paths not only determined but forever intertwined? At dinner, Mrs. Ramsay is struck when he struggles to say "we": " 'We did this, we did that.' They'll say that all their lives, she thought." It's a moving observation, one that highlights the extent to which the very concept of marriage is dependent upon death: "Till death do us part"—that hopeful, fearsome phrase—is what gives matrimony meaning. But just as frightening as seeing one's life laid out before one, stripped in an instant of large chunks of possibility ("his marriage, his children, his house"), are the *unknowns* at work in merging with another person.

Earlier, Mrs. Ramsay feels uneasy as she considers whether she has put too much pressure on Minta to marry. Despite her vague sense that children and wedlock offer an escape from life's hostility, she also knows that good marriages require certain ineffable qualities. "The thing she had with her husband," she thinks. "Had they that?" But that's not a question that Paul and Minta can answer in the affirmative, that *any* couple can answer in the affirmative, without taking a chance that may well prove the opposite is true. ("God, I see the risk in marrying anyone," Leonard acknowledged to Virginia the day after he proposed.)

When I was thirty, I married a man I'd dated for five years; four years later, he left in the middle of the night, and I never saw him again. What on earth did I make, before this experience, of Paul's conviction that asking Minta to marry him had been the worst moment of his life? How could such a claim have held any meaning at all? The truth is that I likely missed it altogether; one of the wonders of Woolf's novel is its seemingly endless capacity to meet you wherever you happen to be, as if, while you were off getting married and divorced, it had been quietly shifting its shape on the bookshelf. It was only after my own rupture that I discovered, embedded in Mrs. Ramsay's reflection that Paul and Minta will say "we" all their lives, what is to me the most resonant of the book's observations about coupling: Marriage precipitates what may well be a splendid new entity, but its price is the supplantation of "I."

In 1938, Virginia wrote to Vanessa bewailing "the complete failure" of her own nuptials; she is unable to visit her sister in France, she says, because she and Leonard are "so unhappy apart that I cant come. Thats the worst failure imaginable—that marriage, as I suddenly for the first time realised walking in the Square, reduces one to damnable servility." *To the Lighthouse* is hardly an antimarriage novel; its portrait of the Ramsays reveals the heights of human connection, imperfect though it may well be. But it also recognizes that marriage is a loss, a sacrifice of self and its expression, and that, contrary to Mrs. Ramsay's beliefs—among them that "an unmarried woman has missed the best of life"—solitude can be an act of preservation. "She liked to be alone," Lily insists, pleading her exemption from that universal law. "She liked to be herself; she was not made for that."

IN THE SUMMER of 1974, in the midst of a worldwide recession, Turkey invaded Cyprus, and my father, who had designed three branches for that island nation's bank, lost his largest client. All of a sudden, there was very little work. At twenty-nine, after two relatively barren years, he decided to shutter his practice and take one of two paths: going to business school or sailing around the world. He was accepted at Harvard, and so put off the sailing.

He arrived in Cambridge in the fall of 1977, carrying two small suitcases and a pair of skis; twenty-four hours later, energized by a day's worth of impressions,

he sat down at the window of his dorm room to write
my mother a letter. It was a hot, humid day, and he
wrote with his feet dangling out beyond the window-
sill, every so often looking up at the ivy-covered court-
yard and watching the other students arrive. "I may
have missed Oxbridge," he wrote, "but what with their
usual combination of panache + gaucheness the Yanks
have done a pretty good job imitating at least part of the
concept." He'd spent the previous evening at the business school pub, where he'd met an Australian ("a super
guy"), a Nigerian ("I begin to see what it's all about.
Imagine being pally with him when he's running his
country"), and an American (his stated "raison d'être
for being here . . . was to make 'oodles of loot.' It was
dropped so unassumingly it sounded lovely"). He found
the United States much changed since his first and only
visit in 1966, and he was impatient to get a feel for its
"heart beat." Before signing off, he drew my mother a
floor plan of his room, complete with a sketch of the skis
propped "ostentatiously" in the corner. In the following
weeks she would send him the Fiorucci prints that later
hung in our house in Boston—huge, semipornographic
photographs of women wearing silver sequins and the
word "Fiorucci" on their bare behinds—but until then
he made do with a copy of *SAIL Magazine*, from which
he cut two orange stickers for his door and mailbox. "If
anyone asks what they represent, the answer is a rising
or setting sun—and I'll let them know which in due
course." This last was a reference to his concern about
how he would fare there—he had been relieved to hear,
in the pub the night before, that only a few students
actually failed.

His next letter to my mother was written at the end

of what he called one of the "most depressing weeks" of his life; it describes eighteen-hour days, impenetrable classes, and awful food. "I spend half the time wondering whether to fly straight home," he wrote. "Got drunk last night—along with everyone else—to cheer myself up. Depressed again this morning. Can't sleep. Bowels in bad shape." A few weeks later he was playing squash when his opponent's racket struck him in the face and smashed his glasses, scratching one eye and driving shards of glass deep into the other. He went to the emergency room alone in an ambulance, believing he would be blind for the rest of his life. He told neither his parents nor my mother, and he stayed in the hospital for two weeks without a single visitor.

This was probably the lowest point in my father's life so far. His trouble with math had already been making it difficult for him to keep up in certain classes, and he was now several weeks behind and unable to read for longer than a few minutes without his good eye tiring. But he continued to write my mother once a week or so, letters that were affectionate if not romantic, and that, in spite of their gloom, retained a certain wit. "I'm back with my feet out the window dropping you a line," he wrote in late October. "It's a beautiful day for a change, and the sports freaks are at it again." In December, his left eye tried to open on its own. "I'm much more cheerful as a result," he wrote. "Someone even commented on my humming as I strolled towards Harvard Square."

Before he left for Cambridge, my father gave my mother a tape recorder so they could exchange spoken letters in addition to writing and occasional phone calls. They hadn't made any promises about the future, but she felt more committed to him than ever. That Christmas, she visited him in Boston, where she hoped he might propose. They went skiing in Vermont and sightseeing in New York; he introduced her to his friends and took her to see *Star Wars* in the theater. He was still wearing an eye patch. For Christmas she gave him a homemade sweater he had designed, a crimson wool pullover with the letters HB$ embroidered in navy on the front; he gave her a calculator, one he'd bought for Harvard that turned out to be the wrong model. It had been a good holiday, but she was disappointed by the gift, and again when he dropped her off at Logan Airport. "You don't want me to wait around until you go, do you?" he asked. "No," she said, though in fact she would have liked it very much.

A few weeks later, he sent my mother a tape, the sole remaining spoken letter they exchanged. "I've just recorded a load of twaddle and subsequently deleted it about you and me," he says. "The intellectual embarrassment is that I'm supposed to be here as a decision maker, and am so inept at making decisions." He seems to be working through the question of whether or not to marry her, striking an uneasy compromise by the end. "The art of survival," he concludes, "which you have practiced far more than I have—you have demonstrated your commitment far more than I have—probably has a lot more significance than some idealized notion of what makes a good relationship and what keeps it going."

Shortly after he uttered these words, he returned to England on spring vacation, and, over dinner at my mother's apartment, proposed. They were married that summer in London, in a civil ceremony at Marylebone Town Hall, followed by a garden party at a friend's house. The thirty or so guests had all received, as invitations, half bottles of champagne with the details of the wedding printed on the label.

WHEN LEONARD WOOLF asked Virginia Stephen to marry him, in January 1912, she had already turned down a handful of proposals, finding her suitors deficient. If only the "earth would open her womb and let some new creature out," she complained to her friend, the writer Lytton Strachey, noting that the men she knew had "grown very stale," and to Clive Bell, Vanessa's husband, that she could not reconcile them with her vision of "the man to whom I shall say certain things." (Lytton's own bungled proposal to Virginia, in 1909, aroused a terror to rival poor Paul's own: "As I did it," he wrote to Leonard, "I saw it would be death if she accepted me.") Virginia's views on marriage itself were also evolving. "I didn't mean to make you think I was against marriage," she wrote to another friend, also in 1912. "Of course I'm not. . . . I began life with a tremendous, absurd, ideal of marriage, then my bird's eye view of many marriages disgusted me, and I thought I must be asking what was not to be had. But that has passed too." Her new criterion for accepting a husband? "Now I only ask for someone to make me vehement, and then I'll marry him!"

Whether or not Leonard made her vehement was still up for debate. She vacillated for months before finally telling him she loved him at the end of May. In the meantime, realizing how painful he found her indecision, she sent him a remarkable letter putting forward her jumbled thoughts. Despite its frankness and

occasional savagery, he saw something in it that convinced him to resign his civil service post in Ceylon and
remain with her in England. "When I am with you,
there is some feeling which is permanent, and growing," she writes of his increasing appeal to her. "Your
caring for me as you do almost overwhelms me. It is so
real, and so strange . . . you have made me very happy
too." And yet her passions pass "from hot to cold in an
instant": "I feel angry sometimes at the strength of your
desire. Possibly, your being a Jew comes in also at this
point. You seem so foreign." Equally concerning is what
she calls "the sexual side of it": "As I told you brutally
the other day, I feel no physical attraction in you. There
are moments—when you kissed me the other day was
one—when I feel no more than a rock."

If one were Leonard, there would be much in this
letter from which to recoil—it lays bare Virginia's vola-
tility, her anti-Semitism, her unresponsiveness to his
advances, all challenges their marriage would hold in
store. But there is also much to admire, for in its candor,
courageousness, and deep reflection, the letter demonstrates her respect for his intelligence and empathy; in
Leonard, it seems, the thirty-year-old Virginia had finally found the man to whom she could "say certain
things."

The letter demonstrates, too, through the serious-
ness with which she treats it, her respect for the ideal
of marriage itself—she is like Paul, who one minute
reacts with horror to his fate and the next resolves to
wake at dawn to prove his love. "We both of us," she
concludes—sliding from "I" into "we" as Paul will do—
"want a marriage that is a tremendous living thing, always alive, always hot, not dead and easy in parts as

most marriages are. We ask a great deal of life, don't we? Perhaps we shall get it; then, how splendid!" In August they were married in a small civil ceremony at St Pancras Town Hall, followed by a lunch party at the house in Gordon Square. The service was so informal that Vanessa interrupted midway through to ask how she might officially change her son's name. "One thing at a time," the registrar apparently replied.

Many years later my father would joke, of the night they were engaged, that my mother had seduced him with a fantastic bottle of Châteauneuf-du-Pape. When he was in a mood more cynical, he would say that he had married on the rebound from Harvard Business School—that he had been so knocked about by his first year in Cambridge that he had returned home and immediately proposed. The one time I asked him about it seriously, he said, affecting nonchalance, "Minty was very loyal and very conscientious and very loving. I was very fond of her, and that was that." As for my mother, she told me once that she was lucky—she married exactly the man she wanted to marry. And maybe she did. Unlike Virginia, who implored Leonard to "go on, as before, letting me find my own way," I think my mother craved the self-sacrifice that Lily so fears. That was the erasure she wanted, that the pact she signed.

5

[They spent their honeymoon with friends, visiting
someone's cousins in a castle near the border of Wales.
The castle might have had a hundred rooms, but the
cousins lived in only three or four of them; the others
were in ruins; you could look up through the fallen ceiling of the billiard room to see blue sky. My parents slept
in a tower room, where their hosts had left a vase of hyacinths—my mother could still remember the smell of
them, she said, even some forty years later, as she stood
at the high window looking out across the countryside,
with its village and its tenant farms bright green after
a rain. What else do you remember? I asked her, but
she had disappeared into her memories. Yes, she said,
distracted, that was almost one of the happiest times of
my life.]

6

Upon graduating from Harvard in 1979, my father took a job at his friend's startup, advising on the adaptive reuse of old buildings. My mother, who had moved to Boston from London six months earlier to discover that her husband's disposable income had gone toward flying lessons, was already settled at an architecture firm in Cambridge. By all accounts, it was a happy time. When I was born, my father took a more lucrative position as vice president at a big real estate company, and my parents, who up till then had stashed me in a drawer at night, began to look for a new house.

My mother sometimes tells the story of how my father had called during his lunch break to say he'd found the perfect home—a large, brick townhouse in the then-rundown neighborhood of Charlestown. When she arrived holding me in her arms, the broker looked nervous. "I don't know if it's wise to bring a baby in here," he said. Built in 1860, the house had most recently been a boarding home; empty for the past year, with neither electricity nor heating, it was filthy and freezing. The rooms were filled with trash and old bedding, and a quintet of abandoned refrigerators reeked of decaying food. Shiny chocolate-brown paint peeled from the woodwork like streamers. There had been a fire in what was to become my parents' bedroom. "Nonsense," my father said, and escorted us inside. When the group entered the basement, stepping over the bodies of two dead rats, an entire section of wainscoting fell to the ground. My mother looked closer and realized the walls were riddled with rot. Just being there made her feel ill, but my father was ecstatic. As soon as the broker turned his back, he looked at her and grinned. "Don't let him see how excited you are!" he whispered.

They signed the papers at the beginning of 1982. My father cleared the house of its overturned refrigerators and moldering furniture; he stripped the walls and painted them yellow, taupe, and mayflower red. He laid new front steps—pressing my bare feet into wet concrete to leave an impression that remains today—and he built a deck that faced the city skyline.

Every night, when his work was done and he was cheerfully exhausted, he would return to the living room, which had a pair of marble fireplaces and ceilings twelve feet high; he would sit for hours on the floor with his back to the wall, holding a cigarette and a glass of wine, simply looking. He had sanded the floors and washed the windows, scrubbed the molding and spray-painted the mirror frames above the mantels with silver automotive paint, but the room was still without furniture, and as he looked across the bare, enormous space—as clean and pale now as a piece of driftwood—he was stunned by its brilliance again and again. "What a beautiful room!" he would call every so often to my mother in the kitchen. "What a beautiful room!"

7

"And here she was, she reflected, feeling life rather sinister again."

"What my mother was like when she was as happy as anyone can be," Virginia Woolf declared, "I have no notion." She was referring to the brief period in which Julia Jackson was married to Herbert Duckworth, a handsome, affluent, charming, and "possibly rather dim" young barrister whom Leslie Stephen, who had known Herbert at Cambridge, would later describe as a "thorough gentleman." Julia—whom as a teenager Virginia suspected of being "aloof," of shedding "a certain silence round her by her very beauty"—first met Herbert at the age of sixteen, in Venice in 1862. In the following years, she would turn down two marriage proposals (one from a painter, the other from a sculptor), choosing instead the more orthodox Herbert, who had been so taken with Julia in Venice that he followed her to Lake Lucerne. She was "head over ears in love with him, he with her," and in 1867, when Julia was twenty-one and Herbert thirty-three, they married. They lived in Bryanston Square in London; Julia quickly gave birth to George, followed by Stella; she was eight months pregnant with Gerald, when, in 1870, three years into their marriage and visiting her sister at Upton Castle in Wales, disaster struck: while plucking Julia a fig, stretching skyward to the hanging fruit, Herbert ruptured an abscess and died just hours later.

Virginia believed that this marriage was "the most important thing that ever happened to" her mother, citing as evidence the "complete collapse" that followed: "She was as unhappy as it is possible for anyone to be." The photographer Julia Margaret Cameron, Julia's aunt—who photographed her often in those years, capturing her niece's anguish at close range and with characteristic soft focus—recalled "her sweet large blue eyes growing larger with swimming tears Oh aunt Julia only pray God that I may die soon, that is what I most want." Stella told Virginia that their mother used to lie on Herbert's grave at Orchardleigh; for a woman so typically restrained, Virginia thought, this seemed "a superlative expression of her grief."

But perhaps most startling to Virginia was the fact that, over the next eight years, during which time Julia devoted herself to caring for her children and the poor, she lost her faith. This loss disappointed Julia's mother, a deeply devout woman, while also convincing Virginia of a capacity for "solitary and independent thinking" that explained how such a woman might next have fallen in love with Leslie Stephen, a very different character from Herbert Duckworth. (It was the religious skepticism that Leslie expressed in his articles, apparently, that first drew Julia to him.) Nevertheless, she declined his first proposal: "I was only 24 when it all seemed a shipwreck," she explained to him in an undated letter.

As for Virginia herself, she remembered her mother as a woman who "looked very sad when she was not talking," a woman with "her own sorrow waiting behind her to dip into privately." That word, "privately"—like Mrs. Ramsay, Julia Stephen almost never discussed her past or the grief she had endured. "I have been as unhappy and as happy as it is possible for a human being to be," she told her friend Kitty Maxse; the phrase stayed with Kitty, Virginia said, because it was "the only time in all their friendship that she ever spoke of what she had felt for Herbert Duckworth."

ALL THE WHILE I was a child, my father wore charcoal-gray suits to work, and colorful ties I selected for him every morning, and black rubber overshoes that on rainy days encased his real shoes like a skin. When he came home at night he would whistle, a piercing, two-tone whistle that was always the same, and as soon as I heard it, I dashed downstairs to meet him. On the days my mother worked late, my school bus dropped me at a pink granite skyscraper in downtown Boston; my father's office, on the thirty-fourth floor, was at the end of a long corridor, and the wall behind his desk a floor-to-ceiling window with shimmering, far-reaching views of the harbor that dizzied me when I pressed my head against the glass. I sat reading at his feet beneath the desk, and later, when he had finished for the day, we gathered up Jack, Chris, and Frank, and took the elevator one floor down to the Bay Club. The waiter brought the men a round of drinks, and for me he brought a martini glass full of maraschino cherries. "They'll dye your stomach red," he always warned.

When I was seven, I answered the phone in my parents' bedroom in Rhode Island—it was Jack, my father's friend from work. On bright days this room fills with heat and sunlight, and, on afternoons when the tide is high, the water outside casts a web of light across the ceiling. So too on that afternoon, as I sat on my parents' bed watching the waves crash above me and waiting for my father to finish his phone call. "Christ," he said, and again, "Christ." When he hung up, he tried to explain: His firm was doing badly, and he and Jack and many others had been laid off. He seemed sad but also calm, and in fact I remember the day warmly. My mother was out, and we played a game of Monopoly. By the time she returned, it had become our news, and he told her I had been a great help.

At first, my father said later, he didn't worry too much about losing his job—he saw it as an opportunity. In the following months, he founded Geoffrey Smyth Associates, a one-person firm specializing in property consulting, investment, and management. But the collapse of the real estate market and ensuing recession made it difficult to find employment. For the next five years, my mother watched as he woke up early every morning, put on a suit, crossed the hall into the study, and sat there searching for a job; he was so good, she said, always striving, always trying. But while I knew this was a taxing time for my parents, it wasn't until I found among my father's papers a document outlining his failed ventures that I truly understood how bleak those years were, and why they produced in him the exhaustion and sourness they did. He lists eighty-four initiatives, alongside increasingly slapdash reasons for their failure: "Banking system crash = no financing available ... It never happened ... No financing; and it never happened ... Left after 8 months; no loans closed! ... We know the rest! ... They have a relationship with Arthur Andersen! ... Got cancer ... Not enough leverage available; Not good enough idea." Taken in full, the document expresses not just my father's determination but also the scope of his defeat. And while I used to wonder whether some mystery lay at the heart of his long unemployment—Did something happen? If so, what?—I now believe, looking at this list, that he was simply unlucky. He concludes by asking himself two questions: "Do something totally different? Give up trying to do something by myself?"

My family's income was cut by roughly three-fourths; my parents began to worry constantly about money. My mother, perpetually frugal, remembers lying awake at night with a stomachache; my father, whose years of flying lessons and BMWs were well in his past, stayed up late making lists with names like "Contacts" and "Existence Variables." The anxiety was soon to have real, tangible effects on both my parents. My mother, who had always been slim, began to put on weight. My father, who may have suffered as much from the boredom of sitting at home as he did from financial concern, became deeply depressed. Always a cynic, he soon grew downright nihilistic—his word—and always a heavy drinker, he began to drink steadily from lunchtime on.

I don't remember when I realized that he was an alcoholic. It wasn't an epiphany that struck me suddenly, but something I one day knew and had known for a long time. Hard, hazy scenes began to snake their way into our lives: We were eating dinner and my parents were fighting. My father slammed his fist on the table and broke a plate; it cut him to the bone and left a gash three inches long. My mother took him to the emergency room, and in the silence they left behind, I mopped up the blood from the family room table. Or the night I returned to a quiet house; I was making tea when my father approached me in the kitchen. "Your mother and I are leaving," he said, and I could tell from the slow, stupid way he said it that he was drunk. "Leaving where?" I asked. "Moving?" He shook his head. "No," he whispered. "Each other. Shhh." Or the evening when my parents picked up a friend and me from school. My father was jaunty, but his eyes were glassy and red. I sat in the back praying he would say nothing to embarrass me, and the moment we dropped my friend off, I yelled at him for acting so foolishly. When we returned home—my mother was still outside, parking the car—he started to shiver so violently that he had to sit down on the steps.

In 1993, when I was eleven and my father forty-six, he was diagnosed with kidney cancer. His doctors said it was probably a direct result of cigarettes: kidney cancer is twice as likely to develop in smokers as nonsmokers. I remember being assured by both parents that he would be fine, I remember believing them, and I remember visiting the hospital after his right kidney had been successfully removed. He was sitting up in bed, pale but smiling as I entered the room. "Lovely to see you, Petal," he said. What I don't remember, and what I recorded in my diary at the time, is how sullen and angry he became in the following months, and my disgust when he continued to smoke in secret, despite having told my mother and me he had quit. My bedroom was directly above the deck, and during the summer evenings when my window was open, I could smell the smoke as strongly as if he were sitting right beside me. That same summer he walked down the dock in his swimsuit, and I saw for the first time the long scar that cut across his abdomen—it was pink and jagged, the skin around it cobbled and lumpy. I asked him if he minded; his stomach was kind of ugly now. "I don't give a damn," he said, climbing down the ladder into the water and pushing off the float with his feet.

Long ago I used to wonder what would have happened if my father hadn't lost his job that afternoon. Would he have smoked less, drunk less? Would he be cancer-free today? But I recently came across some letters that convinced me this thinking was foolish. They were written to my father from his doctor, one year before he'd lose his job and five years before he would be diagnosed with cancer; my father had confessed to him that his "predominant sins" were smoking two and a half packs of cigarettes a day and drinking one bottle of wine at night. "I think you must realize," the doctor wrote, "that you have nearly all the quoted risk factors for premature coronary artery disease." The revelation that my father was already, in 1988, smoking and drinking so heavily came as a surprise, and a challenge to the order I had established in my mind: that before unemployment he was happy and healthy and moderate, and that after it, he was not.

In the coming years, my father would continue with increasing recklessness to abet his own decline. Was there something in him—perhaps given to him at birth, perhaps entrenched in him by some defeat or series of defeats—that made his acquiescence to both alcohol and cigarettes not just characteristic but assured?

It's hard to envision any quantity of joy or satisfaction that would have changed my father's fate; conversely, it's hard to imagine any low that would have struck him as rock bottom.

LIKE JULIA STEPHEN, Mrs. Ramsay appears very sad— "Never did anybody look so sad," we are told again and again—and, like Julia, she possesses a past full of shadows, one informed by some central catastrophe. She "had had experiences which need not happen to every one," she acknowledges at one point, trying to dispel her fear that some calamity awaits her children; significantly, she does not articulate them to herself, a show of reticence that reveals another parallel with Julia. But though it's tempting to assign Mrs. Ramsay the same history as Virginia's mother, particularly when we hear the whispers—"Had he blown his brains out, they asked, had he died the week before they were married?"—the reality remains obscure. All the reader knows for certain is that the events of Mrs. Ramsay's past, coupled with an "instinct for truth" arguably more acute than that of her philosopher husband, have given her a privileged understanding of the world's brutality; and that, again like Julia, she cannot reconcile it with the existence of an omnipotent, benevolent god. "How could any Lord have made this world?" she asks herself in solitude. "She had always seized the fact that there is no reason, order, justice: but suffering, death, the poor. There was no treachery too base for the world to commit; she knew that. No happiness lasted; she knew that."

When I first read *To the Lighthouse* as a moody, impressionable twenty-year-old, I responded viscerally

to Mrs. Ramsay's character. I thrilled to her hasty, incongruous beauty, to her spasms of irritation and glorious epiphanies; I considered tattooing the phrase "It is
enough!" across my forearm. (I still might.) I found myself murmuring the most ordinary of phrases—"Come
in or go out, Cam"—as if they were pieces of poetry; I
was charmed and confounded by the weirdness of her
mode of perception, by her mind raising itself from the
task at hand, by the wedge-shaped core of darkness she
feels herself to be in isolation. "Beneath it is all dark, it
is all spreading," she thinks, "it is unfathomably deep;
but now and again we rise to the surface and that is
what you see us by." I was drawn to that darkness and
depth; it actually *hurt* to read a sentence like the one
above; it was so apt, it was so beautiful; I longed for
Woolf's genius, yes, but I also longed for Mrs. Ramsay
herself, for her as my mother, for her as my friend; I
wanted to *be* her—that's how painful I found the distance between us, the distance between me and that
text. I might have swallowed the page. ("Could loving,"
Lily wonders, "make her and Mrs. Ramsay one?")

For all my enchantment, though, I would have done
well to reflect further upon Mrs. Ramsay's relationship
to life, one I glossed over because I found it puzzling.
Like Virginia, who wondered in her diary why life
was "so tragic; so like a little strip of pavement over an
abyss," Mrs. Ramsay thinks of life as "a little strip of
time presented . . . her fifty years." (Julia Stephen died
at forty-nine.) She thinks of it, too, as an "old antagonist," a formidable opponent with whom she is forever
in combat: "she was always trying to get the better of it,
as it was of her; and sometimes they parleyed (when she
sat alone) . . . but for the most part, oddly enough, she

must admit that she felt this thing that she called life terrible, hostile, and quick to pounce on you if you gave it a chance." I was accustomed to envisioning death and not life in this pugilistic way, accustomed—even when I thought of my father and his illness, *especially* when I thought of that—to celebrating life and not fearing it; I feared death. And I assumed, reading these words in light of Mrs. Ramsay's own imminent departure, that Woolf was conflating the two, or that the distinction (between life ending and death beginning) didn't much matter. But it seems obvious to me now that Mrs. Ramsay isn't thinking of her own mortality, but rather of those experiences she does not name—of the tremendous blows that life has dealt her, that *all* lives are capable of dealing.

Alongside the image of my father as a gregarious young man who never wanted anyone to leave is that of those countless evenings when he retired to the deck after dinner with nothing but a drink and a cigarette and the reach of his own mind. Was he moved? Was he bitter? Was he addled, sad, or scared? Was he dormant, like a machine that's set to sleep; was he distilled, like Mrs. Ramsay, to a core of darkness free to roam? I wouldn't say that he possessed that woman's clarity or rigor, or that he would be roused, as she is, by some "insincerity slipping in among the truths." But I expect that he, too, felt himself locked in a battle with life; that life, which had for decades largely let him be, which he must have thought a loyal friend during those vibrant years in London and beyond, had at long last pounced.

This ambush changed him. His light—that astonishing light—grew noticeably dim. "If there is any good (I doubt it) in these mutilations," Virginia wrote of the death of her mother, and of her oldest sister, Stella, "it is that it sensitises." My father was an alcoholic; I believe that he was born an alcoholic. But seen through the lens of life's antagonism, his utter capitulation to that disease becomes, if not a commonplace attempt at stifling such sensitivity, the battle plan of a mad general: *Pounce if you like. Destroy what you like. I'm way ahead of you.*

8

In the fifteen years since I first misread Mrs. Ramsay's rivalry, I've developed my own private lexicon, my own primitive tally system, for making sense of—or, more accurately, keeping tabs on—that reckless creature life has shown itself to be. I take pride in knowing, truly *knowing*, that however high that tally climbs—however long that list of life's attacks—there's nothing to stop it climbing ever higher. I keep a tally for my friends as well, a small number of whom are still innocents at thirty-five ("she had had experiences which need not happen to every one"), and for Virginia Woolf as well, who lost her mother at thirteen, her sister at fifteen, her father at twenty-two, her brother at twenty-four; whose first and second breakdowns shadowed the second and third of those deaths, respectively; and who, searching vainly for the "good" in this, herself conceived a narrative of combat, one that envisages life as wild, immense, animalistic, and herself as, if not its equal, at least a worthy adversary. "I would see (after Thoby's death) two great grindstones," she wrote of walking London

in the months following her brother's surrender to ty-
phoid, "and myself between them. I would stage a conflict between myself and 'them.' I would reason that if
life were thus made to rear and kick, it was a thing to be
ridden; nobody could say 'they' had fobbed me off with
a weak little feeble slip of the precious matter."

So mutilated, we read even the softest of scenes as a
theater of war. It's been too long since I clipped my cats'
claws, for instance; usually the creatures move about
like ghosts, but now, in the dark, I hear them prowling,
tsk tsk tsk. Last night Thomas jumped up on the bed
and laid his cool paws on my arm; he's an animal loath
to brandish his claws, even in jest, but they're so long
and sharp by now that I could feel their tips like tiny
sabers poking from the fur. And falling asleep, bearing those pricks against my skin—a souvenir—I felt
him grow heavier and heavier, felt him transformed
into a clumsy, ten-ton beast asleep beneath the flowering acacias, whiskers twitching mid-dream before he
wakes restless and ravenous at dawn. What is coming
next for us?

9

"That is the thing itself, she felt, as if there were only one person like that in the world; her mother."

When I think of "mother" (the word, the concept, the thing itself), I think of the scene in *To the Lighthouse* in which Rose and Jasper visit their mother in her bedroom, bearing a message from the cook. Mrs. Ramsay, combing her hair and dressing for dinner, asks if they would like to help her pick her jewelry. Jasper presents her with an opal necklace, Rose with a gold necklace, and she holds the pieces up to her black dress, studying her neck and shoulders in the mirror. (She avoids her face, but her beauty is implicit.) "Choose, dearests, choose," she says, hurrying them through further exploration of her jewelry case, but she is also patient, "for this little ceremony of choosing jewels, which was gone through every night, was what Rose liked best, she knew." As she finds herself wondering *why* Rose attaches such importance to the ritual—Rose whose mouth is too large, Rose who has a wonderful way with her hands—she is reminded of some ineffable emotion that she also possessed, "divining, through her own past, some deep, some buried, some quite speechless feeling that one had for one's mother at Rose's age."

Like so much of *To the Lighthouse*, this scene is loosely based upon Virginia Woolf's own life; she would later recall how she loved to follow the lights in her mother's opal ring during their lessons, and how, after Julia's death, she especially missed their "snatched" private moments—among them, when she got to choose the jewelry her mother would wear. And yet it seems to me that the scene above might be based upon any number of lives, for I, too, remember rifling through my mother's jewelry as a child, sorting her rings and brooches into piles—she had quite a few opals, perhaps because she was Australian—and going through her

closet too, where she kept a pair of red flowering sandals with mock-pearl stamens and a peach-and-gold embroidered dress that I conflated with her wedding dress, a pink flared cotton skirt and matching top. On the rare evenings she went out, I would linger in the warm, carpeted bathroom as she put on makeup; she stood at a vanity mirror with small round lightbulbs running down each side, applying perfume and brown eye shadow that I thought made her eyes look bruised—it was because I wasn't used to it, she said. (One night as my father raged, I met her at this mirror and wrapped my arms around her knees; I told her she looked pretty, a received idea.) And because she always brought me back a treat, some dessert wrapped in a paper napkin, I could envision the parties that she went to, all black and gold and shimmering.

"How did I first become conscious of what was always there," Virginia asks of her mother's "astonishing" beauty. "Perhaps I never became conscious of it; I think I accepted her beauty as the natural quality that a mother—she seemed typical, universal, yet our own in particular—had by virtue of being our mother." That idea, that our mothers are by definition beautiful, must run deep in little girls; I made that assumption about my own before I even knew what beauty was. And yet I was quite a bit younger than Rose when I began to see my mother differently, and began to see differently all that I had mistaken for her glamour. Her perfume had yellowed with age, and the cheap foam applicators with which she daubed her eyelids were crumbling. She almost never went to parties, and her best clothes hung unworn in the closet, still carrying tags from Filene's Basement. Aside from those opals and some silver rings and a string of pearls, the jewelry I loved to organize was most often made of wood or plastic. She had never pierced her ears, and her wedding ring—there was no engagement ring—was a thin rose-gold band she had purchased herself on a lunch break in London. Later, when she began to put on weight, it would have to be snipped from her finger.

"We think back through our mothers if we are women," Woolf writes in *A Room of One's Own*. She is reflecting upon the female novelists of the past, on how the lack of a feminine literary tradition must have exacted a colossal toll upon the work of women. But the sentence also conjures the buried, speechless feeling that Mrs. Ramsay holds for her own mother, and that Rose will one day hold for her—the long chain of motherhood by which all women have been shaped. "You ask how I learned how to fix diesel engines," my father said once. "More to the point is how the hell did your mother learn to be a mother?" I can see the difficulty she faced in being unable to call upon her own experience of being mothered (for my grandmother was a cold and unforgiving woman), and how her strengths as a parent were born in part of her resolve to be her mother's opposite. I never felt perfect growing up, and I certainly don't today, but I always felt *she* thought me perfect, which—and it's a credit to her that this came as a surprise to me—cannot be said of all mothers and their daughters. Never would my mother have thought my mouth too large.

But for all this, I wanted beauty, I wanted glamour; I wanted a mother whom I could look to as a paradigm of the feminine as I myself became a woman. And when I first met Mrs. Ramsay at her dressing table, wearing her black gown and raising to her neck the most beautiful of stones, opals and amethysts, she—so unlike my own mother—seemed to me the perfect surrogate. Here at last was my model.

BY THE TIME I was a teenager, my father was drunk more than he was not. When we sat down to dinner, his eyes were bloodshot and glazed, and his voice deliberate, occasionally slurred. Sometimes he was playful. "Isn't this delicious?" he would ask about a meal he had cooked; he would ask it once, twice, three, four times. If my mother and I indulged him he remained playful, but if we didn't he grew angry—his mood typically shifted from cheerful to silly to sullen to angry to depressed. He would begin to mutter under his breath, my mother would say "What?" too loudly, and he would look at her with hatred for the rest of the meal. If my mother was irritable herself, she would say, "Yes, Geoffrey, the prawns are delicious, but can we please talk about something else?" and his face would twist at what he perceived as her joylessness. Sometimes he was truculent from the beginning, and we ate quickly and silently, trying not to provoke him. And sometimes he was simply stupid, and too sluggish to recognize the condescension with which, after dinner, I rejected his eager, clumsy attempts at conversation. One of the qualities I most admired about my father was his competence, and I found it distasteful to be with him when he was in such a pathetic, insensible state.

When I left for boarding school at fifteen, I considered my father one of my best friends. By the end of that year, I was as distant from him as I had ever been. He

did not like talking on the phone in those days, and during the weekends I spent at home—quite a few of them,
as I was miserable—we barely interacted. I had already
learned how to gauge his moods and, if necessary,
harden myself against them. As the months passed, I
needed to calcify more and more. I think the most difficult aspect of loving my father then, as any child of
an alcoholic could attest, was the way in which nearly
every evening the person I adored simply disappeared.
The man who sat down to dinner was not my father.
His eyes were empty and flat, and looking into them
yielded no sign of recognition or intelligence. Even
were I to shake him, to yell and to scream, I would still
see the same eyes staring coldly back. Before I'd gone
away, we'd had a tradition of sitting on the deck after
dinner; we would stay up late, talking and looking out
at the view of downtown Boston through the trees. Now
I made myself scarce; I shut the door to my room and
talked on the phone with friends or watched movies.

My mother also disappeared, playing solitaire on the
computer upstairs or reading in bed. I rarely went to
her. You would think my father's behavior might have
brought us together; in fact, it drove us apart. She bore
the brunt of my unhappiness, fielding my phone calls
from school as often as six or seven times a day (a curious compulsion on my part, for I refused to tell her anything personal, and our conversations were short and
unsatisfying). But she was also envious—envious of my
relationship with my father, and of his relationship with
me. His conduct sustained a kind of unspoken competition between us, one I should never have won but often
did. (Indeed, although it arouses James's fury, it's entirely *appropriate* that Mr. Ramsay will forever win the

battle for Mrs. Ramsay's attention; the alternative is more disturbing.) Not only did my father turn on my mother more frequently than on me, but he seemed to seek my company more often than he sought her own: it was with me that he sailed and swam, with me that he watched movies and stayed up late at night. I must acknowledge here the pleasure of feeling chosen by him, and the faint insolence toward my mother his actions encouraged. He often impressed on me how terrific she was—how much she doted on me, how lucky I was to have her—but his behavior provided the stronger example. In retrospect, my mother must have found my allegiance to him so unfair: she did everything right, he did everything wrong, and yet it was he who every morning earned my devotion anew. But she must also have understood the excitement of being included in my father's world. The qualities that had originally drawn him to her—loyalty, conscientiousness, a deep capacity to love—stayed with my mother in force. They were her greatest qualities. But they were not qualities that inspired reverence, and my father, for all his tremendous failings, was more commanding and beguiling.

Every so often, moreover, there were stretches of time in which he became the man he'd been before. These were not a result of his drinking less, I don't think, but of periods of external calm—weeks when my mother and he were getting along, or when his work was going well. (He had finally found some success, with a partner, in buying and renovating a commercial building nearby; they were hoping to buy and renovate another soon.) My summer vacation at home was one of these times. Dinners went smoothly night after night, and it wasn't long before I began joining him on the deck again. He would make coffee and take it outside with a glass of brandy while I cleaned up the kitchen; when I had finished, I would make a cup of tea and go outside myself. He was content to sit alone with his drink and a cigarette, but equally happy to have company: my father was never covetous of solitude.

I told him nearly everything that happened in my life—about my friendships and antagonisms; about the parties I had gone to and the trips I had taken. He loved to hear my stories, and with him alone I became a good storyteller. I could make him laugh in a way I couldn't make anyone else laugh, and when I finished he'd say, "Katharine, you must write this stuff down!" If he was feeling expansive, he would misquote Longfellow instead, slowly and with feeling: "Life is real, life is earnest, but the grave is not the goal." He was similarly open with me; we talked about his childhood, his friends, his relationship with my mother, and his work. I often grew bored when he talked about business (though he himself grew animated), but the rest of the time his conversation thrilled me as much as it had thrilled me at thirteen. I was so impressed by the darkness of his worldview. He continued to refer to himself as a nihilist, instructing me to tell anyone who asked that I was a secular humanist, and said again and again, at the age of fifty, how terrible it was to grow old. Sometimes he frightened me with the indifference with which he spoke of death. He didn't care if he lived or died, he said, and seemed never to consider that I might care myself.

On the weekends that summer we went to Rhode Island. In the mornings I lay on the dock in my bathing suit until I was summoned to the deck for lunch, and in the afternoons, when the wind was picking up, I took out the Laser. I wasn't an especially strong sailor, and usually tacked back and forth across the basin, but sometimes I worked up the courage to head out beyond the ruins of the old stone bridge for Gould Island, the uninhabited lozenge of land in the middle of the river. When I was a child, I suspected that the island hid old, weatherworn chests of buried treasure; a thick forest had grown to its shores, and one day my father took me there in the rubber ducky—our name for the orange inflatable dinghy. We landed on a narrow stretch of beach, dragged the boat onto the rocks, and spent the afternoon clambering around its craggy perimeter and unsuccessfully searching for gold. "Don't worry, Poppet," my father said when we were once again bouncing above the waves and headed for home. "We'll find it next time."

By now all that remained of the thick forest on Gould Island were the skeletal boughs of dead trees, and on those boughs, black hard-angled shapes that looked like hand towels hung out to dry: flocks of cormorants airing their water-logged wings. I could see them as I neared the island, their small, sleek heads gleaming in the sunlight. Deep-diving cormorants are one of the few species of waterbird whose feathers are not waterproof; they often kept me company while I sunbathed, standing on the pilings of the dock and holding up their outstretched wings as effortlessly as if invisible strings were pulling them skyward. The harbormaster told us it was they who were responsible for the island's degradation—apparently the accumulation of cormorant guano beneath cormorant nests eventually kills the very trees in which those nests are built. Every time

I circled the island I thought of this, of the fact that one day soon the boughs would fall and the cormorants would move away. I supposed that when this happened the guano would leach into the bay and the forest grow again, and I supposed, too, that then the cormorants would return and the cycle would begin anew. Though perhaps not, I thought, tacking and turning back, in my lifetime.

My father took the Laser on my return. He always left the basin, and sometimes I would stand on the float, still in my life jacket, watching the white sail grow fainter and fainter. ("So much depends," thinks Lily, watching from the lawn as the dull speck that is the Ramsays' sailboat recedes into the bay, "upon distance"; so much depends upon "whether people are near us or far from us.") I knew how exhilarating it was to gather speed as one left the old stone bridge behind, and I often tried to imagine what it was my father saw and felt and thought at that very moment; how funny that he had access to that, while all I had were feet firmly planted and the sight of a tiny white triangle beyond the bridge. But then he would turn back, draw nearer; the sail would grow in size, and with one final tack he would bring the boat alongside the dock and our worlds were once again in line. We went for a swim before it grew dark, diving into water with a surface like tinsel—depending on the tide, it could be emerald green, inky black, dull slate gray, or glistening blue. My father was a neat and capable swimmer. He would stand at the edge of the float, his scarred, knobbly stomach poking out over the top of his bathing suit—his "corporation," he called it, and gave it a pat—and seemed less to dive than to throw himself in all at once. He liked the sidestroke and

I liked the breaststroke; we swam to the boat and back, sometimes climbing aboard for gin and tonics, or else the basin offered up a current so strong that we simply swam in place. By the time we mounted the ladder, the sun was low in the sky, and all it touched was riven by gold.

At the end of that summer I discovered a box of old photographs. The pictures were small, with rounded edges, and their colors strong and saturated. The first showed my parents, in their late twenties, sailing in the Solent. My father was laughing, and my mother looking shyly at the camera; her hair, dyed a vivid red, burned against the bright blue sky. In another, taken at a boat-yard in Sydney, she was crouching with a paintbrush, stenciling letters onto the transom of a dinghy. And in yet another, black-and-white, she was young and smiling in a field of tall grass—in the brilliant sunlight, the ragged stalks appeared ablaze. I was shocked by her loveliness, by her high cheekbones and the light in her blue eyes—I had never seen my mother so happy. It occurs to me now, thinking back to the flesh on display in those pictures, that my mother's body was a book, that my father's body was a book, that written on their skin, and within their skin, was the story of my parents' lives; and that Virginia Woolf, that most incorporeal writer, that writer whose characters drift about like plankton in a soup of consciousness (never, *ever* fucking), is in this respect a pretty useless tour guide. Better someone like John Updike, whose books I flipped through as a kid, looking for sex scenes that would send a flaming arrow up my core, and to whom I returned in an ICU waiting room at twenty-four, reading my way through the Rabbit novels as my father lay comatose next door.

Every time I looked up at the real world after being immersed in those pages, at its textures and shadows and patterns of light, it seemed a more physical, more immediate place; an unpleasant place, yes—grimy, grainy, grubby, tactile—and yet in keeping with the simple fact that we are each of us circumscribed within a body, the shape of which, the scars on which, the holes within which, tell our tale if you care to read it.

That evening I showed the pictures to my father. He thumbed through them; he seemed interested but detached. He paused on one of himself at work, sitting near a striking girl with long white-blond hair and a tight green T-shirt. "My old girlfriend," he said. Vivien. When he saw the one of my mother painting, he paused again. "God, she was skinny," he said. "I remember meeting her at the airport after we were married. I gave her a hug and my arms went right round her. It was 'Where are you,' slipping through my arms." He paused one last time, at a photograph taken at their wedding. My mother was wearing the pink cotton skirt I had found in her closet—too tight for me, even at sixteen—and her curls were tied with ribbons. "Oh yes, that's right," he said. "She had her hair done in this funny style. She went off to the hairdresser's and turned up two hours later with all these stringy things on her head." He reached the bottom of the pile and sniffed. "Right. What's next?"

A few days later I woke to learn that Princess Diana had been killed. The television was blaring news of her death, my mother was emotional, and perhaps my irritation showed, for she angrily accused my friends, who had visited the day before, of using all the newly washed beach towels. We fought. But though my father usually stepped in to take my mother's side, sometimes because he agreed with her and sometimes because it was the politic thing to do, on this day he defended me: "Stop it, Minty—you're being irrational."

She burst into tears. "Stop both of you attacking me," she sobbed. "Stop attacking me!"

"I don't know what the matter is with you," my father yelled. "Maybe it's those drugs you've been taking, but every day, as soon as you wake up, you're in a terrible mood—against the world."

"How dare you!" she screamed. "I'm not on any drugs!"

"Maybe that's the problem then!"

We were going to a Labor Day picnic, and while my father and I loaded the car with salads, sandwiches, and the Sunday papers, my mother sat in the living room and cried. "How dare you!" she occasionally wailed. "How dare you mention my pills in front of Katharine!" (In fact I'd already known about my mother's medications—for depression, for anxiety—but only from the pill bottles that lined the bathroom wall.) All the while the television played in the background, barking about Diana and the accident, and when my mother saw my father carrying the newspapers, she screamed again. "You don't need the papers! You're going to a social event."

"We're taking the papers."

"No, you're not!"

"Fine," he shouted, dumping them on the floor. "Take the papers. I'm sick of your parochial little rules governing your parochial little life. Take the fucking papers."

I'd just received my learner's permit, and was sitting

in the driver's seat adjusting the mirror when my father got in the car. We were about to leave and then my
mother came out on the front porch. She was wearing
an oversized green nightgown. For the first time she did
not scream, but spoke in a low, controlled voice. "If you
don't come back to the house, I'm leaving you," she said.
"I'm serious. You and your alcoholism have driven us to
this." She went inside and shut the door.

"You better go back."

"Yeah," my father said. His voice was subdued. "I
take it we aren't going to the picnic—unload the car,
will you?"

"Sure," I said. I sat there a while longer, looking at
myself in the mirror. I was wearing too much eyeliner.

The house was quiet for the rest of the day. And later,
when this blowup came to nothing, I realized with surprise that I was disappointed. I had wanted my parents
to sever, as one wants storms when sailing.

10

"For nothing was simply one thing."

Over the next few years, I came home to many such fights, arguments fierce and cruel in which my father yelled and swore, and my mother screamed, cried, and retreated upstairs. A sullen response from her, a harsh tone from him—these were enough to unleash a night's worth of bitter accusations. A pattern had developed years before: While my father, unable to remember his hostile conduct of the previous evening, would wake feeling positive and well-disposed toward my mother, she would wake feeling angry and resentful, and as a result be prickly all morning. My father used her morning behavior as evidence that she was the root of the problem, and she used his evening behavior as evidence his drinking was. His drinking *was* the culprit, but I still sided with him more often than with her. Sometimes after their fights I would feel for my mother a surge of love and pity and visit her in the study. "How dare you," she would hiss, "how dare you not defend me," and immediately my feelings of tenderness would vanish.

Meanwhile, my father's health was growing worse. Three months after his kidney was removed, he had returned to the doctor for a routine checkup to find that he had a handful of small benign tumors in his bladder. It was Stage I bladder cancer. The tumors were removed, but six months later the doctors found another one. This too was removed, but three months after that they found a couple more, and three months after that, still more. The tumors were not dangerous in themselves, but they would be if they were to one day break through the bladder wall. And after twenty or so of these procedures—and as the tumors grew more numerous—recovering from each new operation became increasingly traumatic. It seemed like my father was in and out of the hospital every few weeks. Finally it was decided that he should try a round of chemical treatments: once a week for six weeks they would inject his bladder with a potent liquid intended to eliminate the tumors altogether. At that time, the late 1990s, there were three different chemicals available.

It was around the time he tried the first of these that I came home for winter vacation, and, on the day after Christmas, joined my parents for dinner. My father was cheerful; he had been cheerful a lot recently, and I wondered whether it had something to do with the prospect of recovery. But my mother no longer trusted this kind of mirth, and when he tried to engage her in conversation, she flipped through a magazine and ignored him. Gradually his good mood faded—I could see the delight on his face morph into anger—and I steeled myself for yet another argument. He didn't say anything further, though, and after a silent meal my mother stood and brought her plate to the kitchen. As she rummaged for something in the fridge, I happened to look at my father. At that moment, without his seeing me, his face collapsed and he started to cry. He ran to the half bathroom in the hall, and my mother, who either hadn't realized he was crying or was determined to take no notice, went upstairs.

I sat alone at the table; my father's heaving sobs seemed to shake the walls. I didn't go to him—I hoped to give him the illusion of privacy—but I couldn't rid myself of the image of his face, one moment hard and the next crumpled into an expression of despair. How must he see his life? I wondered. He was fifty-one years old, underemployed and an alcoholic. His bladder was strewn with cancerous tumors that needed to be scraped away every three months. His wife was a stranger to him, and he as well to her. My father was not a victim, of course—though unlucky, he must have known that he had largely brought this situation on himself. But I still hated the idea of his isolation, hated that he had tried to communicate his hopefulness and been refused. And I hated too, though it was likely not the subject of his own thoughts, the fact of all his early promise and its mocking contrast to his present.

But how, then, did one reconcile this sadness with the happiness we sometimes had together? For the previous morning, Christmas, my father had popped open a bottle of champagne and poured it into three glasses half-full of orange juice—we always started holidays and birthdays with Buck's Fizz—and we carried them into the living room, which was the color of a seashell, with white plaster molding in the shape of small waves breaking along the ceiling and enormous ornate silver mirrors that reflected this beauty back to itself.

My parents read the newspaper and I read *Pride and Prejudice*—my mother had been begging me to read Jane Austen for years and as a Christmas present to her I had finally obliged—and once I finished I was even mature enough to admit to her that I had loved it. Later that afternoon the three of us curled up on the couch and watched four hours of the BBC production of *Pride and Prejudice*, and when Colin Firth first appeared on screen my parents, independently of each other, began to shriek in mock excitement. "Oh, Darcy!" my mother exclaimed, "Oh, Darcy!" my father exclaimed, and they both fell to their sides as if they had fainted. "Stop it!" I insisted, but I was laughing.

"So that was the Lighthouse, was it?" James asks as the Ramsays' boat approaches the rocks, surprised to find that the beacon, which he remembers as silver and hazy-looking, is now stark and straight and ringed in black and white—a harsher view, as if tragedy had exposed him to a new, more brutal realm. But then he corrects himself: "No, the other was also the Lighthouse. For nothing was simply one thing." Such are the complexities and contradictions of human experience, in which perception is not monolithic, but evanescent, and even an object as steadfast as a lighthouse must wear multiple guises. It was Woolf's genius to express this richness, to never gloss over intricacy or inconsistency, to communicate through her characters her ongoing struggle to find truth and meaning in a world where both are infinitely shifting. "The mind is full of monstrous, hybrid, unmanageable emotions," she wrote once. "That the age of the earth is 3,000,000,000 years; that human life lasts but a second; that the capacity of the human mind is nevertheless boundless; that life is infinitely beautiful yet repulsive; that one's fellow creatures are adorable but disgusting"—such is the "atmosphere of doubt and conflict" in which we find ourselves.

That happy family, that perfect trinity, that enviable and exclusive club we sometimes formed—that was my family too.

11

Claudette's living room was small, and I rearranged her furniture to accommodate a white screen. We sat in darkness as the projector whirred and clicked. Dust swirled in the expanding ray of light. Then a woman—my grandmother, Claudette's great friend—appeared before us, and the narrow apartment receded. She kneeled on a blanket beside a rocky stream; her hair was black and wavy, and she was speaking to a fair-haired little boy. Then she was standing, her hair still black but her lips red, before a diaphanous orange sheet through which shone the sun. It had the weightlessness of a silk parachute. She waved too quickly at someone beyond the frame and a different little boy ran too quickly to her—an effect of early film. He disappeared into her skirts, but then turned back to face the camera, and I could tell from the way his eyes wrinkled at the corners that it was my father, stripped of years.

Then whiteness—the projector whirred and clicked—and the ocean rose up and rolled over. Three older boys ran in; they dove beneath the waves, they shouted soundlessly to those on shore. Then whiteness, and the collision of croquet balls on a green lawn, then whiteness, and a teenager reading in tortoiseshell glasses, then whiteness, and a black silhouette on a mountain-top, then whiteness, and finally a young man. He wore tight-fitting trousers that widened at the knee; he was showing off a bright red caravan he had built in a field ringed with trees. The colors were bleached and textured, like watercolors on a windowpane. He held a cigarette in one hand, a tool of some kind in the other, and his nostrils flared slightly as he turned once more to face the camera. He was a serious, imposing figure, but then he was proud, and then he was excited, and then he smiled, and in that instant his face relaxed and his eyes filled up with light.

I went to sleep that night in Claudette's guest room, a tiny, old-fashioned bedroom with a dressmaker's dummy in the corner. The space was too dark—the wooden shutters fit too neatly across the panes of glass—and the uneasiness borne by the films gathered and intensified until it was a crushing grief. I don't know him well enough, I thought, panicking. I should have spent more time trying to know him. I turned on the light and took out my diary. *He is going to die soon.* As soon as I wrote it, I longed to take it back.

12

"It had flashed upon her that she would move the tree
to the middle, and need never marry anybody, and she
had felt an enormous exaltation."

Shall we check in on Paul and Minta Rayley, that young couple of Mrs. Ramsay's creation? Neither returns to the Hebrides in the novel's final section, but we do hear news of them from Lily, who over the years has paid some visits to their cottage north of London, where Paul breeds Belgian hares and Minta, singing, bored, presses her arm upon her husband's shoulder—a call for his discretion. Last time we saw Minta, she was wearing her golden haze; last time we saw Paul, he was burning and glowing and bound for adventure; it swept over Lily too, seated next to Paul at dinner, "the emotion, the vibration, of love." But during one visit, the couple's relations are unbearably tense, and from a single phrase—that Paul plays "chess in coffee-houses"—Lily pieces together a narrative, one in which Minta, "wreathed, tinted, garish," comes home at three a.m. and stands on the staircase eating a sandwich, while Paul in his pajamas brandishes a poker and shouts "something violent, abusing her . . . saying she had ruined his life."

Paul with his exquisite profile; golden-reddish, wild Minta—in marriage, he has grown "withered, drawn; she flamboyant, careless. For things had worked loose after the first year or so; the marriage had turned out rather badly."

A little while ago, I had lunch with my father's friend Zette at her home on Water Street beneath the shadow of the Brooklyn Bridge. Over homemade squash soup, she caught me up on her retirement, and I caught her up on my failed marriage, and perhaps because marriage led to marriage (Zette herself had never married), she asked if I had ever heard about the weeklong sailing trip she had taken with my parents—it had been, she said, like something out of a film. They sailed all around Rhode Island and Connecticut; the weather was perfect; and yet all the while she felt my mother straining to keep things together. She wondered why they had invited her. Then, at the very end, all the cracks opened up. "I was trying not to hear," she said, "but on a boat you can't get very far away. And I thought, *That's* why I was invited—to keep them apart." I apologized, lamely, some twenty years later; I could easily imagine such a scene. My father yelling, throwing things about the cabin; my mother begging him to keep his voice down.

As she stands painting on the lawn, Lily contemplates the story she has drawn up in her mind about the Rayleys. This "is what we call 'knowing' people," she muses, " 'thinking' of them, 'being fond' of them! Not a word of it was true; she had made it up; but it was what she knew them by all the same." She is reflecting not just on the limits of knowledge but also on the opacity of other people's marriages; the little scene I just created—my father throwing things; my mother pleading with him to be quiet—is no more real than Lily's image of Paul as he waves a poker on the stairs. Even Zette, hiding in her cabin and trying not to listen, a single data point that has for decades shaped her understanding of my parents' union, was in possession of no more than some crude approximation of the truth. A marriage is a secret, an alliance so private that even one's closest friends are privy only to its contours, to the performance that it becomes in public; no one on the outside could know the precise nature of its dynamics within. And it's telling that when Zette recounted the sailing trip, I was surprised not that my parents had fought but that I had lost track of a whole week they'd spent at sea; even at thirty-five, I keep forgetting that the bulk of their marriage was invisible to me, and my understanding of those gaps a fiction. In *To the Lighthouse*, Lily imagines how she would take satisfaction in telling Mrs. Ramsay that Paul and Minta's marriage was a failure; as a teenager, I would have summed up my parents' union similarly. And yet coupled with their misery was potent connection, one that bound them to each other—irrevocably, it seemed—and that neither Zette nor I could ever hope to fathom.

After we had finished our soup, Zette told another sailing story: how many years later, out of the blue, my father called her from the East River to say that he was right outside. She ran up to the roof of her apartment building, the same apartment where we were having lunch, and they waved to each other just as he and *Solent* were passing beneath the Brooklyn Bridge. They kept waving until the boat was out of sight. It was the last time she saw him.

BY THE TIME I was a senior in high school, my father turned from silly to angry so quickly that I was frightened to be around him after six o'clock. At dinner he did everything too hard: he placed silverware on the table with a bang, he chewed fiercely, he cut violently into slabs of butter. Conversations were strained and dangerous. If we didn't humor him—sometimes my mother didn't humor him—his face would grow tight and he would stand up. Grabbing his wineglass, he would open the screen door to the deck and slam it shut behind him. Later, when he had installed a mechanism to stop it on its hinges, the door would bounce back, and slowly, quietly, close itself. It was a silence more sinister than the banging had been.

I'm sure an onlooker would wonder, as Zette wondered, why my parents didn't get divorced. They spoke of it often. They announced several times in those years that they would be separating, and it was always said with such finality that I believed it to be true. But I had noticed something about my parents, which is that the older they got, the less full their lives became, and the less individuality they seemed to possess. They had plenty of friends in England and Australia, but in America they rarely socialized. My mother blamed this on my father's drinking; my father on her "neuroses." She had quit her job at the architecture firm when he finally found employment, and later took the part-time position of managing his buildings. They both worked from home, from the same office, and on many days they did not leave the house; when they did, it was often to go to the bank, post office, or grocery store. Unlike my friends' parents, who seemed to lead lives as individuated as my own, my parents' lives were so inextricably entwined that were they to separate, it would be as two people not quite whole. They were rarely apart for longer than three hours at a time. They shared everything they possessed. Most significant, the life they had created in America was a shared life. They did not belong here as individuals. They had no extended family here and few friends; they had only a daughter and each other.

Shortly after Paul asks Minta to marry him, he has that vision: of "how they would retreat into solitude together," of how they would "walk on and on, he always leading her, and she pressing close to his side." I see my parents in that image, and see too how paradoxically it was their retreat into solitude, their very closeness—the way they clung to each other even as they clawed at each other—that most divided them. Were they whole, my parents could have parted; were they whole, they might not have needed to. Lily is cognizant of such risks; as she watches Paul and Minta at dinner, flinching at the "fangs" of love to which Minta is exposed, she feels grateful that she may still elude their fate: "She need not marry, thank Heaven: she need not undergo that degradation. She was saved from that dilution." It's a dark view of marriage, but one that's not so different, really, from Mrs. Ramsay's observation that Paul and Minta will say "we" all their lives—both characters are grappling with the ways in which wedlock promises an erosion of the self.

That spring, as my parents and I were finishing

dinner one night, my father stood up and opened the liquor cabinet. Then, without warning, he slammed the cabinet door and struck the table. "Stop playing silly games, Minty!" he yelled.

He left the room, hurling the door closed behind him. When he was gone, my mother told me she had poured the bottle of brandy down the sink without telling him. We waited. He returned with his shoes; he was going to the liquor store. At first he was silent, his face hardened into an expression of rage, and then he began to yell.

"Stop playing these fucking games," he shouted. "You never stop eating yourself stupid—do I throw out your food?" Earlier that day, during a rare moment of intimacy, my mother had told me she'd lost fifteen pounds.

"You're such a jerk," I said quietly. I was almost never the object of my father's anger, but when I said this, he turned to me furiously and struck me across the neck with his shoe. It didn't hurt. I had the sense he'd stopped his swing at the last moment.

"Geoffrey!" my mother screamed, rising from her chair.

"You mind your own business!" he shouted at me. "You're a fucking spoiled brat." He left again, and when he returned he was carrying the heavy-duty, plastic garbage can from the driveway. It barely fit through the door frame. "I've never thrown out your food," he continued to shout at my mother. "Let's start now." He carried the garbage can into the kitchen, shoving her out of the way and trapping her behind the fridge door. "What is it? Rice? Potatoes?" He began to grab at bottles, chunks of cheese, chicken breasts, and Tupperware containers, dumping them all into the trash. It was only when he had emptied most of the fridge that he returned the can to the driveway, poured himself some wine, and disappeared outside.

My mother was tearful, and I went to hug her. I hadn't hugged her properly in a long time, and her body was simultaneously known and unfamiliar.

"Mom," I pleaded. She smiled at me wistfully, and I held her again. Her face was wet.

"Did you know it was ten years ago today that he was laid off?" she asked. She began to talk and talk—about his alcoholism, how he could only get better when he wanted to—and it occurred to me that she never discussed my father with anyone.

When I returned to my room, my overwhelming sensation was one of exhaustion and even boredom—I was sick of spending evenings like this. From then on I began to avoid him at night even more deliberately than I had before. I remember an exchange in Rhode Island, at the end of a day spent watching Antonioni films for my art history class. I was brushing my teeth when my father appeared at the bathroom door. He was hunched over, and his own teeth were stained gray from red wine. His hair (I suddenly noticed) had also grayed. He was smiling shyly and holding one of his beloved Patrick O'Brian novels—its cover showed a wooden ship thrashing on enormous waves. "What?" I asked. He'd been drunk at eight o'clock and it was midnight. "How did you like *L'Avventura*?" he asked. "It was fine," I said. "I'll talk to you about it in the morning." He wanted to talk now—he said something about Monica Vitti. "Good night," I said. "I'm tired." He looked hurt, but finally turned around and went downstairs. And yet how much I wanted to talk to him too! How much I wanted to stay up late and hear his thoughts on Antonioni, whom he had loved when he was younger. And how badly it hurt to send him away like that, evening after evening, terrified, *terrified*, that we didn't have much time together, that he would soon be gone.

13

People sometimes ask me if I'm angry with my father. When I say I'm not, they think I'm lying to myself. I don't think I am. When I look back on his worst acts, I can remember my wrath and hatred, certainly—so violent, so complete; so *inexorable*, I thought at times, that I could barely stand to be in my own skin. But I can also remember the way in which, within a week or two, such vehemence had faded to nothing; how that brutish stranger was again and again vanquished by that other, most gentle and lovable being: my father. And the truth is that neither memory—neither the loathing nor the absolution—feels especially familiar now. They feel like stories attached to someone else.

14

"A shutter, like the leathern eyelid of a lizard, flickered
over the intensity of his gaze and obscured the letter
R.... He would never reach R. On to R, once more.
R—"

My father's first assignment at the Architectural Association was called the Primitive Hut Project. The
conceit was that one was stranded on a deserted, rocky
island in the Hebrides—one much like the Ramsays'
own, perhaps—and needed to build a settlement out
of the available resources. But it was a pathetic assignment, my father said later, because if there was nothing
on this island but rocks and sod, and maybe a couple of
trees, then the only thing you could really build was
stone huts. There were a few design issues—you could
build huts of different sizes, or a hut for the chieftain,
or a communal hut, or a kitchen hut set apart from
the residential huts—but that was about it. Nevertheless, the students were given over a month to complete
the project, and my father spent weeks constructing a
model from layered cork sheet cut in contour and white
plaster molded into the shape of parabolic domes. ("For
structurally," he said, interrupting himself, "if you're
building a hut without any mortar, because of the effect of the structural profile, it has to be a parabola.")

"The thing was exquisite," he said. "There was nothing intrinsically wonderful about the design—there wasn't any design to be done. But it was absolutely beautiful."

When he turned up on the day it was due, however, he found he was the only one who had taken the assignment literally. Everyone else had produced designs for baronial halls, for manor houses, for citadels with castellated turrets.

"Were they made out of stone?" I asked.

"God knows what they were made of," he said. "No one seemed to know or care. But my model got no recognition whatsoever, and I realized that reality didn't enter into it. So I think I just sort of lost it at that point, and said, Oh, well, if this is the way it's going to be . . ."

I first heard about the Primitive Hut Project when I was in college—my father told the story as a sympathetic response to some academic trauma of my own. Yet he continued to refer to it in the coming years, and I began to understand that the assignment had become for him symbolic, the perceived foundation of a gradual, pervasive disappointment.

A few months after handing in his model, though, he published, in *Architects' Journal* and *Building Design*, a handful of impassioned articles that belie his portrait of himself as an increasingly cynical young man. He may well have given up trying in earnest (his final thesis, after five years of study, was a detailed design for a hovercraft), but he was, nevertheless, wholly absorbed in art, architecture, and design. His professors were the members of the avant-garde group Archigram (antiheroic, pro-capitalist, hooked on futurism; walking cities and living pods), and my father, who described himself as a kind of fringe hanger-on to the movement, seems from his writings to have zealously embraced their ideas. He was equally galvanized by new developments in fine art—many years later, when he would dismiss Archigram as a load of old rubbish, he spoke with wonder of a show at the ICA in London called *The Popular Image*, of seeing for the first time paintings by Warhol, Lichtenstein, and Rauschenberg. (As Woolf would later write of December 1910, alluding to the *Manet and the Post-Impressionists* exhibit curated by her friend Roger Fry, this was arguably another moment at which "human character changed.") All of which is to say that my father's time in architecture school, *not* a primary source of skepticism, seems rather to have been a period of great personal growth; and that his conception of these years was inherently flawed. He came to misunderstand them, I think, and misunderstood in turn a feeling of disillusionment that was no doubt very real, and very much more complicated than he made it out to be.

Perhaps the best evidence of this is *Clip-Kit*, the magazine my father started with his friend Peter in his second year. *Clip-Kit* was intended to promote new technologies in architecture; its manifesto argued that the "narrow preoccupations of both architects and students" were at odds with "an era of unprecedented technological advance." ("What was the idea behind it?" I asked him once. "Oh, there wasn't any idea," he said.) Somehow the launch party attracted the attention of the architectural establishment, including that of Reyner Banham, the influential critic. Banham was an enfant terrible, my father said, and he liked his protégés, and though my father wasn't typically one for having mentors, Banham became the exception. That spring my father entered an IBM-funded design competition; the top ten applicants would be awarded an invitation to the Aspen Design Conference, a return ticket to England, and $2,000 in cash. As Banham was the competition adjudicator, my father figured he had a good shot. He was on holiday in Scotland with his mother when he learned he'd been selected. A telegram came to the hotel that read, simply, "You've got America." They celebrated with a long, lavish meal, and my grandmother remembers how generous my father was with his tip. "He was on top of the world," she said.

I suppose it's impossible to judge to what extent a single event has changed a life, but it has always seemed to me that the 1966 Aspen Design Conference was to transform the lives of a good many people I know. Old friends, yes, and I doubt my father would have settled in the United States otherwise, but also: there he met Rosamind and Leslie Julius, renowned English furniture makers who had brought with them their daughter, Corinne, a bright young art student who would one day marry my father's younger brother, Andrew. Rosamind always recalled her first impression of my father. Young, handsome, the cynosure of all eyes, he entered the conference tent grinning and wearing an all-white suit and silver tie. His girlfriend had made the tie and he carried more of the same kind with him in a bag. They were two dollars apiece, and that batch sold out within minutes. He spent the next week selling more ties, taking photographs, peddling *Clip-Kit*, and going to parties. Unabashed and unself-conscious, he was that summer just nineteen years old.

From Aspen he headed to Denver, from Denver to San Francisco; with $2,000 he was able to travel for months, staying with people (students, professionals, academics) he had met at the conference. In Los Angeles someone lent him a gold 1958 T-Bird convertible, and he was cruising along the Sunset Strip with the top down, wearing a crimson Levi's suit, when he spotted David Hockney, a former neighbor, in the next car. Hockney invited him back to his house, later the scene of *A Bigger Splash*, but all my father could remember was lots of turquoise water and lots of young men. He left LA for San Diego, for Tijuana (where he stocked up on Ovalados cigarettes), for twenty-four hours and nearly as many rolls of film in Las Vegas. Next was Chicago, where his host, the dean of the University of Chicago architecture school, hired him to give a slide show and lecture on his travels. That night, still wearing his crimson suit, he set off on a Frank Lloyd Wright walking tour of Hyde Park. There he was befriended by an elderly black man, who, certain he would be mugged, insisted my father return home and waited with him till the bus came.

From Chicago to New Hampshire to Boston to New Haven: at Yale he crashed with a prime mover like himself, an architecture student he'd met in Aspen. They stayed up all night and then the prime mover said, "We've got to go." "Where are we going?" my father asked. "We're going to Philadelphia," the prime mover said. They climbed into his Mini Cooper S and drove through the dawn; they got there at daybreak and toured the city as the sun rose. Finally, just before he was to fly back home, my father stopped in New York. "New York," he said, "was unbelievable. New York was fantastic, it was all happening in New York. It was all happening everywhere. America was cultural overload, it was like having an excess of exquisite desserts, just crammed at you over a three-month period."

Of his final years at architecture school, he remembered little. Upon graduating he joined a small, up-and-coming firm, and left two years later having been project architect for three buildings—one in Bath, one in Runnymede, one in Maryland. This was a terrific amount of responsibility for someone so young, and he later attributed his success to the very pragmatism that at other times he described as his downfall. "I was never the world's greatest designer," he said, "but I was practical and a good manager. I could do useful work for people, and I was promoted on that basis." At twenty-five he started his own firm; it was 1972, the year he met my mother.

EARLY ON IN *To the Lighthouse*, we learn that Mr. Ramsay is "one of those men who do their best work before they are forty"—that, as his old friend Mr. Bankes puts it, he "had made a definite contribution to philosophy in one little book when he was only five and twenty," and that the labors that followed were essentially "amplification, repetition." Mrs. Ramsay fears something similar, worrying that her husband "might guess, what she a little suspected, that his last book was not quite his best book." She's right to worry, for it's Mr. Ramsay's paralyzing belief in his own failure that gives rise to his worst qualities, which are considerable; he is, as Lily attests, "petty, selfish, vain, egotistical; he is spoilt; he is a tyrant; he wears Mrs. Ramsay to death."

Woolf adopts the seemingly simplistic analogy of an alphabet to convey her patriarch's intellectual development: "his splendid mind had no sort of difficulty in running over those letters one by one, firmly and accurately, until it had reached, say, the letter Q. . . . But after Q? What comes next? . . . In that flash of darkness he heard people saying—he was a failure—that R was beyond him." The analogy is likely grounded in Leslie Stephen's own titanic efforts to finish the *Dictionary of National Biography*, a project that spanned nearly a decade; at any rate, Mr. Ramsay's anxiety about his legacy certainly evokes that of Virginia's father. "Despite his obvious eminence," Hermione Lee writes in her biography, "Leslie read himself as a failure, a 'jack of all trades' whose name would only be mentioned in the footnotes of 'the history of English thought.'"

And yet Mr. Ramsay's obsession with failure is drawn as much from Virginia's experience as from her father's own. Her diaries and letters are full of self-doubt, most often about her work, occasionally about her childlessness; struggling to finish her first novel—"you wont like it," she wrote to her friend Violet Dickinson, "you'll tell me I'm a failure as a writer, as well as a failure as a woman"—was partly responsible for her breakdown in 1913. Her distress on revising *The Years* some twenty years later was equally severe, nearly giving rise to another mental collapse and inspiring thoughts of suicide. "I have never suffered, since *The Voyage Out*, such acute despair on re-reading," she wrote in 1936. "On Saturday for instance: there I was, faced with complete failure." In response, Leonard planned a trip to Cornwall, her first in six years, hoping that its happy memories would calm her; as he later recalled, they "crept into the garden of Talland House and in the dusk Virginia peered through the ground-floor windows to see the ghosts

of her childhood." But while the Cornish visit did al-
leviate her headaches, their return to London and the
specter of additional revision was debilitating. Writing
in her diary in June—one of only a handful of entries
from that time—she described "a week of intense suffering . . . a feeling of complete despair and failure."

Even *To the Lighthouse*, which she called "easily the
best of my books," was a source of anxiety. She worried
it was "rather thin," that readers would find it "sentimental," that "it will be too like father, or mother," that
"all my facts about Lighthouses are wrong." Concerns
about the work's inherent value weave their way into
the novel itself—Lily associates the moment at which
she first picks up her brush with a child's fear of the
dark, and later, returning to her picture, thinks it so bad
she wants to weep. Like Mr. Ramsay himself, moreover,
who is always fretting over his readership, she can't stop
dwelling upon the fate of her canvas, painfully aware it
will be relegated to an attic somewhere. ("Although to
be fair," said my Oxford tutor Shane, meditating upon
the picture's "brown running nervous lines," its stew of
red, gray, green, and blue, "it does sound like an absolutely dreadful painting.")

"Failure" is also the term by which, as early as fifteen
or sixteen, I had come to understand my father's own career. He was finally earning good money from his commercial properties, but I couldn't stop comparing the man
he might have been—a great architect—with the indifferent real estate developer he had become; I couldn't stop
wondering what had befallen that whirlwind of energy,
passion, and ambition. Was his defeat, as I then saw it,
a by-product of alcoholism or depression? A function of
aging? An outgrowth of that creeping disillusionment

he always cited? Was it the case, as my uncle Andrew once suggested, that life threw at him more than his fair share of challenges, challenges for which his native enthusiasm had left him ill-equipped? Did he make a mistake in abandoning England? "I always thought America would be good for him because he was so enterprising," my mother said, "but in a way he was too English and eccentric. I often wonder what he would have been like if he'd gone back—would he have started his own firm? Sometimes I think it was all wrong what we did." The men who know my father best cite, and this surprised me, a crisis of confidence, a deep-seated doubt about his own abilities; he believed there was some inner core of creativity that was essential to becoming a successful architect, they say, and that he didn't have it—that, if we are to borrow Woolf's analogy, he knew he would never reach R.

Maybe he was right. Maybe I'm being too hard on him. It takes a certain courage to recognize one's gifts or lack thereof and act accordingly—to face the truth that, as Mr. Bankes acknowledges, "we can't all be Titians and we can't all be Darwins." Besides, "failure" is my word, and not one I ever heard my father utter; what right have I to label him thus? In *To the Lighthouse*, Lily and Mr. Bankes lament Mr. Ramsay's inability to accept his true nature—they wonder why, rather than admitting the pleasure he takes in his work, in his family, in the accolades he receives, he must instead dismiss their importance to him. The answer? "All had to be deprecated and concealed under the phrase 'talking nonsense,' because, in effect, he had not done the thing he might have done. It was a disguise; it was the refuge of a man afraid to own his own feelings, who could not say, This is what I like—this is what I am."

So why not laud my father's admission that, as he told me once, he was perfectly happy with no particular ambitions or objectives, just muddling through on a hedonistic path? Why not celebrate his ability to say aloud, "This is what I like—this is what I am"?

WHEN I WAS nineteen, I spent a summer in London working for Peter, my father's university friend and *Clip-Kit* cofounder. Following a successful career in magazine publishing, Peter had started an architectural branding company; on arrival I was given some busywork and a desk across from Peter's son, who dated an editor at *British Vogue* and turned up each morning carrying a silver motorcycle helmet under his arm. I was slightly in love with him, and slightly in awe of his father, whose sporadic appearances at the office always gave rise to a low hum of excitement. Which is not to say that Peter was mesmeric: he was quiet and thoughtful, and his employees were responding not to some great personal magnetism, but to talent fulfilled.

In late August my parents came to visit, and one night we went to Peter's house for dinner. I had never met his wife, but heard she was stylish, clever, and cutting. Indeed: Jane opened the door wearing a tight white tank top, black pants, and hot-pink high-heeled shoes. She was dark and very thin, and her black hair was cast in a sharp, implacable bob. We settled in the living room—art covered every inch of the walls—and within minutes Jane had us laughing, telling funny

stories that won't be funny now. Her oldest son was a terror, she said, shagging every man, woman, and goat in
sight. Her oldest daughter was shy, but nevertheless up
at Oxford snogging the Prince of Canterbury (or someone like that). Her other son worked for Peter—"The
heartthrob!" my father exclaimed, and I flushed—and
Alice, her youngest, was my age. Alice bounded down
the stairs a few minutes later. She wanted to be a doctor,
and she called her parents by their first names.

In time Peter turned to my mother. How was she, he
asked, and listened intently to her answer. He seemed
to like her, and to like my father too—for a little while
my father had made Peter's family laugh in turn. But
he'd been drinking since noon, and as the night wore on
I watched him toughen and grow surly. He declined to
speak about the buildings he had renovated; he shrugged
off questions about his health. My mother asked after
Peter. He told her about the book he was writing on
the Sydney Opera House, about biking across France.
"My goodness!" said my mother, who was nervous. "All
that way!" Peter enthused about new developments in
high-rise architecture and then glanced at my father,
who was pouring himself another glass of wine. Had he
been following any of this stuff?

"Come off it, Peter," he said. "You know it's all completely specious." Earlier in the evening he had won
Jane over, but now she turned on him.

"What *do* you care about, Geoffrey?"

He stared at her. "Nothing much," he said. "I'm a
nihilist, aren't I, Katharine?"

I shrugged, embarrassed. "I don't know," I said.

Jane stood up. "Right. Let's eat." She led us to the

table, where soon enough we enjoyed ourselves again. But to my father, she didn't say anything further.

After dinner he went outside to smoke a cigarette, and Peter joined him in the garden. The women sat at the table drinking coffee. Alice laid her head on her mother's shoulder. She purred and yelped. "We speak to each other in cat language," Jane explained.

"Peter hates it!" Alice said. "He begs us to stop," and they laughed. They were so exotic, I thought, so wonderful.

In the car on the way home I asked my father if he and Peter had had a good conversation. "No, not really," he said.

"How come?"

"Well, I'd had too much to drink, and he was being boring."

"Oh," I said, and turned to the window. At dinner Peter had produced an old black-and-white photograph of my father and himself at university, a publicity shot taken for *Clip-Kit*. In it they were staring sternly at the camera, my father holding a copy of the magazine—it was clear they were trying to look as serious as possible. (For what they were doing was important! New technologies in architecture!) But instead they just looked young. I cringed, imagining their exchange in the garden. Peter would have tried to engage my father, once, twice, three times: he was tolerant and kind, and as passionate and driven as he had been at nineteen. And my father—*he* was the boring one—would have disparaged everything that Peter said.

I can't celebrate my father's declarations of happiness at having renounced his ambitions because I don't believe him. Words like "rubbish" and "specious" were his own attempt at deprecating and concealing that which moved him most, at making light of the fact he had not done the things he might have done. He *wasn't* happy, and giving up—on architecture, on life itself, even—was, far from an honest acceptance of his limitations, a betrayal of that uncommon radiance he once possessed.

Mr. Ramsay's fear of insignificance is so great that an offhand remark about nobody reading Scott anymore incites him to pick up *The Antiquary* so as to prove it untrue. But rather than hiding behind illusions of permanence, he bravely questions their validity. Man's "fame lasts how long?" he asks himself. "His fame lasts perhaps two thousand years. And what are two thousand years? . . . The very stone one kicks with one's boot will outlast Shakespeare." Such interrogation is just one example of what Woolf calls his "power, his gift," and it's one to which he will remain forever faithful: "he would not die lying down; he would find some crag of rock, and there, his eyes fixed on the storm, trying to the end to pierce the darkness, he would die standing." Something similar is true of Lily, who banishes her doubts by taking up her brush again, and of Virginia herself, who went on to write eight novels after her first nearly drove her to suicide.

Such is the nature of Woolfian failure, which, despite my urge to conflate them, turns out to be a different breed from my father's own. We see Mr. Ramsay stretch often in *To the Lighthouse*—to reach R, to pierce the darkness, toward his vanished wife; in our final view of him, he stands up "very straight and tall" in his boat, stretching his body toward the lighthouse. He will not grasp what he is seeking. R remains inaccessible, and darkness won't give way to light; Mrs. Ramsay is dead, and the novel ends before he can set foot upon the lighthouse rock. But the vigor with which he continues to strive is a triumph, and one that breaks my heart when I compare it to my father's own surrender. Striving would have nourished my father, I think. Striving might have even saved him.

IN 2006, MY father received a call from Peter. Peter had been invited to speak in New York, at the opening of an exhibition called *Clip/Stamp/Fold: The Radical Architecture of Little Magazines.* The show featured *Clip-Kit*—would my father be interested in coming? No, thanks, he said. He wasn't really up to it, and anyway, it sounded dead boring. A few weeks later, in New York, I saw a poster for the exhibition taped to a wall. There indeed was *Clip-Kit*, a great-looking magazine, its pink-and-white cover bound by a red clip.

The exhibition was in a long narrow room, and the magazines were displayed chronologically on the walls and inside plastic globes. A prerecorded voice was talking over a loudspeaker; with a pleasant shock I realized it was Peter. When I got to *Clip-Kit*, I paused to read the blurb. "After transferring from Bristol University to the Architectural Association (AA) in London," it read, "former *Megascope* editor Peter Murray began collaborating with fellow AA student Geoffrey Smythe [*sic*] to produce *Clip-Kit: Studies in Environmental Design.*" Before leaving I took a few photographs of the exhibition with my cell phone. I tried to show them to my father, but they were too small and blurry for him to make out.

15

I never met my father's father—he died of heart disease mere months before my birth—and for many years my only knowledge of him was a large framed photograph that sat upon my grandmother's desk. In it, he was reclining in the cockpit of a sailboat, and he looked a kindly person, with white hair, glasses, and tanned skin. Even as a child I had looked at this picture with interest, feeling a kind of condescending sorrow for the old man from my grandmother's other life who had had the bad luck to die. ("Oh, the dead!" thinks Lily, "one pitied them, one brushed them aside, one had even a little contempt for them.") But my understanding of Charles Smyth expanded somewhat when, rummaging through my grandmother's cellar one night, I found a newspaper article written on the occasion of his memorial service, an event attended by hundreds of people. He had been education officer for Slough and Eton—a service for which he was awarded an Order of the British Empire and a visit with the queen—and much loved, apparently, by his former colleagues and students. My grandmother read an excerpt from John Donne's "Meditation XVII," a reflection written at a time of illness: "Any man's death diminishes me, because I am involved in mankind," she quoted and then said, "I am quite sure it would be true to say of Charles that above all he was involved in mankind."

What struck me most on reading the article, however, was the text of a short note my grandmother had found among her husband's papers. *No grief, please*, he had written. *I've had a good innings.* I was deeply affected by those words, not really for the man I'd never met, but because I hoped, and yet was doubtful, that when the time came my father would be able to say something similar.

16

"It is enough! It is enough!"

My favorite sentence in all of *To the Lighthouse* comes at the end of Mrs. Ramsay's episode of solitude. As she sits alone, feeling herself aligned with the lighthouse's third stroke, her serene acknowledgment of death—"It will come, it will come"—becomes an exalted affirmation of happiness and the value of the moment:

> With some irony in her interrogation, for when one woke at all, one's relations changed, she looked at the steady light, the pitiless, the remorseless, which was so much her, yet so little her, which had her at its beck and call (she woke in the night and saw it bent across their bed, stroking the floor), but for all that she thought, watching it with fascination, hypnotised, as if it were stroking with its silver fingers some sealed vessel in her brain whose bursting would flood her with delight, she had known happiness, exquisite happiness, intense happiness, and it silvered the rough waves a little more brightly, as

daylight faded, and the blue went out of the sea
and it rolled in waves of pure lemon which curved
and swelled and broke upon the beach and the ecstasy burst in her eyes and waves of pure delight
raced over the floor of her mind and she felt, It is
enough! It is enough!

I love this sentence for its beauty, its strangeness—what
are waves of pure lemon?—its splendor and its surging
exultation; I love it too for what I see as its encapsula-
tion of the book itself, its evocation of Woolf's unrelenting search for meaning in the face of death. At the same
time as her novel was beginning to take shape—and as
a deep depression was again beginning to govern her
mood—she found herself reflecting on a recent trip to
France. "L. & I were too too happy, as they say," she
wrote in April 1925, "if it were now to die &c. Nobody
shall say of me that I have not known perfect happiness." The sentiment prefigures Mrs. Ramsay's own
revelation, of course, getting at how—for Virginia, as
for Othello—perfect happiness (such a simple concept!)
is bound up in death in ways both good and bad; it forces
us to confront our own mortality, yes, the fact that *all* is
fleeting, but it also provides what may be the best and
only consolation for these truths. Indeed, central to Mrs.
Ramsay's discovery is the idea that—despite its pitiless-
ness, despite its remorselessness—the passage of time is
ultimately unable to efface the great gift of a moment,
and that a moment is enough.

Yet Mrs. Ramsay's words, while far from a capitulation to her predicament, are not exactly a celebration
of it either. Hung about with exclamation points—
marvelous on the page, but the reason I'll probably steer

clear of that tattoo—the word "enough" appears triumphant, an instance of genuine victory over life, that
old antagonist. But "enough" is mere adequacy, mere
sufficiency—not abundance, undoubtedly not ideal fulfillment. Mrs. Ramsay's happiness may partake of eter-
nity, but she herself will die within the year. Here, then,
is the most Woolfian of epiphanies: ambiguous, equivo-
cal, and wholly fitting of a writer whose work is charac-
terized above all by inconclusiveness, and who, like Lily
in "The Lighthouse," the novel's third section, found
herself longing for a great revelation that would almost
certainly remain elusive. "I enjoy almost everything,"
Virginia wrote in February 1926, a time at which *To the
Lighthouse* was pouring from her with uncommon ease.
"Yet I have some restless searcher in me. Why is there
not a discovery in life? Something one can lay hands on
& say 'This is it?' My depression is a harassed feeling—
I'm looking; but that's not it—thats not it. What is it?
And shall I die before I find it?"

A FEW MONTHS after our dinner at Peter's house, in the
fall of 2000, my father underwent the last of the three
chemical treatments aimed at curing his bladder cancer.
The first two treatments had failed. We were warned it
was unlikely the third would succeed, but in November
he called me, his voice alight. He'd just had his checkup,
he said, and for the first time in all his years as a cancer
patient, his doctors hadn't found a single tumor. "We're
going out to dinner to celebrate."

By February, the tumors had returned. No further
treatments were available; the only option was for my
father to continue to go to the hospital at three-month

intervals to have the growths removed. Meanwhile, however, I was happy—truly happy—for the first time in years. From the very beginning of freshman fall, when I'd spent the night with a senior and walked home barefoot at sunrise, heels in hand and laughing out loud at the thrill of it, college had felt like it held space for me in a way that high school never had. I didn't think much of the English department and its New Historicist bent, but I made great friends; I took up Italian; I discovered comparative literature, enrolling in courses on Strindberg and Ibsen. As a sophomore, I even fell in love.

It was against this backdrop that my father, who must have reconciled himself to small surgeries every three months for the rest of his life, became the unexpected beneficiary of that operation—revolutionary in those days—to remove his bladder entirely. He was only fifty-four, and his body free of cancer for the first time in nearly a decade. But he was not at peace.

"He's changed, you know," my mother reported while I was still at Oxford.

"What do you mean?" I said. Ever since his bout with delirium tremens, any reference to my father's condition had roused in me a feeling of alarm.

"He's . . . I don't know. Calmer. Less excited than he was. Less funny. A bit remote." And then, "I'll be interested to see what you think." As if he were a book she was recommending, I thought, or a movie. Her obliqueness frustrated me, but at the same time I thought I knew what she meant. I was used to speaking to my father on the phone for well over an hour. He would take the receiver out on the deck, along with a drink and his cigarettes (every so often I'd hear the click of a lighter, a slight pause, his deep inhale). I would tell him stories; he would laugh and say, "It's lovely chatting with you, I feel we haven't had a chat in ages." Since the operation, though, we hadn't spoken for longer than five minutes. My mother would have trouble finding him, and on taking the phone he was unfocused and abrupt. I would speak, he would listen, and then he would say, determinedly, "I must go. I've got to finish my lunch." Or "set the table" or "make some calls" or "water the plants"—any number of excuses for "ringing off."

Aside from our Virginia Woolf pilgrimage that spring and a few long weekends over the summer, I didn't see my parents again at any length until the following Christmas, which we spent visiting family in Australia. My father seemed well, I thought, and, if drinking, drinking less. Each night we stayed up late, talking and reading. He had started *To the Lighthouse*, to please me, but found it detached, hazy, delicate. He was too insensitive, he said. He liked Dickens, Trollope, and Raymond Chandler. The place we were staying was overrun with wallabies and possums, and every evening the possums dropped down from the eucalyptus trees and landed at our feet. If we did not raise our legs, they tried to climb into our laps, and later, once I had left my father and gone to bed, I could hear through the screen his ongoing conversations with them. "Hel-lo!" he would call, in the same warm voice with which he would one day speak to my cats, and sometimes, when the creatures sought to jump onto his shoulders, "Look, you *are* a nuisance," or "Stop it, you silly thing." Animals and children: they loved my father.

By Christmas Eve his mood had changed. We spent

the holiday at a distant cousin's sheep farm in Tasmania, and over dinner I watched as he helped himself to glass after glass of wine. I watched the cousin and his wife, neither of whom had ever met my father, watch him too. ("If he drinks again, he'll drink himself to death.") Outside the light was fading, and through the window I could see the low hills across the lane, at sunset a pretty gilded green, turn dark purple, then dark gray. We spoke of wool, of irrigation, of hanging laundry on a line—he was so grateful, my cousin said, that he had had the courage to give up engineering and city life. Hostile, my father opened another bottle of wine.

The next day, Christmas, we left for Tasmania's west coast, once considered the end of the world. For years it had been accessible only by sea—a wild sea, a sea still known for its shipwrecks. My father continued to drink; there was a tense Christmas dinner, a terrible fight, that freighted silence. I sat alone in the bedroom. My father is destroying himself, I thought. I tried to read, my mind skittering over the pages; I put down my book and went out to the deck.

His shape was barely visible against the dim gray harbor. "Hey," he said when he saw me crying. He put his arms around me. The night was cool, misty; I could hear waves slopping at the seawall below. "Let's go inside," he finally said, putting out his cigarette.

He followed me into the bedroom. "Don't worry," he said as he shut the door. "This isn't your life."

"It *is* my life," I said. I sat down on the bed; he sat facing me. I remember the aseptic bedspread, the sheen of oak veneer. "I'm crying about your drinking," I said. "It's ruined my life since your surgery." I was stilted, as always during these kinds of conversations. I was so worried I would alienate him that I spoke in shorthand, using words that cast mere shadows of the truth.

"How?" he asked. His tone was dismissive, and I realized then how drunk he was.

"I'm depressed, I'm unhappy," I said. "I'm petrified of your dying."

"You never told me that." He took my hand and pressed it.

"But why do you do it?" I finally asked. "When you know . . . Why do you do it?"

He looked right at me. "Because I don't care that much."

Those words—I felt like I'd been punched.

The bathroom door opened; my mother had finished her bath. He rolled his eyes. "We'll talk later," he said, withdrawing to the deck.

The following day we went by boat to the shallow, treacherous mouth of the harbor—Hells Gates, they call it—and my father stood upright and apart. He wore a black windbreaker and mirrored wraparound sunglasses we had found on the street, and where his eyes should have been was the battered bronze of the sea. I thought him evil then, and impenetrable, and so too later when he clasped my hand again and said, "We will talk soon." That evening he pulled over without explanation and threw up on the side of the road.

A FEW WEEKS later, back in Sydney, we went for a swim and afterward sat on beach towels in the sun. "Shall we have our talk now?" he asked, surprising me. "I guess so," I said.

I faltered at first, and he became facetious, claiming yet again that there was no medical reason why he should not drink. His excuses were evasive and familiar. He needed some hobby to keep him occupied; his work was not demanding enough. I grew frustrated. He was so transparent, I thought, so *gutless*. When I said again how terrified I was that he would die, he simply looked puzzled. "Why?"

"Because I love you!" I yelled. "Because you are my favorite person!"

"Oh, well, I suppose I always think of myself as being a bit superfluous."

I was looking, when he said that, at a narrow dock that cut into the harbor, at white paint peeling from its pylons, at water turning muddy at the shore. When he spoke again, it was as if some tide had changed its course.

"I don't want to upset you," he said, his voice suddenly sincere. "You're the most important person in the world to me." And then: "I'm sorry. I love you so much." It was the only time I heard him say it, that he loved me, and it was what I wanted. He never explained for what he was apologizing, and when I told him how terrible I thought those words—*Because I don't care that much*—he did not take them back but held more tightly to my hand. It did little to console me. But I was so close to him then, and he to me, and with it I was joyful, and with it whatever had happened, and whatever was to happen, had a kind of unreality. *This* was the mean level of the sea, this the zero point, and all the rest was only rise and fall.

Before we got up from the beach, he told me he had been thinking about sailing to Cuba. It was a long haul, he said, and a bloody expensive one at that, but he figured that he (and I, if I wanted to come along) might be able to leave in the spring. "Wouldn't it be neat!" he cried, becoming a younger version of himself. "Wouldn't it be fantastic?" His excitement was electrifying; I recognized it from another time. And now, remembering its resonance, it occurs to me that my father at fifty-five had forgotten how to be well, and forgotten how to access the particular ease—the particular complacency, even—that wellness brings.

Virginia Woolf was well acquainted with the unique psychology of sickness, sending regular dispatches from those foreign lands to which our maladies expose us. An attack of influenza brings to light the "wastes and deserts of the soul," she writes; a trip to the dentist's chair carries us "down into the pit of death." She may be exaggerating for effect—though her own episodes of madness almost certainly bared her to such chasms—and yet hers is a serious argument for how illness separates us from the healthy, whom she calls "the army of the upright," and how, for the invalid, "the whole landscape of life lies remote and fair, like the shore seen from a ship far out at sea." My father's operation had taken place nearly a year before—he had been cancer-free for almost twelve months—but he still behaved as if he were stuck aboard that ship. It must be so difficult to bid farewell to one's secret world of illness, and perhaps more difficult still to reclaim and trust in one's new place among the living. When my father spoke of sailing to Cuba, though, it was as the promise of passage ashore.

———

IN THE MONTHS that followed, I started worrying less about his death. He refused to attend the AA meetings his doctors recommended, but he did go to Faulkner three times in the next three years. (His returns from rehab were always excruciating—I couldn't speak to him on the phone without searching his voice for traces of alcohol, and if I was home I found myself sneaking sips of his cranberry juice to see if it was spiked. It never was.) I always nurtured a sliver of hope that this time his sobriety would last, but it was almost a relief when—in two weeks' or two months' time—I watched him pour himself a glass of wine. To *know* he was drinking was less exhausting than being suspicious, and less agonizing.

Shortly after Christmas, he decided to sell our first boat, *Mistral*, and buy a sailboat my parents named *Solent*, for the strait where they'd first sailed together. On the weekends I spent in Rhode Island that summer, I found him flushing water through the bilges or scrubbing weed from the propeller; in the evenings we went for spins around the island. Then, while my mother took the wheel, he and I threw overboard the yellow polypropylene line and let ourselves be towed downriver as we had done when I was little. He was consistently contented and relaxed—he even put on weight—and the gloominess that had for the past year governed his mood was largely gone. Was the rediscovered pleasure of messing about in boats a necessary piece in making real to my father the verity of his own good health? I can't say for sure. But while it would be a mistake to align this acceptance, whatever its cause, too closely with Mrs. Ramsay's own epiphany, there's something about her recognition that our moments of joy are sufficient to sustain us in the face of death that feels enlightening. I believe my father found a kind of happiness during those hours spent on board, and perhaps even that it, too, was enough.

At the end of the summer we sailed to Newport; it was the only overnight trip I ever took on *Solent*. I was already in bed when my mother called me up on deck. She was standing at the stern looking down, and when I joined her I saw below the shape of my father, halfway through a late-night swim, floating on his back and buoyed by a cloud of brilliant violet light. Jellyfish. Tiny globes that flushed and flared in the blackness, their purple cilia like longitude lines, trembling and collapsed. Burned, burned out, and burned again; the ocean flickered on and off. At first I pretended I was not moved, but then warmed slowly at the beauty of it: my father's pale, healthy body in the raven sea, carrying with it a fragile lavender halo, now this way, now that, and he grinning, kicking his arms and legs, stirring, whipping the water into a churn of light.

17

In St Ives, the fury of the sea is at the heart of things. If you take a cruise to Seal Island, hugging the crumpled, lime-green Cornish cliffs, your guide might be a lifeboat captain, retired now, who remembers climbing the seal-strewn rocks as a child and being stranded as the tide rushed in. If you dine at Alba, a restaurant named for a 1938 shipwreck that drowned five sailors (and would have drowned many more had not people waded in with torches), you might see through the window the rituals of the current lifeboat crew—they hold up beers and laugh and flirt while hosing down a blue-and-orange vessel on the wharf. If you stop in at the coastguard station, where you can buy used paperbacks for twenty-five pence to benefit the cause, you'll find the latest incident report tacked to a bulletin board and full of small-town drama: "Reported large drifting object to Coastguard. RNLI Lifeboat returning from another incident confirmed it as a dead seal." And if you roam the town's twisting cobblestone streets, you will probably chance upon a large bronze plaque, tarnished and

sweetly wordy: IN MEMORY OF THE MEN OF SAINT IVES WHO
LOST THEIR LIVES IN THE PURSUIT OF THEIR PROFESSION
OF FISHERMEN WHILE WORKING IN VESSELS REGISTERED IN
THE PORT OF SAINT IVES. It offers up a long list of the de-
parted: brothers and cousins, it seems, and perhaps also
fathers and sons.

Later, reading up on Godrevy Lighthouse—which
sits upon a long, treacherous reef they call the Stones,
and which Virginia Stephen visited in 1892, signing a
guestbook that would later fetch £10,250 at auction—
you'll learn of dozens of additional disasters, among
them my favorite: the 1649 wreck of the *Garland*, a ship
carrying the clothing and furniture of newly beheaded
King Charles I and his fugitive queen. Of the sixty or so
passengers, a man, a boy, and a wolf-dog were the sole
survivors; they scrambled up Godrevy Island, where
they briefly lived on seaweed and rain. For years afterward, it was said, gold buttons would wash up on the
beach at Hayle. Or another: the 1939 wreck of the *John
and Sarah Eliza Stych*, a lifeboat that capsized three
times while trying to rescue an unfamiliar vessel in a
storm. The only surviving crewmember was William
Freeman, who managed to swim ashore near Gwith-
ian; in his youth, he had worked as a boatman for the
Stephens. ("On Saturday morning," wrote ten-year-old
Virginia in the family newspaper, "Master Hilary Hunt
and Master Basil Smith came up to Talland House and
asked Master Thoby and Miss Virginia to accompany
them to the light-house as Freeman the boatman said
that there was a perfect tide and wind for going there."
Then, with casual brutality suggestive of her future
writing, "On arriving at the light-house Miss Virginia
Stephen saw a small and dilapidated bird standing on

one leg on the light-house. Mrs Hunt called the man
and asked him how it had got there. He said that it had
been blown there and they then saw that its eyes had
been picked out.")

And if, on your last morning, you clamber up the
steep path to the headland known as the Island, you
will reach St Nicholas Chapel, a stone sanctuary built
in the early fifteenth century for the patron saint of
sailors. Its silhouette dominates the landscape—it may
have stirred you with its mystery that first night when,
stumbling upon an unknown beach, you looked up to
see it glowing high and yellow on the cliff, a lighthouse
of a different kind—and now, astride the threshold, you
will find yourself startled by its smallness and simplicity. The day is somehow bright and cloudy all at once;
sea pinks blanket the hillside like clumps of melting
snow, and the beaches below are radiant and white as
bone. ("It's because of the sand," says your proprietor of
Cornwall's famous light, "it's made of silica and blinding at low tide.") And looking out on the ocean, soft
as velvet today and just as dull, and murmuring those
rousing lines, *We perished, each alone*, Mr. Ramsay's
lines, *But I beneath a rougher sea*, you will marvel that
it could hold such violence, that such a pacific-looking
body would take from us even a single man.

18

"But it would be a mistake, she thought, thinking how they walked off together, arm in arm, past the greenhouse, to simplify their relationship."

My father had been free of cancer for nearly four years when my parents decided to join me for Thanksgiving in New York, where I had settled after college. I was looking forward to seeing them, and particularly to seeing my father—recently returned from a visit to rehab, he hadn't had a drink in two months. On the evening before their arrival, I tripped across a dead mouse that was lying on my carpet. It was on its back, its little teeth bared; its gray fur was matted, as though chewed on, and one of its hind legs was bloody. I yelped, and that night dreamed that the walls and windowsills of the house in Rhode Island were swarming with rats.

The following day my father carried up the bags and promptly stepped on a second dead mouse that was prostrate in the entryway. "Ah—a nest!" he exclaimed. We put the turkey in the fridge next to the nonalcoholic beer, went for a walk along the river, and then sat in my living room waiting for the kettle to boil. When there was a lull in the conversation, my mother looked at my father, then at me. "We have some bad news, I'm afraid."

I looked at my father. "You're sick."

"Yes," he said.

Several weeks before, his routine CAT scan had revealed black spots on his lungs. There were three possibilities: lung cancer, which was untreatable; kidney cancer, which was untreatable; or bladder cancer, which could be contained with chemotherapy. Because my father's oncologist had recently retired, it took nearly a month to schedule and receive the results of a biopsy. My parents had learned only the day before that the spots were bladder cancer.

"But bladder cancer is good?" I asked.

They hesitated. In the past few weeks, my father had also been complaining of back pain, and his new doctor thought that the disease—which, I suddenly realized, must have been lurking in his body all along—might have already spread to his bones. If that were the case, then his chances of survival were much lower: bladder cancer patients with metastatic deposits in the lungs often respond well to treatment, but those with bone metastasis have an average life expectancy of one year. A bone scan was scheduled for the following week.

That night we rented *March of the Penguins*—eggs cracking in the cold and fluffy chicks being carried off by vultures. We were still watching the opening credits when there was a scrabbling in the kitchen: Oscar, my cat, had caught a third mouse. He held it tightly in his mouth and ran in excited circles around a kitchen chair. The mouse was only a baby; still trapped between Oscar's jaws, it waved its tiny legs and a minute later died. My father scooped it up and dropped it down the garbage chute, and we continued with the film. But the incident had left me distracted. When Oscar later sat on my lap, I was repulsed—I couldn't expel the image of the animal struggling inside his mouth.

My parents left as soon as the movie ended. I was brushing my teeth and Oscar hovering by the stove when he suddenly lunged at something underneath it. He emerged with a fourth mouse that was very dark gray and even smaller than the third. "Okay, Oscar, drop it," I said, assuming he would kill it as quickly as he had the one before. But instead he carried it into the bathroom, and when I followed him, he turned on me, crouched low, and hissed. I was frightened—I'd never heard him make such a sound before. "Please, Oscar, just kill it," I pleaded. "Please just kill it, please." I watched as again and again he let the mouse run alongside the bathtub, only to attack it when it reached the wall. In its brief moments of freedom, the mouse sat motionless on hind legs, front paws raised. Finally it made a break for the living room: it refused to die. There Oscar caught it again and batted it across the wooden floor; he caught it again, and this time succeeded at lifting it into the air with his two front paws. When he finally dropped it, the mouse ran into the closet and inside one of my boots. I sat on the floor and wept.

Eventually Oscar retrieved his prey and carried it back to the bathroom. The mouse had grown weak; now when he dropped it on the floor, it simply lay there. It was still alive when, forty-five minutes after the initial pounce, I could stand the game no longer and swept it into a dustpan. Once inside, the mouse curled up with its eyes closed. No wounds were visible, so it looked peaceful, as though it were sleeping. I was still crying when I took it out into the hall.

I called my father soon afterward to say that Oscar had caught mouse number four. "Tomorrow we'll block up the mouse hole," he said. I told him I felt sorry for it. "Oh, Katharine," he said. "Your heart's too large. You saw the movie—nature's cruel."

MY FATHER DID not have cancer in his bones, which is why his doctor gave my parents permission to postpone chemotherapy and travel to Australia. Once there, though, he began to feel very ill. He made an appointment with a second doctor, and the resulting X-ray—taken just six weeks after the original CAT scan—showed that the tumors in his lungs were dramatically enlarged. "If I were you," the Australian doctor said, "I'd get on the next plane home." So my parents flew back to Boston, where my father would start chemotherapy just after Christmas. They said that the speed with which the tumors had grown was not necessarily bad news—according to a third doctor, chemotherapy is more successful at treating fast-growing cancers than slow ones. I clung to the comment, as I did to a statistic that someone had mentioned in passing: bladder cancer is successfully contained in two-thirds of cases. But these were just words.

The imprecise nature of treatment became even clearer when, during winter vacation, I went with my parents to meet my father's new nurse. Erika gave us what she called "Chemo 101"—the treatment would last six months; it would be two weeks on and two weeks off; the most significant side effect would be fatigue;

my father would lose his hair. She was careful to stress that we were not in a curative mode, but a maintenance mode: the cancer would never go away, but with luck it could be put into remission. Earlier that day I had happened upon my father's list of questions for the meeting. "Side effects?" he had written. "Time frame?" And at the end, "Worst case? When?" When he asked Erika for a prognosis, though, she said only that it was too soon to tell.

Meanwhile, it was the most peaceful time I had spent with my parents in years. My father was tired from the chemotherapy, and his face drawn and aged, but he was also sober, and consistently tender and kind. And as his two temperate months turned into three, four, five, six—I didn't know how or why—I started to forget the terrible fights, the bloodshot eyes, the silly, sinister moods: all that life had been before. Within a few weeks his hair had fallen out—"I'm a little baldicoot!" he told me cheerfully over the phone, for by that time I had returned to New York. But he was not in pain, and even when he did start drinking again—of course he started drinking again—my parents remained a different couple from the pair they'd been before. My mother attributed the change in him to lorazepam, the anti-anxiety medication he'd been prescribed. They called them his "Be Nice to Minty" pills.

One night, around the time we were expecting the treatment's initial results, I called my father at home. It was too late to phone, but my urge to speak with him was strong and sudden. His voice was small. He had not been asleep, he said, but he was in bed, reading Trollope. I asked if he had heard from the doctor; he said, no, they were doing the tests on Tuesday. Finally I mentioned something I was working on for grad school, an essay about him. I assumed he would be pleased.

"Oh, god," he said. "The lengths we go to getting you educated." I laughed, but his tone made me uneasy. "It's not the money," he said, "it's the ignominy."

"I'm not sure I know what 'ignominy' means," I admitted.

"My voice is croaky," he said. "You'll have to look it up."

As soon as we stopped speaking, I went to my dictionary. The definition left me surprised and chastened. My father—of whom I expected imperviousness—was ashamed.

WE RECEIVED THE test results a few weeks later. Erika had said we should consider it good news even if the number of tumors in his lungs remained constant, but in fact the scans had shown a marked improvement—"A new lease on life," he told me over the phone. The tests that followed showed the same. My family's peaceful period endured. When the doctors discovered a cancerous growth on my father's spine, and suggested he suspend chemotherapy for a month's worth of targeted radiation, it seemed just one more obstacle to overcome.

Then, in August, my mother called to say that my father was in the ER. He'd had chemotherapy the previous morning, but, ignoring instructions to take it easy, had spent the afternoon working on the boat. He was unable to make it home before throwing up—my mother said later that his vomit looked like wet coffee grinds strewn across the front steps. She took him to the hospital, where the doctors eventually concluded that dehydration, coupled with too little wine to drink at lunch, had triggered a second case of delirium tremens.

I returned to Boston the next morning. My father had been moved to intensive care, to a long room with a window at the far end, though the glass was blocked by too many pieces of hospital equipment to let in much light. These machines—sixteen in total—beeped and flashed; one displayed the green scrawl of his heartbeat, another his blood pressure, and another his body temperature. The intravenous drips, when they were about to empty, ping-pinged forlornly; when he later acquired a breathing tube, its papery lung inhaled and exhaled like a scuttling octopus. He might have been sleeping when we first walked in, but for his right eye, which was open and staring at the ceiling. The nurses had tried gluing the eyelid closed—a clear crust of adhesive lined his lashes—but it kept popping open. I approached him and kissed his forehead; it smelled medicinal. Then a team of radiologists came to install a PICC—a twenty-four-inch tube that would wind its way from my father's inner elbow to his heart. I returned two hours later to find crimson, coin-sized drops of blood speckling the linoleum floor; no one bothered to mop them up, so they dried there and turned rusty.

It was several days before my father woke. I was excited to see him sitting up, but he looked at my mother and me with no sign of recognition. He shifted in bed; I noticed that his wrists were now restrained. "How are you?" I asked. Accusingly, he turned to me. *Who are you*, he mouthed. "I'm Katharine," I said. "I'm your daughter." I touched his arm. "Who are you?" he asked again, and fell asleep. My mother joined me at his bedside. Alone in the big, empty Boston house we had been fighting like dogs, but now, seeing her bent over her husband, smoothing his thin hair, I found myself moved. "Poor Geoffy," she said. "I hope he's not miserable."

The look of love on her face was humbling—in all this time, I hadn't once thought of my father's experience. Nor of my mother's own, for that matter. "You know, it's been so long," she said later, "thirteen years of this, that sometimes I feel like I'm going to die first." The words surprised me. But the day my father was diagnosed with cancer in his lungs was the day she turned sixty—of course she must ponder her mortality along with his.

"But to go on with their story," Lily thinks of Paul and Minta Rayley toward the end of *To the Lighthouse*, "they had got through the dangerous stage by now." She recalls how Paul has taken up with a mistress—a solemn woman with braided hair whom Minta describes with admiration—and how, from the friendliness and pragmatism with which Minta handed Paul his tools when their car broke down, it was clear that everything would be okay. "Far from breaking up the marriage, that alliance had righted it. They were excellent friends, obviously." The anecdote gives Lily a sense of triumph over Mrs. Ramsay and her antiquated notions—"It has all gone against your wishes," she imagines telling her. "They're happy like that; I'm happy like this"—and yet the story also makes a case for the plasticity of marriage, for its capacity to continually evolve. The Rayleys' union could be considered the foil to the Ramsays' own, but I think it's more imaginative to view those two relationships not as "good" or "bad," but as differing examples, out of a countless number of examples, of the idiosyncratic, often unwieldy bonds we forge in wedlock, and as yet another reminder that, in marriage as in life, nothing is simply one thing.

When Lily sees the Ramsays walking on the lawn, her impulse is to turn an alliance of boundless complexity into a symbol: "So that is marriage," she thinks, "a man and a woman looking at a girl throwing a ball." This moment, in which Mrs. Ramsay, sensing her husband's wish to protect her, shakes herself from solitude to join him, is my favorite that the couple shares. They engage in easy conversation—"Pray Heaven he won't fall in love with Prue," she says of the odious Charles Tansley, to which Mr. Ramsay replies that he'd disinherit her if she wedded him—but they brave, too, a painful episode in which Mrs. Ramsay cannot confide her private thoughts: "He did not like to see her look so sad, he said. Only wool gathering, she protested, flushing a little. . . . No, they could not share that; they could not say that." But though "the inadequacy of human relationships"—Mrs. Ramsay's phrase—runs deep here, it doesn't diminish the couple's intimacy. Later in the walk, she guesses that her husband is thinking of the books he might have written had he never married. But he "was not complaining, he said. . . . And he seized her hand and raised it to his lips and kissed it with an intensity that brought the tears to her eyes, and quickly he dropped it."

Following on the heels of Mrs. Ramsay's self-protectiveness, this gesture shows us what we *can* share, what we *can* say; it's a testament to the glory of love *and* the glory of marriage, inadequate though both may be. And while the exchange is likely based upon the Stephens' marriage, one that instilled in Virginia that "tremendous, absurd, ideal of marriage" with which she began life, I expect she took inspiration from her own as well. Marriage to Leonard may at times have felt like servitude, but it could also be an overwhelming source of joy. "I was overcome with happiness," she wrote when, in 1937, he implored her not to leave him for the weekend. "Then we walked round the square love making—after 25 years cant bear to be separate . . . it is an enormous pleasure, being wanted: a wife. And our marriage so complete."

My parents had been married for over twenty-eight years on the day my mother stood at my father's bedside, smoothing his hair and worrying about his comfort. Maybe they would have been better off apart, maybe each would have had a greater shot at fulfillment had they found the force of will to separate. But the fact is that they *didn't* separate; that for nearly half their lives they were as entangled as it's possible for two human beings to be; and that, though I used to feel inclined to scorn their marriage, to do so was as mistaken as to simplify the Ramsays' own. My parents' connection was infinitely more complex than I gave it credit for; it was a living thing that sometimes shrank and sometimes grew. It was tender, it was vicious; it adapted itself to the facts on the ground. It held majesty in addition to its heartache, and its most vile moments could not negate its best.

I WENT TO the hospital every day that August, and every day I stayed for eight hours. I worried sometimes that the nurses would think me naive, for my father, still sedated, would remember nothing of it. But, I thought later, lying in bed in Rhode Island, listening to the whisper of the waves outside and finally approaching sleep myself, the reason I spent so much time at the hospital was not that I thought it would soothe my father. I went to the hospital because I liked it. I liked stacking my cafeteria tray with prepackaged salads and cups of tea, and the soft rainbow of scrubs worn by nurses, and the way these scrubs draped over brown and black clogs. I liked the barren beauty of words such as cannula and catheter, so at odds with the drama requiring their use, and the brisk foreign language spoken by doctors who swept so quickly through the halls that they seemed to leave a wake. And I liked the hospital's efficiency, its sterility, its impersonality, and I liked, most of all, the illusion that I was an integral part of that enormous, well-oiled mechanism that was keeping my father and so many others alive.

Sometimes he opened his eyes. Sometimes he even smiled. Once he opened his eyes and looked at me questioningly. "Cancer?" he whispered. "Yes, Dad, you have cancer," I said, and he started to cry. "But you're fine," I said. "You'll be fine." By now all four of his limbs were restrained; the head nurse, Jim, said he had been trying to climb out of bed in the middle of the night. Every few minutes he asked for a pair of scissors, and the words returned me each time to the nightmarish precision of his request years earlier—*Get me a short, sharp knife.* "Get me out of here," he whispered now, and "Take me away, take me away, take me away." I stood by his bedside, and the machines—sixteen in total—beeped and flashed: his guts, spilled from his body and made anew, from metal and from plastic. Was the body merely an appliance, indifferent and supplantable? Or was it something else entirely? The days passed and the monitors were switched off, one by one, until at last he was deemed stable enough to move to a regular hospital room, though even there he was in shackles half the time.

The final connection was a catheter that ran from his neobladder to the Foley attached to the bed; for days its contents had been a bloody light pink, the flesh of a grapefruit, but eventually the tube ran clear and a urologist ordered its removal. "Your urine looks absolutely beautiful," he told my father. "You could drink it." Soon we would drive to Rhode Island, where the specter of a hurricane was passing through, where I would catch my father smoking on the hammock, and where, later, lying in bed, I would consider the weeks lost to the hospital—their small horrors and small triumphs. I knew the sense of accomplishment I felt at our having survived them was misguided: this ordeal had been merely a digression, the trials that mattered yet to come. But it was still an extraordinary place, the hospital; a rare, incomparable place. And perhaps my father was thinking something similar, for on the morning he was to leave it I found him sitting in a chair, looking out the window. The catheter had been removed; he was unfettered once again. Beyond the glass was the low swell of Beacon Hill, and behind it, the higher swell of downtown, and then, just visible behind another building, the silhouette of the pink granite skyscraper where I had, some twenty years before, ascended thirty-four stories to meet my father—a dark-haired young man in a dark suit who swung me into his arms, took me with him to the cocktail lounge, ordered me a glass of bright red maraschino cherries. His defiance was gone now, so too his raw sorrow—he was himself. "It's amazing they've even kept me going this long," he said.

When I think of the changes we witnessed in just twenty years of waterfront living, I am reminded of the summer I began crossing paths with a certain mallard duck. The first time I saw her, I was reading on the front porch. A red pickup truck came to a sudden stop in the middle of the street, and the driver laughed as he watched her lead eight ducklings toward the water. She quacked, and pretended to ignore him; the ducklings, some still emerging from the tall yellow grass that lines the hill opposite, struggled to keep up. The next morning I was still in bed when I heard the sound again. Throwing off the covers, I went to the window and watched as one by one the ducklings, now returning to their nest, slipped between the pale stalks. From then on I was attuned to her call, which, though quiet, was so distinctive and persistent that once it even carried over the blare of the radio as I was driving home. I slowed when I heard it and then I saw a solitary duckling, brown, downy, no larger than an apple, bobbing down the road before me. I stepped out of the car and waved him toward the beach; like a windup toy he spun in a circle and carried off in the direction I had sent him. Then I spotted his mother, watching us uneasily from beside an overturned dinghy.

I saw her for the last time one evening, when, sitting down to dinner, I heard her song rising from the beach below. Leaving my own food, I grabbed some stale bread and walked a little ways down the dock. The sun had already set behind the houses and a line of peach light fading to blue ran along the treetops. To the south, a slow-moving slab of cloud blazed a brilliant hot pink. The water was mirror-smooth, and in its surface, broken only by the silhouettes of sailboats, was reflected this line of peach, this faded blue, this blazing hot pink wall of cloud. I tore off pieces of bread and threw them in the water. The mother duck swam toward me. Her ducklings had been resting on the shore—in the twilight, with their legs tucked beneath them, they'd looked no different from the stones of the beach—and now they hurried to the water, happily braving the miniature waves. That night, I saw with a shock, there were only two.

I thought I was alone, but then I heard someone on the next dock say hello. It was John, our neighbor, returning from a swim. I felt embarrassed at being discovered. "Just feeding the ducks," I said, and he said, "Oh!" He hadn't seen them until now.

"Do you remember," he asked, "when we used to have big birds? The swans that would come in the morning?"

"Yes," I said, "and there were those seven geese that swam in a line up and down the basin."

"That was ages ago, wasn't it?"

I nodded. "I'm worried," I said then, of the ducklings, "because there were at least eight of them a few
days ago."

"They do disappear," he said.

Later I poured myself a glass of wine and sat outside on the deck. The cloud to the south was gray now,
and ordinary, and the salmon light over the treetops
shrinking and intensifying as the sky grew dim. A few
mature ducks were floating near the dock, their bodies
black against the blackening water, and as I watched
they were joined by more ducks and still more. By the
time the sky had darkened completely, there were several dozen of them, a navy protecting the seashore, and
their low, relentless call—the same call I had grown
accustomed to hearing from the mother duck, now mul-
tiplied by fifty—made a chorus that was amplified by
the water. I looked hard for any miniature shapes that
might signify a duckling, but saw none.

I had never seen so many ducks in the basin, nor
had I seen them gather in this way. But the waterfront
is perpetually evolving. The year we arrived, hermit
crabs furrowed the sand, and petite, haughty-looking
sea horses could be found darting and hovering in the
shadows beneath the docks. A large oyster bed grew in
the mud, and our neighbor, a young clam fisherman,
helped to cultivate it with his children by gathering
stray oysters and adding them to the pile. A seagull we
named Sally liked to walk the length of the seawall,
and to seize the clothing we had left out to dry. She
would take a sock in her beak, carry it with her as she
rose, and drop it on the beach as other seagulls will drop
crabs. Sally's greatest trick was knowing when someone
was taking a bath upstairs; then she would land on the

sloping roof above the dining room, peer through the window that is eye level with the tub, and tap her yellow beak upon the glass.

I don't remember when I realized that the oyster bed was gone; that I had seen neither a sea horse nor a hermit crab in several summers; that Sally had not returned. I would say it takes time to become aware of an absence, but then again, the year the clam fisherman killed himself and his family moved away, that loss was immediate and engulfing. The geese I'd mentioned to John disappeared over ten years ago, and I haven't seen one since, but last summer, walking up the dock, I saw beneath me the remains of a dead goose drifting downstream. Its plump body was still afloat, but its long, thin neck hung straight down in the water, occasionally dragging along the basin floor.

One summer we had great blue herons, and another summer we had lion's mane jellyfish, tangled, reddish fiends up to a foot in diameter whose sting is like a terrible sunburn. I rarely swam that year, too fearful to enjoy myself, but my father did, and kept on hand a jar of meat tenderizer to neutralize the venom. Horseshoe crabs have come and gone, and egrets, and the summer my father ended up in the ICU we had more starfish than ever before. If a starfish is left in the sun too long, it will ossify to a crispy brown and die, and I got in the habit of climbing down the seawall ladder at low tide and tossing into the water those creatures left behind. There would be over a hundred baking slowly in the heat, and I liked the work of picking them up by their dense, scratchy, dark-pinked limbs and skipping them, like stones, into the sea. The task reminded me of a story I had read as a child, about a woman who walks along a vast beach throwing stranded starfish out into the waves. "Why bother?" a stranger asks her. "You'll never be able to save them all." The woman pauses, picks up a single starfish, and casts it into the ocean. "Yes," she says, "but I just saved that one." I had always hated that story, had always felt irritated by its cloying sentimentality, and it bothered me, as I tossed star after star back into the basin, that I could not banish from my mind that vacuous phrase—*I just saved that one.*

PART TWO

1

It was the day after Christmas, a winter morning that began as mornings often did: waking, walking downstairs, seeing my father bent over the newspaper through the doorway to the family room; his hearing me in the hall and saying to my mother, "Do I hear the pitter-patter of little feet?" As I made tea they read aloud small pieces of news that pleased or provoked them and then we talked vaguely about going to Rhode Island. A pale day pressed against the windowpanes—Rhode Island would be cold—but we decided that we would go, after all, and my mother rose to pack some food.

My father rose too, to pour himself another cup of coffee, but he stumbled and fell against a chair. He held up a hand to calm us, yet his face was tight with fear. "I can't breathe," he whispered. He began to pace, staring down at the carpet and inhaling raggedly. "I can't breathe," he said again, more to himself than to us.

"Katharine, take him to the clinic," my mother said. She went to page Erika.

I led my father through the hall and into the

brightness of the street. He was gasping, clutching my arm, but ignoring me completely. In the family room I had assumed the fit would pass, but now—the remoteness of his mind was startling—I had the feeling we had crossed into new territory, a wilderness terrible and undefined.

At the clinic, the nurses gave him oxygen and fixed wires to his chest and arms; his oxygen absorption, even with assistance, was just 70 percent. For some minutes he continued to gasp, concentrating on the floor, but then he returned to himself and was even able to protest when the doctor insisted he go to the emergency room. "Not again," he moaned. "I couldn't face it." Soon afterward, he was carried on a stretcher into the back of an ambulance.

At the hospital, they wheeled him into a long queue; a mask was strapped to his face, and he had lost color, but he smiled when he saw me and held out his hand. We were still waiting to be admitted when Erika sprinted down the ER hallway—not to offer assistance, but to confirm his living will. "Geoffrey, I know we've talked about this," she said, "but I need to make sure. Should the need arise, you don't want any heroic measures, right?"

"No, absolutely not," he said. He could hardly speak.

I didn't understand then what heroic measures were. I would never have expected my father to agree to life support, but the phrase seemed to suggest something different—a challenging operation, perhaps. And because everything was happening so quickly (an hour ago we were packing for Rhode Island), I reacted with the panic of a child.

"Dad, why not?" I cried. He didn't say anything, but Erika looked at me sadly. "It wouldn't be appropriate," she said.

Nurses came and went, doctors came and went. The hours elapsed. It was already nighttime when an unfamiliar doctor appeared; he was handsome and officious. My father in turn was a veteran patient, one whose alternating charm and mordancy either pleased or affronted his doctors. In this case, neither seemed enamored of the other.

"When did this all start?" the doctor asked, flipping through his chart.

"Forty years ago, when I started smoking."

The doctor didn't acknowledge the joke. "What are your symptoms?"

"I can't bloody breathe." By this time my father's mask had been replaced by an oxygen tube. I could see from a monitor in the corner that his intake was stable at 90 percent, though his blood pressure was half what it should have been.

"I need to ask you an important question," the doctor said. "Should the situation become acute, which is a distinct possibility, do we have your permission to use an intubator?"

"Christ, we've already been through this," my father said. "No heroic measures."

Hearing the phrase for the second time that day, I started to cry. The doctor ignored me as he repeated what we had already been told: there were three possible causes for the collapse, a blood clot in the lungs, an infection like pneumonia, or the cancer itself. Eventually, he left.

"Asshole," my father said. "How many times do we need to go through it?"

A group of radiologists wheeled in an X-ray machine. My mother went for a cup of coffee while I sobbed in the hallway, distressed enough that a teenage burn victim and her mother—the girl confined to a wheelchair, one side of her face red and textured, like mashed strawberries—felt the need to console me. "Is that your father in there?" the mother asked when I had pulled myself together. "Oh sweetheart, I'm so sorry."

When I returned to the room, my father looked up and smiled. "Hello, lovey," he said. He was sitting up, the arms of his sweater draped over his hospital gown and a pair of glasses dangling from his neck. A sailing magazine was open on his lap. Aside from the tube running beneath his nose, he looked as he always did: relentlessly alive.

I sat down in the chair beside his bed. "Are you scared?" I finally asked.

He shook his head. "No."

By then it was well past midnight. We tried to nap, we tried to read. "You know the more I think about it," he said at one point, "the more I think that doctor was nuts."

"Which doctor?" my mother asked.

"Exactly," he said. "Witch doctor!"

My mother and I laughed, and I thought how difficult it was to believe in death for more than a few minutes at a time.

Somewhere outside the sun was rising. My mother had gone to get some sleep; my father was still sitting up, his sweater tied around his shoulders. I told him how frightened I was and then I told him he was my best friend.

"That's a lovely thing to say," he said. "I think I thought I was just a silly bee."

"No, Dad, I mean it," I said, trying to make him understand.

"Look, you're making me cry." I looked at him and saw his eyes were watering. He gave me his hand and I took it, and as we sat there holding hands against the sheet, I felt, together with my grief, a strange elation at how moved he was. "I've been shedding a few tears myself here and there," he said. And then, "I think it was only this fall that I realized how sick I was."

"I think I only just realized," I said.

It was true, and later, once it became clear that everyone else had known all along, I thought how surprising it was that my father and I were the last to know.

The next day my parents and I met with Erika and Dr. Kaufman, my father's oncologist. His loss of breath was not caused by a blood clot, they said, nor by an infection like pneumonia. It was caused by the cancer itself, which, in the two weeks since his last scan, had colonized his body completely. As we could see from the X-rays they held up to the light, his lungs were riddled with new black shadows. He had been scheduled to begin an experimental chemotherapy treatment in just a few days, but now, said Dr. Kaufman, it was no longer a good idea. Paradoxically, Erika explained, the sicker you are, the less effective chemotherapy becomes. No one in the room said what this meant, exactly, but this is what it meant: after fourteen years, we were done trying to save my father.

2

Shortly before the start of "Time Passes," Mrs. Ramsay visits her youngest children in the nursery, where, to her annoyance, she finds them sitting up in bed, quarreling over the boar's skull that their uncle sent them from the colonies and that she foolishly allowed them to hang from the nursery wall. Although James shrieks whenever his nurse tries to remove it, Cam is terrified of the horrid shadows that it casts across the room. "Well then, we will cover it up," says Mrs. Ramsay, who, trying and failing to find something suitable in the children's drawers, takes off her shawl and winds it round the skull, transforming its jagged bone into a soft shape upon which to project the most enchanting fantasies. She "laid her head almost flat on the pillow beside Cam's and said how lovely it looked now; how the fairies would love it; it was like a bird's nest; it was like a beautiful mountain such as she had seen abroad, with valleys and flowers and bells ringing and birds singing . . ." When these words, echoing ever more rhythmically, finally succeed at sending her daughter to sleep, she crosses to James's side of the room to assure him that his beloved skull remains intact. "See, she said, the boar's skull was still there; they had not touched it; they had done just what he wanted; it was there quite unhurt." James hops from bed to make certain and then, once he too is tucked in, Mrs. Ramsay pulls down the window, gets "a breath of the perfectly indifferent chill night air," and steals downstairs to meet her husband.

I first learned of her death exactly five years before my father's collapse. It was the night after Christmas, and I was curled up on a cot in my grandmother's study.

The others had gone to bed long before, and, rather like the novel's poet, Mr. Carmichael—who stays up late reading Virgil but eventually blows out his candle, as if to say that unlike Dante we must navigate this hell without assistance—I was reading well into the early hours. I can still remember my grief and indignation at the revelation; what shocked me most, at least at first, was its detached and oddly graceless language, trapped between the bars of a parenthetical aside: "[Mr. Ramsay, stumbling along a passage one dark morning, stretched his arms out, but Mrs. Ramsay having died rather suddenly the night before, his arms, though stretched out, remained empty.]" These words were appalling. I loved Mrs. Ramsay deeply, already, and I saw her death— not only bracketed, but the subject of a subordinate clause!—as a cruel trick; it made me want to toss the book aside, in anger and sadness, yes, but also because the prospect of confronting the next ninety pages without her seemed intolerably dull. I understood even then that it was life's cruel trick and not Woolf's own—that, as the premature deaths of Stella Duckworth and Julia and Thoby Stephen attest, the universe is eminently capable of dealing out the "holocaust on such a scale" that Mrs. Ramsay thinks improbable in "The Window." But it is only now I realize just how accurately "Time Passes"—in the indifference that it flaunts, in the desperation it arouses, even in the boredom that it promises—replicates the experience of severing from the person we love.

Shortly after Mrs. Ramsay's death, the shawl she wrapped around the skull begins to slacken, a tiny movement that is nevertheless likened in its violence to the fracturing of a mountain: "in the middle of the night with a roar, with a rupture, as after centuries of quiescence, a rock rends itself from the mountain and hurtles crashing into the valley, one fold of the shawl loosened and swung to and fro." This is the fairy-tale world that Mrs. Ramsay created for Cam, with its beautiful mountains and valleys, but now on the brink of collapse; and, with it, the collapse of Cam and her siblings' childhood illusions. For as the wrap that has been an emblem of Mrs. Ramsay's protection continues to unwind—a few pages later, "the rock was rent asunder; another fold of the shawl loosened; there it hung, and swayed"—it becomes clear that there is no escaping the horrors it once veiled. The unraveling shawl: I can think of no better metaphor, not just for Mrs. Ramsay's vanishing but also for the stretch of days, concentrated and raw, that followed my father's fall, with their gradual baring of the bone beneath his skin, and of those savage truths from which, up until then, he had largely succeeded at protecting me.

3

At home, we made up a room for him to die in. The study where I had been staying seemed the most sensible. I cleared a space for the oxygen machine and organized stray books into piles. I vacuumed the rug and dusted the gray-veined marble mantelpiece. I moved my things to the living room, putting down sheets for myself on the couch, and when I'd finished, I felt better than I had in days.

A hospice nurse arrived soon afterward. She described the symptoms my father could expect in the coming weeks; she listed the medications he would take and the numbers he could call in case of emergency. To my mother she handed a bottle of liquid morphine to store in the fridge, and to me, a little blue book called *Gone from My Sight: The Dying Experience*. She said, when he asked, that she expected my father to live for another three to six months. "Six months!" he exclaimed. "What a bore."

The days following her visit blur together now, and perhaps this is odd but I remember them fondly. I spent New Year's with friends who were visiting Boston; we watched fireworks from their waterfront hotel and drank too much of the unlimited champagne included in our prix fixe dinner. My father was still well enough to pick me up the next morning, and I made him pull over so I could throw up in the street. "Poor Poppet," he said and then, "What a neat little thrower-upper you are!" But the temperature was falling, and that was the last time we went outside; instead we stayed indoors and watched movies. He wore the black fleece pants and red fleece bathrobe my mother had given him for Christmas along with a fleece hat, fleece mittens, black silk long underwear, and a fleece electric blanket for the car.

This new wardrobe, which made my father satisfying to hug, disguised his thinning, disappearing body. He didn't speak often of the fact he was dying—death appeared in wry asides, and in conversations with friends overseas. Nor did he begin to speak emotionally. And yet he did become more physically affectionate, and it was rare that he would pass my mother or me without folding us into his arms.

He spent a lot of time in the kitchen, standing next to the exhaust fan with a newspaper spread open on the counter and a cup of coffee at his hand. This was the only place in the house where my mother permitted smoking, though by then she would have let him smoke wherever he wanted. I sat on the counter next to him, or on the floor with my cats, in whom he took a lot of pleasure. It no longer bothered me when he smoked, except when he grew careless and walked too near the oxygen tube with a lit cigarette. And I did think about how absurd it was that the prospect of my father lighting himself on fire could inspire such conventional fear, the kind of fear that should have belonged properly to the past. It all comes to the same thing, I reminded myself. Death is death. Yet we retained the instinct for preservation; my father winced when, on New Year's Day, he swerved to avoid a car accident, even though the night before he had spoken of suicide. We have little capacity, it seems, for drawing connections.

I spent the days making my father cups of coffee, watching television, deciding whether or not to take a term off school. It was only at night, when I woke with a start to the vast, tenebrous living room, that I had a sense of the wildness that encroached. I lay awake remembering what it was to sit on the deck in Rhode Island; I thought about the ways in which the world had darkened and enlarged, how being a human being had suddenly become a more serious occupation than it once seemed. I thought of strangers I had seen on the street, of how many of them had endured this and worse. How could people be asked to endure this?

And yet all the while I had the sense that I was perceiving only the shadow of the thing and not the thing itself—that I had as yet no idea what enduring was.

Because before I'd gone to sleep I had sat with my father in the study, listening to him talk; soon it would grow light and I would hear him creep downstairs and retrieve the paper from the front steps. I would open the door to the family room and find him bent over the news, and at the moment I saw him, my body would loosen and relax, and the terror of the night become unreal. As long as this continued, as long as he was here, it was impossible to fathom what it meant that one day soon he wouldn't be.

4

"But what after all is one night? A short space, especially when the darkness dims so soon, and so soon a bird sings, a cock crows . . ." We may easily survive one night, Woolf assures us; the trouble is that night follows night follows night, that "the winter holds a pack of them in store and deals them equally, evenly, with indefatigable fingers." They were simply biding their time, those forces that gave me the gift of a morning that was so soothing in its sameness, those forces that seemed to respect human life sufficiently as to leave the Ramsays sleeping undisturbed. ("Whatever else may perish and disappear," says the speaker of those dormant bodies in their beds, "what lies here is steadfast.")

For it's only a matter of days before the outside world that during Mrs. Ramsay's dinner party had seemed so safely banished begins its full assault. The succeeding nights are rife with "wind and destruction," the trees "plunge and bend," the sea "tosses itself and breaks itself." Mrs. Ramsay dies abruptly in the middle of the night, and her husband, arms outstretched, lurches down the hall without her. And if, in the midst of this tumult, a solitary sleeper wakes in the small hours, throws off his covers, and descends to the beach to seek "an answer to his doubts," he will be bitterly disappointed, for he will find there nothing that can "bring the night to order" and make "the world reflect the compass of the soul."

I used not to know what to make of this sleeper or those nameless others who haunt the pages of "Time Passes." I believed I grasped their formal function, but— and this is the heart of it—I could not bring myself to care about them; and so too the section as a whole, in fact, which was dizzying in its ambition ("this impersonal thing, which I'm dared to do by my friends, the flight of time, & the consequent break of unity in my design," Woolf called her radical experiment), but which also left me cold and longing for the pathos of the Ramsays' private lives. But I see now that this longing is the point; that these sleepers are not mere bloodless wraiths; that they are you and they are me; that catastrophe transforms us in that way; that it momentarily connects us, ordinary people, to the bones beneath the shawl and sends us on a search for answers in the dead of night that is archetypal and inexorable but that if we try to talk about it sounds at best symbolic or overwrought at worst. And that the answers prove elusive is a lonely, frightening thing. But the search itself? "Almost it would appear that it is useless in such confusion to ask the night those questions as to what, and why, and wherefore, which tempt the sleeper from his bed to seek an answer." Almost.

5

Hospice had been under way for nearly a week when we remembered *Gone from My Sight.* The book was still sitting on the table where the nurse had left it. "One to Three Months Prior to Death" sounded almost pleasant—it was a time of sleepiness, of diminished interest in food and the newspaper, of "withdrawing from everything outside of one's self and going inside." But we did not like the sound of "One to Two Weeks Prior to Death," which described disorientation, plucking at sheets, conversations with ghosts, a body temperature that oscillates between chill and fever, and a blue pallor to the nail beds, hands, and feet. We liked "One to Two Days to Hours Prior to Death" even less; it was a time of restiveness, erratic breathing, glazed, unseeing eyes, magenta limbs, mottled buttocks, and, finally, unresponsiveness. "What appears to be the last breath," the book said, "is often followed by one or two long spaced breaths and then the physical body is empty."

For the first time, it occurred to me to dread the stretch of hours between my father's death and his cremation, that weird limbo in which his body would persist without him in it. I struggled to picture how blank and baggy his skin would seem, how empty I too might then become.

One day I woke him from a nap, helped him sit up, and heard him cry out in pain more loudly and desperately than ever before. We had been introduced years ago to the oncologist's pain scale, a scale on which "one" signifies no pain and "ten" signifies the worst pain one can imagine. My father had always scoffed at the subjectivity of the pain scale, had always assigned his pain a modest four, but now, and on the nights that followed, he screamed and howled and pushed my hand away when I tried to touch him. "Ten!" he wailed. "Ten, ten, oh god, ten!" He was taking 160 mg of OxyContin a day then, but he might as well have been taking nothing. I sat with him on the bed while he cried, and I looked at the bookshelves that lined the walls. Sometimes I thought how strange it was that I could neither see nor feel the violence that was wracking his body, and sometimes I thought, in spite of myself, that this was the way that dying should be. How grim and gruesome and apt, I thought, that leaving life should look like this.

After some hours, the pain had passed. It had taken a frantic phone call to hospice and a trip to a twenty-four-hour pharmacy, but now we were sitting calmly on the living room couch. At my father's request, we were trying to write a prospectus of the boat for the broker who would sell it after his death. In the past week he had developed an obsession with organizing his affairs; he'd even expressed feelings of inadequacy for not yet building the bookshelves my mother had requested in the fall. (I'm reminded of "The Window" and its sense of thwarted action—of Mrs. Ramsay's half-knit stocking, of Lily's unfinished painting, of James's aborted journey to the lighthouse.) But my father's desire to leave things in order was greater than his ability, and as we sat there—I with a pen in hand, waiting for him to dictate; he staring blankly at the measurements of the engine he had installed the summer before—I could see how tired he was, how hard he was working just to wrap his head around ideas that a week ago would have been simple. I could see his mind failing.

"I do miss my energy," he finally said.

"Let's take a break, Dad."

"It's the most peculiar experience," he said. "I've never in my life . . . it's just not wanting to do anything."

So we rested instead. The reigning sounds of the living room were the heaviness of his breathing and the occasional rustle of the newspaper open on his lap. He was wearing his reading glasses and fleece robe; as at the hospital, the oxygen tube passing beneath his nose gave the only clue to his condition. It had been twenty-five years since he'd restored this room himself, and even now I was moved by its beauty. I let my eyes rest on its Victorian moldings, on its wide silver mirrors and marble mantles and walls the color of seashell. The phone rang. It was hospice, calling to ask whether his pain was under control. "It is," he told them cheerfully. "I may be dead in a few weeks, but I'm not dead yet." Later he closed his eyes, and eventually I drew my laptop to my knees and started to write. "What are you doing?" he murmured.

"I'm just typing away."

"Oh, that's nice, keep doing it. I find it very soothing."

He fell asleep; every so often I looked up to see the rise and fall of his chest. I was amazed at the calm that spread throughout the night—how different it was from the agony of the previous hours, and yet how different, too, from the ugliness of so much of our earlier lives. I didn't know it at the time, but this was a kind of happiness.

The following morning I left for New York, where I had decided to remain a student; when I returned to Boston three days later, I found a man significantly changed. He looked at me from across the room, gave a distant wave, and scuttled to the kitchen. "How are you?" I called. "Yes, yes," he said, and lit a cigarette. I followed him and he patted me on the head; his eyes were distant, and as he moved I noticed his curious new gait—a cross between a limp and a strut. He muttered to himself as he smoked. My mother had warned me that he was worse, that he was in pain and taking more medication than ever before, but I hadn't understood what that meant.

Looking after him then was exhausting. He darted through the house, crowing and babbling in response to imaginary voices; he stopped only when he became transfixed by the faces he saw in the folds of fabric. Then he would call me over and point them out, and the odd thing was that after a while I could see them too—enclosed in the creases of couch cushions were the long, thin visages of old men with drooping eyes and elongated chins. His pleasure when I finally did see the faces he saw was childlike and disarming.

Putting him to sleep was most difficult. It took hours to convince him to go to bed and just as I was looping the oxygen tube over his head and covering him with the blanket, he would decide he needed a cup of coffee or a final cigarette. Then he threw off the covers and hobbled downstairs; by the time he reached the kitchen, he had forgotten why he was there and we would have to prepare for bed all over again. This happened three or four times a night.

For the first time, it felt as if we were waiting for him to die.

We had been waiting all along, of course, but now he was no longer well enough to be conscious of waiting himself. Most of my attention went to caring for him, but I also spent a great deal of time willing myself to remember what he had been like just three days earlier. It was remarkable to me that this present self could occlude the selves that came before, and I was frightened death would do the same.

Time passed. His moments of agony became more and more frequent, and more and more severe, and one day hospice admitted his case was beyond their capabilities; he needed to return to the hospital, they said, to be treated by doctors who could monitor and respond to his pain full-time. So, less than three weeks after that lazy December morning on which my father stood for a second cup of coffee and stumbled from shortness of breath, we returned one last time to the hospital with this man too sick to die at home.

6

In the pages that follow Mrs. Ramsay's death, it appears as if the spirit of the Scottish home will continue to endure without her. "Loveliness and stillness" rule within the house itself, and even the potency of nature is unable to dethrone them: "the prying of the wind, and the soft nose of the clammy sea airs, rubbing, snuffling, iterating, and reiterating their questions—'Will you fade? Will you perish?'—scarcely disturbed the peace, the indifference, the air of pure integrity." Yes, the shawl will soon begin unraveling, and a floorboard comes untethered on the landing, but such threats cannot match the pluck of loveliness, or the fury of Mrs. McNab, the Ramsays' indomitable housekeeper.

Here, then, is a manageable view of death, one that suggests it need not hack away at our foundations and even endows it with some poetry, as if there were something romantic, something pure even, about the void left behind by the people we love. And so it was that, still reading in my grandmother's study, still grieving Mrs. Ramsay, I began to actually take solace in time's passage, in the progress it enables, as spring returns to the Hebrides, laying a veil of green upon its fields, and Prue Ramsay is married in another parenthetical aside, taking her father's arm as they walk down the aisle. It's against this setting—"how beautiful she looked!"—that we join the solitary sleepers as they venture once more to the shore, where summer approaches, the evenings grow longer (in June it's nearly ten before the last light leaves the basin, making it feel as if we have all the time in the world), and it becomes "impossible to resist the strange intimation . . . that good triumphs, happiness prevails, order rules." It's difficult to believe in death for more than a few minutes at a time.

But Woolf's ruse in "Time Passes" is to again and again give the lie to our complacency, just as life itself, that pouncing beast, always gives the lie to our complacency. In yet another parenthetical aside, we are reminded—how could we forget so soon?—that nothing is steadfast, neither good nor happiness nor order: "[Prue Ramsay died that summer in some illness connected with childbirth, which was indeed a tragedy, people said, everything, they said, had promised so well.]" The indifference of the announcement is horrifyingly familiar, as is the anguish it awakens (though less so the banality that replaces the peculiar, suggestive language that heralded Mrs. Ramsay's end—the brackets I kept scouring for the warmth and wit of "The Window" tell us nothing of the true cost of death). Then, on the following page, twenty or thirty young men are blown up by an exploding shell in France, "among them Andrew Ramsay, whose death, mercifully, was instantaneous." Prue who left one breathless with her beauty; Andrew with his extraordinary gift for mathematics—just gone. I felt tempted, first reading of that blasted shell, to fault Woolf for excess, for trampling the bounds of plausibility. But then I remembered: this *happened* to her.

(Oh, and that loveliness that once went hand in hand with stillness? It will fade and perish too. The Ramsays' home, forsaken now, is as vulnerable as the family it once sheltered.)

MY FATHER'S NEW hospital room was large and often bright. There was a window that looked across the river to Cambridge, and as the days passed I watched this river freeze from above, waxen ice spreading over its surface. Then the river was white, covered in a thin layer of snow, but inside the room it was seventy-six degrees, sunlight spilled across the floor, and my mother's narcissus bulbs burst and her tulips unfurled. Erika had laughed about the way this wing of the hospital looked like a hotel, and perhaps too much was made of this, for later, once my father had started to hallucinate, his most constant preoccupation was of persecution by a hotel staff. But Erika was right: as I looked around me at the turquoise lamps with their ruffled white shades, at the imitation Sargent hanging on the wall, at the faux-mahogany side tables and gray-blue foldout couch, it was hard not to imagine a Holiday Inn. As I had thought while transforming the study to a bedroom weeks before, How strange that *this* is where my father will die.

When he wore the nasal cannula that looped over his ears and under his nose, delivering six liters of oxygen per minute, his O2 saturation hovered at around 91 percent; when he didn't, it fell to 73 or 74. There were pills, of course: on an average day, he took 300 mg of Colace, 10 mg of Dulcolax, 17 g of MiraLAX, 20 mg of Celexa, 200 mg of Provigil, 15 mg of oxazepam, 75 mg of methadone, 10 mg of Decadron, 300 mg of Neurontin, 40 mg of Nexium, 30 mg of Compazine, and six tabs of senna; one 21 mg nicotine patch was affixed to his upper arm. These medications were intended to treat constipation, depression, anxiety, lethargy, insomnia, pain, bone pain, nerve pain, breakthrough pain, stomach acid, nausea, and nicotine withdrawal. At any given hour he was visited by an oncologist, a pain specialist, a team from palliative care, a doctor from the floor, a nurse from the floor, a chaplain, a social worker, a case manager, a nursing assistant, or Ham, the beaming Nigerian who bathed and shaved him.

And yet these placatory measures—the oxygen, the medicine, and the host of parishioning specialists—were largely invisible to the onlooker. Unlike my father's ICU bedside, which had four months before been a jungle of machinery, all beeping and flashing, this, his deathbed bedside, was vacant. A new bag of gleaming saline sat off to one side; the monitor that would once have displayed his vital signs was dark. He wore pajamas from home rather than the standard-issue paisley-print hospital gowns, and the sleeves of these pajamas slid easily down his bare forearms, unimpeded by plastic tubing or butterfly needles. Of course they did, for chemotherapy had failed. The goal had changed.

The day my father arrived, he was given an opiate nine times stronger than morphine through an intravenous drip; within hours he was no longer lucid, and within days he was hallucinating. I liked the hospital less then—realized quickly that my previous attraction to it had been inextricably bound up in the belief my father would get well there—but I still found comfort in its repetitions: in the steady stream of doctors, in the hot meals delivered to the room, in the young blond nurses with pretty names like Ashleigh and Isabelle, and in the act of pushing again and again through the lobby's revolving doors and ascending twenty stories to a high-shine, fake-wood-clad wing that offered sweeping, frozen river views.

Sometimes my father saw planes exploding through the walls and sometimes he held animated conversations with friends he hadn't seen in years. Sometimes he cowered before the nurses who tried to boost him up in bed. "Please don't leave me, Katharine," he begged then. He was in pain—he often clutched at his left shoulder, where a large tumor was encroaching on his spinal cord—and gradually, inexplicably, his left hand swelled so much that his fingers lost all definition and became cartoonish. He hadn't eaten in over a week. He hadn't had a bowel movement in over a week. Every morning he threw up yellow, sour-smelling bile; it spilled out in a rush and splashed against the sides of the pink plastic bowl we kept near the bed. Every few minutes he coughed up a lump of bloody mucus and slowly, methodically, folded it into a tissue and placed it on the table beside him. The tidiness of the gesture was his own—he folded the newspaper the same way.

There was little sense of urgency. Days passed quickly and unproductively; I spent my time holding cups of water to his lips, talking to nurses, or climbing into the hospital bed and lying by his side. Sometimes, when I put my head on his chest, he would, even though he was barely conscious, raise his hand and stroke my hair as he had done when I was a child. At other times he grew exasperated and elbowed me out of the bed. "It's not a bloody car park!" he exclaimed, and I laughed out loud. His mood was generally amiable and confused. He winked at me often, as if to suggest this was an inside joke we shared, and asked frequent questions, nodding his head in agreement at answers he did not understand. "I want to go home," he said, again and again. "We're here because they can monitor your pain better than we can at home," I said, again and again. "So we're better off here?" "Yes." "Okay then." A few minutes later: "Are we going home?" "No, we're staying here." Nodding, "Okay, that's fine." And again: "That's it—let's go home. Let's go home." "We can't go home." "Tomorrow? We can sail all day tomorrow?" "Yes, we can sail all day tomorrow." And then again: "I don't know if we're going to London or Paris tonight." "Not tonight." "We're going home instead, are we?" "No, it's the middle of the night." Nodding, "Oh, okay. But I'm never doing this again. Never ever." And the next day: "I'm getting fed up with this place." "Well, at home you were in so much pain, and here you're better." "I'll say." "But perhaps you can go home in a few days," I said. "And then I won't be ill," my father said. "Right,"

I said, holding back sudden tears. "And then you won't be ill."

One afternoon the doctors called my mother and me at home and advised us to return as soon as possible. His breathing had slowed, they said. He was dying very quickly now. We were at his bedside in thirty minutes; his eyes were open but unseeing, and his breath, warm and sweet, smelled like burnt caramel. His chest moved up and down more slowly than it had before: he would inhale, raggedly, then hold it, waiting full minutes before exhaling. Sometimes he held his breath for so long that I forced myself to believe that it was time. Then his chest would fall again, and I would relax. I was aware of a feeling of *wanting* it to happen, and when I felt this I would chide myself. Stupid, stupid, I said. Don't you understand that this— this sitting here—is all you have left? At one point I whispered in his ear that he was brave, and to this he said, "Rubbish." I worried until he spoke again that it would be his last word. To my mother he said, "Sorry, love"—said it as plainly and easily as he had when he was well—and with it she began to glow. "Did you hear that?" she asked.

At midnight he requested a pencil and a piece of paper. The pencil kept slipping from his hand, but eventually he grasped it and began to sketch, rapidly, as though he had something of utmost importance to chronicle. He drew a grid-like pattern that looked at first like a tic-tac-toe board and next like a ladder. Every so often he stopped and stared upward, searchingly, before returning to the page. He added a rectangle, a circle, another rectangle, and finally a wide U-shape across the entire design, and as he drew he continued to look upward at something neither my mother nor I could see. I began to feel nervous. Then my mother thought to follow his gaze, and when she did she exclaimed, "Look, he's drawing the ceiling!" I turned my face up, and immediately recognized the white acoustic tiles, the rectangular air-conditioning vents, the round light fixtures and U-shaped metal rack from which hung the bed curtain. He looked at us, when my mother said this, and rolled his eyes. Obviously, he seemed to say.

He continued for nearly an hour; he wrote the words "glass or plastic?" along the top, next to an arrow pointing at the lights. When he finally grew tired and dropped the pencil in his lap, my mother quickly took the pad and put it in her bag. I could tell it pleased her to think that the person he had once been—an architect—was still somewhere inside. It pleased me too, even as I sensed we were applying rules of sanity to madness: that my father was sketching the ceiling, as opposed to some dreamscape, did not make his performance any less alien. In time I began to scrawl every phrase he uttered, no matter how nonsensical, into the pages of the book I was reading. "This hospital, they control the clamshell," he said, and "Let's have a beer!" and to an imaginary friend in the corner, "I'm sorry, Jack, I'm a bit . . ." I thought he would never speak to us as himself again, and grasping at fragments and hallucinations seemed the only way to glimpse the contents of his mind.

We slept at the hospital that night—my mother on the couch and I beside him in the bed—and again the following night; over twenty-four hours had passed since the doctors had said he would die in minutes. Sitting in that room came to feel like traveling across an enormous ocean in an airplane. The air was hot and dry; the bottled oxygen hissed loudly in our ears. The intercom blared, its words coated in static, and fluorescent light from the hall crept beneath the door, preventing the room from ever becoming fully dark. It gets to the point, my mother said, where one feels one has never done anything else, and will never do anything else again. Against this arid backdrop were the images, crowding and repeating: light dappling the green and lilac of our porcelain vine; my father pickling lemons in oil and salt. Draped across his shoulders, my cat; and the deep red of the sail cover against the sky. The impressions were so remote, their scope so narrow, and I wondered whether remembering would be easier when I was no longer faced with his body on the bed before me. I looked forward to when I could gather every last piece of him into a pile: photographs, letters, scraps of paper. I was convinced that the hoarding of these artifacts would be almost as good as having him back.

On the second night I woke to the sound of his breathing. He had asked us not to draw the curtains, and the lights across the river floated up and in, bathing the bed and the floor in a pale, watery glow. My mother was asleep, her face to the wall, but my father was awake and staring out the window. I sat on the edge of the bed; he did not look at me, but past me, and his breathing was even slower than before. A breath and a silence. A breath and a silence. He jerked his head toward the door, then back toward to the window; he saw me, and, recognizing me, gave a quick, troubled smile. He seemed frightened, and I became frightened myself, sitting with him, waiting, beneath the bluish light. An hour passed, maybe two hours, until, suddenly—he had been searching for something out the window—he sat upright in bed, clutched at my hand, and stared straight at me with wide open eyes. "We're floating!" he shouted. "Grab the line! We're floating free!" His voice was full of horror. He pulled at my arm, begging me to understand, and I was shocked by his strength. "We're floating free," he shouted again. "For god's sake, Katharine, you and I are finished!" I tried to speak, but he stopped me. "No, listen to me," he cried. "We've broken away from the pylons and we're floating free. We're finished, you and I. We're finished!"

"No," I said. "No, Daddy, listen to me. We're at the hospital, we're fine. We'll be fine."

I could feel him slacken when I said that. "We're at the hospital?" he said. "Yes," I said. "We're at the hospital."

"Oh," he said quietly. He was very small then, a child. "Oh," he said again.

I continued to sit with him, and it was not long before he retreated back into himself, his breathing slow and halting again. A breath and a silence. A breath and a silence. The longer I stayed there, the longer it seemed that the high bed on which we sat drifted on the surface of the slick blue floor, and the longer it seemed, too, that the night outside was summoning us to it, that we had torn free of the pylons that were holding us to earth. I thought then that after all these years the time had finally come, and I was scared, and it was too soon: No, I thought, not yet, I thought, please not yet, I need to do more, say more, please. But as we held fast to that boat-like bed, floating now out over the river, I remembered, and was calmed by, a line about a weary sailor who after

circling round and round in stormy seas at last sinks to
the floor of the ocean with a feeling of immense relief.
It was Mrs. Ramsay's line, I realized later. *To the
Lighthouse* was already lighting my way forward.

7

Imagine your childhood home, abandoned in the wake
of some apocalypse. ("I could hardly bear to look at it
again," said Leslie Stephen of the impossibility of returning to Talland House without his wife.) Might the
books go moldy, the coats and dresses hanging in the
bedrooms disintegrate amid a plague of moths? Might
a rain pipe blocked with fallen leaves direct its stream
into the study, spoiling the carpets, and a mischief of
rats scamper through the attics where, long ago, you
had pinned strips of seaweed to the wall? Might hail
and damp accost the nursery, dislodging plaster from
the ceiling and rotting its weird souvenirs—"Whatever
did they want to hang a beast's skull there?" your em-
battled housekeeper might ask, noticing the bone's gone
moldy too. And when this same housekeeper finally
concludes that the job is too much for one woman, when
she shuts the door and turns the key, leaving the house
to fill with sand like a discarded shell and the shawl
to "idly, aimlessly . . . swing to and fro," is there *any*
power that might "prevent the fertility, the insensibility of nature" from triumph absolute?

Before she departed, the housekeeper had taken your
mother's gray gardening cloak between her fingers, had
observed her comb and brush upon the table; and from

these numb objects, the memories began to flow—the lady bending over her flowers with the washing; caring for one or other of her many children; reserving for the housekeeper a bowl of soup. For one hopeful moment you wonder if they, the memories, might themselves be equal to the force of nature; and, if not the memories, the objects, for how could an errant vine or thistle compete with the legacy of glass and china that has sat upon a dining table laid for fourteen guests? But the housekeeper's memories, far from lasting, "had wavered over the walls like a spot of sunlight and vanished." She had shut the door and turned the key. And realizing that "nothing now" withstands "the thistle and the swallow, the rat and the straw," that nothing now opposes them, you may even find yourself *courting* the destruction of that which you love most, that which once seemed indestructible. "Let the wind blow. . . . Let the swallow build in the drawing-room. . . . Let the broken glass and the china lie out on the lawn." *Sometimes*, says my friend who lost her mother years ago, *full months will pass without my thinking of her.*

And so it is that your abandoned home will one day reach a tipping point, a moment at which the whole house, grazed by the weight of just one feather, would have "turned and pitched downwards to the depths of darkness," would have "plunged to the depths to lie upon the sands of oblivion." This is an ageless vision; one day it will come to pass. But even should it rouse you with its terror now—Stupid, stupid, you might think, remembering the way you coveted disaster—so that you hurriedly write to the housekeeper to say you'll be back soon; so that she and a companion arrive with pails and mops, sponges and brooms, evicting spiders from their webs and lifting from the floor thick layers of filth; beating carpets, airing out long rows of books, polishing the baths and taps until they gleam; so that builders come to mend the fallen ceilings, and plumbers to replace the failed pipes; painters to refresh the walls stained brown by rain, and a gardener to mow the lawn and poison the rats; so that after seemingly endless weeks of labor this groaning army finally gathers up its tools and declares the task complete, even then this house upon its battered seascape will be a stranger to you. "Ah," said the housekeeper before she left, breaking at teatime and rubbing her face with sooty hands, remembering the marvelous parties that your mother used to throw, as many as twenty ladies and gentlemen gathered in the dining room, resplendent in their evening clothes and glittering jewels, "they'd find it changed."

8

For hours I sat on the edge of the hospital bed, waiting for my father to die. I waited so long that eventually the room began to brighten and then to flood with light. My mother rose, my father continued to breathe, and that afternoon he turned onto his side and slept, soundly, for nearly nine hours. He rustled the sheets when he woke, and my mother and I went to him; he opened his eyes and smiled in recognition. "Hello," he said. "I couldn't have some orange juice, could I?" He sucked the juice vigorously through a straw, finished it, and asked for some limeade. He finished that, asked for rice pudding and next for half a grapefruit. It was the first time he had eaten anything since his arrival. "I've been on the most amazing odyssey," he said, and spent the following hour recounting, in a voice that was confident and clear, tales of abduction, bobbing gold animals, and sulky bugs the size of tennis balls.

In the middle of the night he woke again. I had started to sleep with the wariness of an animal, and the moment I heard him stir I leapt up and approached his side. "What are you doing here?" he said when he saw me. "You poor thing. This is no life for a twenty-five-year-old, sleeping at the hospital." I liked the hospital, I said—I was thrilled at how himself he was—and offered him a cranberry juice. "For some reason I'm off cranberry," he said. "How about some coffee?" I ran down the hall to make a pot; when I returned, he asked for another rice pudding, coupled with a new concoction, a blend of blueberries, Jell-O pudding, and ice cream. I fed the mixture to him with a plastic spoon. On finishing, he asked for the second half of the grapefruit and finally to lower the bed. "I've enjoyed our midnight feast," he said.

The next morning Ham came to wash his hair. "Katharine," my father said, even more cogent than he had been the night before, "this is my hairdresser, Ham."

"I know Ham," I said.

"I can't believe you know my name!" Ham exclaimed to my father. "You're doing so good this morning!"

"Of course I know your name," my father said. Two days earlier, he had accused Ham of trying to kidnap him. The doctors concurred with Ham's assessment, though—with some surprise, they told me that my father's blood pressure and heart rate were both up.

That day I still held the pink plastic bowl to his mouth to collect his bile, and took from him the tissues in which he folded his bloody mucus. I helped him shuffle to the bathroom and slide off his diaper, trying not to look at his wasted legs. But I also poured endless varieties of fruit juice—"I like a degustation," he insisted—fed him meals bite by bite, and raised and lowered the hospital bed. I sliced pears into requested sixteenths and microwaved old cups of coffee; I made new pots of coffee and retrieved cartons of vanilla ice cream from the kitchen. At first I performed these tasks gladly, and with energy, but as the days passed and my father continued to improve, I began to feel irritated by his infinite demands. Then, seven days after the day the doctors told us he had mere minutes to live, they changed their minds and said it would more likely be six to eight weeks. What's more, they said, he would soon be able to go home.

I continued to sleep at the hospital, but now when I woke in the night to the sound of rustling sheets, my exhaustion struck me like a sickness. I squeezed my eyes closed and pretended not to notice that he was awake. But then I would hear the mechanical whir of the bed being raised—he had learned how to do it himself—and finally a meek voice: "Petal? You wouldn't bring me a little cup of coffee, would you?" The hospital hallways were bright and largely deserted then, the kitchen empty. I stood by the bed while he sipped the stale liquid—he was strong enough now to hold the mug on his own—and finally, liquid gone, bed lowered, I would turn him onto his right side and build a wall of pillows along the length of his back. Sleeping in this position was the only way he could avoid the tumor that continued to press against his spinal cord. He fell asleep easily, but I never could; long after I had turned off the lights and returned to the couch, I lay awake thinking.

His becoming unexpectedly better, and my being proven wrong once again about the room in which he would die, was reinforcing a secret suspicion I had carried with me for fourteen years now, a suspicion that, as close as we were, as close as we continued to get, it, his death, would never actually happen. When I considered what it was like, this waiting, I thought again and again of that old paradox, the one that says a runner approaching the finish line must necessarily run half the distance to that line, and half of that distance, and half of that and half again, so that he will never in fact arrive but simply continue to split the space left to travel; and I thought of the way in which my father's hospital stays—now piling atop one another at an almost exponential rate—seemed to halve the distance to death each time, and to nevertheless each time prevent him, evermore, from actually reaching the end.

In the days that followed, he was restless, disoriented, and good-natured. He was fascinated by the experience of being ill, and he wanted to entertain; he described at length his hallucinations and insisted I record them in my notebook. ("Try to have a nap, darling," my mother said. "I can't," he said. "Katharine and I are writing my memoirs.") His confusion meant that we didn't discuss anything "meaningful," as I thought of it then, but also that our time was unclouded by the grimness of previous weeks. We talked about rice pudding, methadone, and the best position for sleeping—he wouldn't trust the construction of his pillow-wall to anyone but me. "Katharine and I have a system, don't we, Katharine?"

he would say, waving the nurses away. We talked about ice cream, and whether or not doctors should have tattoos, and the joys of having a bowel movement for the first time in nine days. ("It's just the highlight," he exclaimed, "a major deal.") He fell in love with the word "bolus," the term for each new opioid injection and repeated it over and over: "Bolus, bolus, bolus." His vitality was seductive, and I think there were moments when I, too, forgot that he was ill. I know that when I later saw photographs of those weeks, I was shocked by how sick he looked. His skin was blotchy, his head too large for his emaciated frame, and his hair was so wispy and white that you could see through it to the outline of his skull. He had posed for the pictures with confidence, and I expect he thought he looked just fine, but his smile was feeble and expectant, as though the very act of raising his lips was a struggle. Returning to those pictures made me uncomfortable and ashamed; I had the sense I was looking at something too private, too obscene to be photographed.

One day his business partner came to the hospital, and for several hours the two men pored over papers and plans, my father trying to pass on all the knowledge Chris would need when he was gone. I doubt they accomplished anything, and I remember thinking how curious it was that the contents of my father's mind would so soon disappear—not just thoughts, feelings, and memories but also concrete information. Across the river from the hospital was a building that emitted a steady, balloon-shaped cloud of white smoke. "What is that?" I had asked my father one morning, assuming it was pollution. "Water vapor," he said, and explained that a such-and-such machine produced it for such-and-such a reason. ("He said it so wisely," Cam marvels of her own father, "as if he knew so well all the things that happened in the world.") It was startling to realize that these lessons, my education about the way things worked, were coming to an end.

My father was greatly tired by Chris's visit. "Tee-tee," he finally said, bidding his partner good-bye. I helped him prepare for a nap and walked Chris to the elevator. "It's amazing to see him so much better," he said as we waited for the doors to open.

The doctors were similarly astonished by my father's recovery—having predicted he would die the week before, they couldn't understand his new fortitude. The only one who wasn't surprised was my father's primary care doctor: he had known my father for years, and to him it made perfect sense that he would be clinging so scrappily to life. In the hallway my mother begged him for answers, for some inkling of what we could expect; he told us it could be weeks or even months before my father died. "You forget what a remarkable liver Geoffrey has," he said. "What a remarkable metabolism."

My father's persistence made sense to me as well, but I couldn't put my finger on *why* it made sense. It wasn't that he was spiritual, or that he believed life inviolable in some way. Nor did he love life absolutely; if he had, I thought, he wouldn't have lived it so recklessly. There was no doubt something in him—an energy, a restlessness of uncommon force, perhaps—that made him a singularly uncooperative victim. It was the thing that had for fourteen years allowed him to hold fast, the thing that even now was capable of delaying his departure for weeks and months on end. But what I still can't understand is how someone so self-destructive—so *anti-*

life, it sometimes seemed—could also kick and rear and hold such life within; how a man who claimed to have so little attachment to the world could nevertheless possess a body and perhaps even a soul that cleaved so determinedly to it. Why was my father so intransigent? Why was he still here?

9

Just after the death of Andrew Ramsay, the solitary sleepers, still roaming the beach in search of solace, catch sight of an "ashen-coloured ship" on the horizon, of "a purplish stain upon the bland surface of the sea as if something had boiled and bled, invisibly, beneath." Such mutilations of the landscape give these searchers pause; if once they found themselves placated by the majesty of sea and sky, now they must again confront the possibility that nature, no less ruthless than war-waging men, will not provide them with the answers that they seek. This may be the greatest shock of all: I know that I rarely feel more alone, more forsaken, than when I return to Rhode Island—that cathedral with its watery pews and vault of clouds, that portal (it sounds silly) to all that is most good and holy in this world—and it meets me not with revelation but with cool, unyielding silence; as if all those evenings on the deck when I felt myself so full of light that I thought that I might float away were counterfeit. "To pace the beach was impossible," the sleepers conclude. "Contemplation was unendurable; the mirror was broken."

"Time Passes" is Woolf's most pessimistic take on the likelihood of locating what she calls "the clear words of truth," but she does offer an alternative that, though it seems lofty at first, should resonate with anyone who—in pursuit of clarity or consolation or simply the deliciousness of feeling known and understood—has found herself crawling into bed with a good book. If we can't find meaning in the natural world, she reasons, if the relief it offers is mere artifice, then maybe we must turn to art instead. In one of the novel's final parentheticals, we learn that Mr. Carmichael's new collection has enjoyed surprising success, that the war has revived people's interest in poetry. Mr. Carmichael adored Andrew Ramsay; Mrs. Ramsay thinks with deference of the old man's devotion to her son, and Lily remembers hearing that when he learned of Andrew's death, he "lost all interest in life," a deprivation she senses in him as they share the lawn. But the poems he wrote in response to that loss—as *To the Lighthouse* itself grew out of loss—offer comfort to a population scarred by war; art may not give us the unequivocal truths that we desire from our world, but it can provide a stay against its chaos and confusion.

"Most fiction . . . makes us more aware of ourselves," Woolf wrote, while yet other of it fulfills our "desire to be steeped in imagination." Small wonder, then, that Scott's Waverley novels are among the first objects that Mrs. McNab rescues from the house; or that I drowned myself in *The Red and the Black* and *Wuthering Heights* during those long hospital weeks, escaping to the tower prison where Mathilde pays Julien Sorel a visit in disguise, and to the misty, rutted moors that so confound Mr. Lockwood as he makes his way to Thrushcross Grange; or that, at the very moment I believed my father to be dying, my mind alighted, quite involuntarily, upon the pages of my favorite novel, taking solace not just in its lessons but its language, in the rhythm and beauty of phrases as familiar to me as the sound of the waves that break in Rhode Island. "Who am I, what am I, & so on: these questions are always floating about in me," Virginia wrote while at work on *To the Lighthouse*, aligning herself with the restless sleepers who demand of the stone and the puddle, " 'What am I,' 'What is this?' " It was books—reading them, writing them—that would bring her closest to an answer.

WE HAD BEEN at the hospital for nearly a month when my grandmother and uncle Andrew arrived from England. They stayed at a hotel nearby, and every morning and evening visited my father in his room. They had come to say good-bye, of course, but we didn't talk about that; nor did we talk about the fact that for ten years—the result of a falling-out over something long forgotten—Andrew and my father had barely spoken.

On their last night, my grandmother and I went out to dinner, leaving my father and his brother alone. Andrew was still there when I returned three hours later; I could hear his loud English voice from halfway down the hall. He was sitting on the couch with a beer, gesticulating wildly about something, and my father was sitting up in bed and laughing. The hospital room, typically so sterile, seemed bright and warm; they had been great friends once. When I entered they looked up without seeing me, and Andrew kept talking. I could sense their reluctance to let the night go, and I was sorry to make them.

The following evening—the last my father would

spend at the hospital before going home—he woke from a nap feeling cheerful. I fed him a dinner of spaghetti, green beans, and tapioca, then climbed onto his hospital bed with a notebook. This time, however, he had no interest in recounting his hallucinations; he wanted to talk about business. He reached for the pen and drew a shaky, three-circle Venn diagram. In the center he wrote "DEAL," and in the first and second circles he wrote "PEOPLE" and "PROPERTY," respectively. But he couldn't remember what went in the third circle. "Money?" I offered. He laughed. "That's a good idea," he said. The answer didn't satisfy him, though, and we kept thinking. "Fate?" I said next. He laughed again, a real laugh, so that when I looked at him, his shoulders were shaking and his eyes all scrunched up. But "Fate" wasn't right either, and the longer we waited, the more palpably I could feel him straining. "Dad, I think it has to be money," I finally said, and with a start he agreed with me. "Of course!" he said. "Finance!" He wrote "FINANCE" in the third circle. "Gosh, you're good, Katharine," he said, and I felt ridiculously proud.

It was getting late, and I suggested he call my mother at home to say good night. "Katharine and I have written a book!" he exclaimed when she picked up. "We've written a book!" His delight was profound, and I can't help parsing it now—what is the legacy promised by such scribbling, the bridge that it builds to the future? What relief, what reward, that of imprinting ourselves on the page? My father paused, listening to her. "Well, at this rate I could have years and years to run," he said at last. "At this rate I could have forever. We may still be waving good-bye in another forty, fifty years' time."

I wasn't sleeping at the hospital that night. I fed my

father his pills, pressing each one into a spoonful of applesauce, then lowered the bed and turned him on his side. I lined the length of his back with pillows and drew the cotton covers to his shoulder; I closed the curtains and set a cup of tangerine juice on the bedside table. I turned off the lights and put on my coat, and finally I bent to kiss his cheek. It was warm and slightly bristly, and also slack and soft.

"You'll have a couple of fluffies waiting for you at home," he said sleepily, of my cats.

"Yes," I said. "I'll tell them you said hello." And then, "Good night, Dad. Sleep well."

"Mmm," he said, without opening his eyes. "Night-night, lovey. It was lovely having you."

He died two days later, in a rented hospital bed that sat in the middle of our living room. He was fifty-nine years old, the same age as Virginia Woolf when she died in 1941. My mother said that his last few breaths were slow, each one several minutes apart. Everyone who had seen my father at the hospital was stunned—"He seemed so well," they said afterward—but the doctors and nurses were unsurprised. "It often happens like this," they said.

10

In August 1905, Virginia Woolf and her siblings returned to Cornwall for the first time since childhood. On the night of their arrival, they—Vanessa, Thoby, Virginia, and Adrian, each in their twenties and newly orphaned after their father's death from cancer the previous year—decided to climb the hill from Carbis Bay

to Talland House, a distance of several miles. Julia Stephen had died a decade earlier, and their home sold soon
afterward, but as they approached the site of so much
early happiness, it was at first as if no time had passed
at all. "It was dusk when we came, so that there still
seemed to be a film between us & the reality," Virginia
wrote in her diary the next morning. "We could fancy
that we were but coming home along the high road
after some long day's outing, & that when we reached
the gate at Talland House, we should thrust it open, &
find ourselves among the familiar sights again." In this
fantasy, the years have collapsed and the house is still
home to that Victorian family of ten, but it's a fantasy
that transforms the living Stephens into phantoms, into
children homeless not just in space but time: "As we
knew well," Virginia concludes, "we could go no further; if we advanced the spell was broken. The lights
were not our lights; the voices were the voices of strangers. We hung there like ghosts in the shade of the hedge,
& at the sound of footsteps we turned away."

It was months after my father's death before I returned to the house in Rhode Island. Once there, I
treated it like a museum, touching nothing, as if the
same film that seemed to separate Virginia from her
reality had rendered me invisible, ineffectual, an apparition. In my parents' bedroom I avoided my father's
brown leather sandals, looking from afar at the glossy
imprint of dirt where his heels had been. When I hung
up my coat, I made sure it did not brush his sea-colored
down vest. Most disconcerting were the cigarette butts
I saw through the window to the deck. They could have
been smoked that morning. I felt something akin then
to what I had first felt on visiting Pompeii: the voyeuris-

tic sensation of stumbling upon that unexpectedly private thing, an ordinary day interrupted and preserved. So too here, where, for a short while at least, my father's death had petrified his life, preserving it with uncanny clarity, and in a form both recognizable and alien.

It was a wet day in April when I first arrived. The sky was gray, the sea was silver and gray, and as I felt the underside of the steps for the house key, I could see small circles bloom and bloom and bloom where rain hit the water beyond the seawall. The basin was empty of boats—deserted pink buoys glowed brighter than they should have beneath the lightless clouds—and the line of land across the way was bleak and brown, its faraway trees slight puffs of smoke. The island to the south was barely visible through the mist.

My mother had warned me the house was a mess. After emptying the boat for the broker, she said, she had dumped everything on the floor and gone back to Boston. That's fine, I had said, but as I walked through the rooms, turning on lights and opening blinds, I was stunned. The floors were strewn with stacks of paper and old sailing magazines, with pots and pans and cans of food. In the living room I found foul-weather gear and crinkled cotton distress flags; on the table, plastic mugs and a couple half-used bars of soap. In the billiard room—bereft now of a billiard table, for we had sold that, too—were life jackets, fenders, and tattered white sail bags. At the kitchen counter I nudged aside a tool kit to make room for the kettle and saw that my mother had forgotten to empty the coffeepot: mold grew in green and white rings on the black skin. A few weeks ago, in Boston, I had found her cell phone in the fridge.

I'd left New York to do some writing, or so I told

myself, and when my cup of tea was ready, I settled down to work, curled over a desk in the studio that feels at high tide as though it were cantilevered out over the water. But it wasn't long before my attention wandered—first to a dry, leggy spider's corpse that had been there since the summer and next to a seagull that I could see out the window. I watched as she plunged into the icy water, surfacing instantly in possession of a large, hairy crab; then she floated, complacently arranging and rearranging the wings along her back, and seemed almost to forget the crustacean writhing in her beak. But eventually she rose, flew in a compact circle above the beach, and finally, climbing as high as the house and pausing, suspended, let drop her prey onto the rocks below. The crab made a noise like a gunshot as it hit the ground, but the seagull was unsatisfied, and, picking it up, rose once more, circled once more—this orbit slightly larger and spanning the space between the docks—and again dropped the crab onto the beach. This effort went on for some time, the circle always widening, the seagull's wings always pumping harder, until I lost sight of her altogether and concluded she had found another, better beach. Minutes later, I heard a sharp crack—the gull was back, the crab shattered, and for the next half hour she gorged herself, picking and tugging at the flesh within the shell.

When the rain stopped, I put on a coat and walked to the end of the dock. A length of hose trailed in the water, and I coiled it up and looped it around a cleat. Seaweed grew thickly on the tubing that had been submerged. Different seagull hunger had scattered the float with the broken remains of mussels, crabs, and starfish, and I spent a while tossing back each leg, each

claw, each jagged shell. It was difficult, that day, to believe that sunlight had ever fallen there, or would ever
fall there again. In summer, when a cloud passes across
the sun and the walls of the house turn momentarily
to bone, I feel the same. ("What's it like in winter?" I
would ask the hotel owner in St Ives, looking out the
window at the mild, luminous beach. "Wild," he said,
"and wet. The wind slams at the windowpanes.") And
yet how many evenings had I spent on this float, at the
hour when the sun was setting and turning yellow all
in sight? How many times had I called to my father
and waited for him to pad down the dock in his purple
swimsuit? He always dove without hesitation, and after
surfacing swam a few strokes away from the house.
"Toasty warm!" he exclaimed of the water, and I would
dive in myself and be shocked by the chill. Sometimes
we swam to the boat; sometimes we swam from dock to
dock, greeting the neighbors who were sitting outside.
We crawled back against the current and climbed out,
he first, into the cooling evening air. By the time I had
taken an outdoor shower and dressed, the sky was pink,
the lights were on, and sounds of classical music filled
the house.

At dusk I took a bath in the claw-footed tub upstairs.
The walls of this bathroom are painted yellow, and a
white wicker armchair sits in the corner beside a low,
rectangular window—the same window on which
Sally, the seagull, used to tap her beak. During the day
its glass had revealed the basin, but now, as the sun set
somewhere behind the clouds, it was slowly becoming
a blackened mirror. The water pooling and steaming
around my knees was a faint turquoise against the
white enamel of the tub; for as long as I could remember

I had thought it beautiful, and for as long as I could remember I had liked to tilt my head back and watch it play as lines of light along the ceiling. All day the house had been to me a hideous scrap heap, a failed plot, a universe collapsed and cold. But this, I thought—pushing the surface of the bathwater away to create chaos on the ceiling—this is kind of the same.

After my bath, I put on a flannel robe, knotted my hair in a towel, and lay down in the blue room. I wasn't intending to fall asleep, but I did, and as I slept I had the most vivid dream yet. It was a hot, bright day and my father and I were sitting in a garden full of flowers. He stood up to leave, and I stood up to say good-bye. He put his arms around me, loosely at first, but gradually his grip grew tighter, and he started to shake, and I knew, though I could not see his face, that he was crying. He hugged me harder and then the cries began to rise in me as well, for suddenly I understood.

PART THREE

1

"For really, what did she feel, come back after all these
years and Mrs. Ramsay dead? Nothing, nothing—
nothing that she could express at all."

I once saw a well-dressed woman on the street receive a phone call. She listened for a moment, then her eyes widened and her mouth opened in a wail; her face and body crumpled, and she fell to her knees on the sidewalk. I knew that the worst that could happen had happened to her, and I was impressed and envious of her single-mindedness—of how tidally she had been taken over by her sorrow. I had often wondered what it would feel like when my father died, and here now was my model: *I* would be felled as this woman was felled.

But when it finally happened, it felt like nothing at all.

I was standing in a university hallway between classes. "Darling?" my mother said when I called her at home. "Dad's dead." "Oh," I said, and cried a bit—not because I wanted or needed to, but because it seemed the thing to do. My classmates flocked to me; I pushed them away; I was conscious of a woman I'd never liked who seemed to watch me from afar. I gathered up my things, feeling melodramatic, feeling floaty. On my way out, I bumped into the man whom I would one day marry and divorce; we had just spent our fourth night together. I wanted to bawl, to collapse in his arms, or rather, I wanted to want these things, but it was so cold outside, and his front, when he hugged me, was hard. I made jokes as he hailed me a cab. A few minutes later, I called to say I felt anxious about the way we had parted—I didn't like how it was going, this moment I had been imagining for fourteen years. Then my phone died, and I was alone.

Within the hour I found myself on a train to Boston, rocking with its back-and-forth and holding a copy of the *New York Times*. My father was dead. How completely strange. I had seen him the previous morning, when I stopped by the hospital on my way to New York. He had been so wild, so full of manic energy—I'd gone to the kitchen to make him a cup of coffee, and when I turned in to the hall, he was standing specter-like at the other end of it. It was the first time he had been out of bed in days, and he wasn't wearing his oxygen; he staggered toward me, smiling oddly, and he was so thin that he needed to hold up the waistband of his black silk long underwear with both hands. I yelled at him to lie down, and he gave me a cheeky look and darted away, perching eventually on the arm of a nearby chair. When I dragged him back to bed, he spilled the coffee I had made him down his front. It was with relief that I quickly kissed him good-bye and left the hospital for good. In retrospect, it was obvious how little his mind was working, but it had never occurred to me it would be the last time I would see him—we'd been promised weeks and weeks. Nor did it occur to me when I spoke to him on the phone that evening (I was in a cab, going up

the West Side Highway) that it would be our last conversation. What had I said? Something about how we
could talk later, how I was just calling to say hello. The
receiver kept slipping from his hand. An ambulance
had brought him home that afternoon, and he was sitting up in bed while my mother cooked him an omelet.
She said later that he got up every few minutes to smoke
cigarettes by the exhaust fan. I had cut the conversation short, embarrassed by the extravagance of taking a
taxi—I hadn't wanted him to know.

Now, on the train, I bought a microwave pizza from
the café car and read the entire newspaper. Both the
newsagent and the vendor had behaved as if it were an
ordinary day. My father is dead, I said to myself, my father is dead. I was fascinated by the scarcity of any emotion; was I in shock? I felt quite sane. There was plenty
that I could have done to bring on feeling, but bemused
oblivion arrived more readily.

He had been in a coma all morning, my mother had
said. He took a breath and then seemed not to breathe.
He took another and then he died. Do I regret not being
there? I asked myself. Perhaps, but not too much. I
closed my eyes and tried to sleep. I opened them and
asked my seatmate for the time. We were still hours
away, and I willed the seconds to pass, even as I had
an image then of the death moment as a fracture that
had split my life in two, and every minute, every mile,
a measure of the growing distance between me and the
part of life I much preferred. Some ten years later, I'm
still on that train.

Virginia Woolf called her mother's death "the greatest disaster that could happen," and she returned again
and again in her writing to the morning on which it

came to pass. But the common thread between these scenes is not her devastating grief, but rather an anxiety similar to the one that had already begun to plague me: the insufficiency of her emotions in the face of such disaster, her inability to feel much of anything at all. Twenty-nine years later, she recalled how, visiting her mother's body for the first time, she "laughed . . . behind the hand which was meant to hide my tears; & through the fingers saw the nurses sobbing." And in a different entry over a decade on: "I remember turning aside at mother's bed . . . to laugh, secretly, at the nurse crying. She's pretending, I said: aged 13. & was afraid I was not feeling enough." The crumpling of the well-dressed woman on the street is a form of loss we recognize, a portrait of despair congruent with our expectations; it appeases in a way insensibility cannot. And it occurs to me now that those awful parentheses—the ones announcing Mrs. Ramsay's death; the ones that breed dissatisfaction in a reader longing for a scene that will instead spell out the moment's horror—serve to enact not just life's fickleness but also the dissatisfaction of the child who, try as she might, cannot adequately feel her parent's passing. Woolf's decision to forgo such a scene is a protest, a declaration that truth often flees from the deathbed, that the figure of the sobbing nurse obscures far more than it reveals.

At last the train pulled into South Station, and I caught a cab to Charlestown. I paused outside the house, as if to enter were to break a seal of some kind, and finally climbed the steps and rang our bell. My mother came gratefully to the door. We clung to each other. Then, passing the closed doors of the living room, we stood together in the kitchen while the kettle boiled.

The house seemed extraordinarily silent, our lowered voices an intrusion.

"You don't have to see him," she said. She found it comforting, though—she had been giving him pats all afternoon.

"I want to," I said, and eventually, holding a mug of tea, I opened the living room door. The lights were dimmed, the heat turned way down. My father lay in a hospital bed where the dining table had been, a white sheet drawn to his shoulders. From the threshold he looked himself, but when I went closer his face morphed into something other, something so simultaneously like and *un*like the person he had been the day before. Virginia recorded how, on visiting her mother's body for the second time—someone had turned Julia from her side onto her back—her face appeared "immeasurably distant, hollow and stern," and how, when she bent to kiss her cheek, it was like "kissing cold iron" and she jumped back. Her account is eerily familiar—I know that sense of distance, that cold rigidity, that flight response; they must be hallmarks of mixing with the dead.

My father was pale, and his eyes and mouth were open; his skin was slack, but he gave the impression of being immensely hard all over, as if the skin were made of wax. I found myself waiting for movement—some twitch, some rise and fall. But of course there was nothing, and for a moment it was as if I, too, had stopped breathing, so transfixed was I by his utter quiescence. Then I moved closer still and saw the top of his head. His hair was matted and oily, thinner than I remembered it, and suddenly I didn't want to touch him; I hated being in that room with him and, compelled, I fled. But later, once the door was closed, I was comforted to know that he was still near.

Before going to sleep we called the crematorium, and shortly afterward two polite, somber men in black overcoats arrived at the front door. My mother showed them in; from afar I saw my father for the last time—he seemed to lie at the end of a long telescope—and then we let them wrap him up and take him. I watched from the living room window as they loaded his body into the back of a minivan, and I thought how altered was a world in which my father's place was not with us but in the street with strangers; that with strangers, he would burn at two thousand degrees. Then they drove away, and I was left alone in that cold, echoing room, where weeks before my typing had soothed him to sleep, where as a child I had danced on the tops of his feet, and where, in the beginning, he had sat on the bare wooden floor with a cigarette and a glass of wine, marveling at the great, unfurnished space and calling out every so often to my mother in the kitchen, "Oh, Mint, what a beautiful room!"

"She was dead. The step where she used to sit
was empty. She was dead."

Virginia described the days before her mother's funeral as a period of "astonishing intensity." She and
her siblings "lived through them in hush, in artificial
light. Rooms were shut. People were creeping in and
out. People were coming to the door all the time. . . .
The hall reeked of flowers. They were piled on the
hall table." It was the spring of 1895 in London, but it
may as well have been the winter of 2007 in Boston,
a stretch of weeks I remember above all as crepuscu-
lar and silent, shot through with the cold beauty of
a hundred pounds of flowers and the hollow chiming
of the doorbell. I couldn't shake that crystalline, hy-
peraware feeling one gets on important occasions—on
birthdays, for instance, or on losing one's virginity.
My father is dead, I said to myself, my father is dead.
Again and again I said it, and still I failed to grasp
what it meant.

The first night I slept badly and at five in the
morning got up to use the bathroom; the sky outside
was not yet light, and I had the sudden impression

that the space around me was thick with ghosts, or rather one ghost, who, gigantic, permeated the whole room. It was an alarming sensation, and I felt it several times before never feeling it again. (On the day after Julia died, Virginia told Stella she had seen an apparition, a man sitting with her mother on the bed. Stella—the daughter of Herbert Duckworth, Julia's first husband—looked frightened. "It's nice that she shouldn't be alone," she finally said.) Later, on trying to pretend my father could see and hear me from above, I grew exhausted.

The house continued to fill with cards and flowers— death will mobilize even the most distant of relations, it seems. My mother, who loved flowers but worried at the excess, longed for a rationing system that would allot her one bouquet a week instead of fifty all at once. She also saw the ringing doorbell as an interruption at a time when she wanted to be alone with my father. But I liked hearing from the outside world: grief is rapacious, and cards and flowers functioned as its fuel. As long as they continued to proliferate, the experience of loss was active, almost diverting. It was only when their numbers dwindled, then ceased altogether, that a kind of dullish hunger set in.

My mother was resistant, too, to a commemoration of any kind. My father was still alive when she began objecting to a funeral with fierce, panicky resolve, and though he had concurred—and had, at her urging, warned friends who visited the hospital not to expect one (so it became *his* decree)—I remember thinking that she hadn't given him much choice. I expect her opposition lay in her inclination for privacy, her pos-

sessiveness of his memory, her aversion to public vul-
nerability; and yet, being vulnerable, she was unable
to mount an effective protest when some friends insisted: several weeks after the cremation, we invited
seventy-five people to our house for champagne and
orange juice. In anticipation, she made the nearly ca-
lamitous decision to try to stall the flowers, moving
the bouquets to the living room and turning down
the heat. That night, the temperature dropped forty
degrees and the pipes froze; her next day was spent
crawling around with a hairdryer, an attempt to prevent the metal from cracking and water from flooding
the floor.

But the party went well. Several of my father's friends
gave toasts, and my mother, impressing me with a talent for public speaking, read an excerpt from Edward
St. Aubyn's *Never Mind.* I hadn't planned on talking
myself, but at the last minute scrawled down a speech
about my father and Rhode Island. At its center were
words that he had said to me that fall: "I've had a damn
nice life." During my mother's toast I had laughed, but
when I tried to give my own, I cried so helplessly that
my friend Jessa had to read the first paragraph in my
place.

Eventually, that hypersaturated feeling began to
fade. On first returning to my apartment, I had been
met by a spectacular flurry of death-related activity. My
friends' parents sent flowers; acquaintances sent cards.
Jessa gave me some DVDs of TV shows. Another friend,
Laura, an Orthodox Jew, invited me to her parents'
apartment for a kind of mini sitting shiva. For several
hours she and her mother listened as I talked about my

father's life; I loved that neither was cowed by death's awkwardness. After a while, though, the distractions stopped. In their absence, I found grief unsatisfying. There was nothing to cling to. My father is dead, I continued to say, my father is dead. My appetite for wishes had atrophied. I would ignore the clock at 11:11 and unthinkingly flick an eyelash from my cheek—there was not a single thing I wanted.

I drifted through my days with an unfamiliar sense of alterity. I was enrolled in an education class for a new teaching position; I didn't know the other students, and I remember the dreaminess and alienation with which I sat at the back of the room, watching from my high-up perch—or so it seemed—and saying, over and over again, My father is dead. I spent an absurd amount of time imagining the moment at which various acquaintances had learned of my loss, and I basked in the special haze that now must cling to me (much as Virginia, dreaming she had been diagnosed with a terminal illness, enjoyed what she called "a luxurious dwelling upon my friends [sic] sorrow"). Above all, I disliked the passing of time, disliked the thought that every minute carried me further from my father. This was impossible to reconcile with the feeling of waiting, with the sense that something on the horizon would soon give substance to this stupid vagueness.

Virginia described a similar malaise, recalling how the intensity of those first few days gave way to a "muffled dulness that then closed over" her and her family: "we seemed to sit all together cooped up, sad, solemn, unreal, under a haze of heavy emotion. It seemed impossible to break through. It was not merely dull; it was unreal." She chafed beneath the suffocating mourning conventions espoused by Queen Victoria—the parties ceased; the laughter ceased; for months, the family wore black from head to foot. Even their notecards were ringed with black. Hand in hand, they marched to Kensington Gardens to sit beneath the trees, and once there the silence was oppressive—it was, she said, as if a "finger was laid on our lips." Leslie Stephen's groans resounded through the tall, dark house; he paced up and down in the drawing room, exacting pity from Stella and his female children, waving his arms, wailing that he had never told Julia how much he loved her.

At thirteen, Virginia did not recognize the root of her disquiet; when Thoby, speaking of the dissonance between the siblings' inward experience and outward behavior, remarked that it was "silly going on like this"—"sobbing, sitting shrouded, he meant"—she was appalled. But in retrospect she saw that he was right. The tragedy of her mother's death, she said, "was not that it made one, now and then and very intensely, unhappy. It was that it made her unreal; and us solemn, and self-conscious. We were made to act parts that we did not feel; to fumble for words that we did not know. . . . It made one hypocritical and immeshed in the conventions of sorrow."

I lacked the kinds of elaborate customs that governed the Stephens' behavior, of course; thanks to my era, and to my father's hostility to organized religion, I lacked any customs at all. But while I wouldn't have traded the freedom to mourn as I liked for those claustrophobic, false-feeling Victorian practices, or even the comfort of a god I didn't believe in—how gratifying,

that afternoon of sitting shiva!—I did find myself longing for ritual, for structure, for some organizing principle by which to counter the awful shapelessness of loss.
The conventions of sorrow may give rise to hypocrisy,
but sorrow uncontained holds its own perils.

THE BEGINNING OF "The Lighthouse" finds Lily sitting alone at the breakfast table, awkwardly wondering whether to pour herself another cup of coffee
and struggling to summon the appropriate emotions.
"How aimless it was," she thinks, forty-four years old,
still unmarried, and returned to the Hebridean house
for the first time in a decade. "How chaotic, how unreal . . . Mrs. Ramsay dead; Andrew killed; Prue dead
too—repeat it as she might, it roused no feeling in
her." In place of sorrow is her vacant mind; in place of
familiarity a morning on which "the link that usually
bound things together had been cut." A family fight
is under way—Mr. Ramsay demands a voyage to the
lighthouse, but Nancy has forgotten the sandwiches
and Cam and James are running late—and to Lily at
the table, still straining to make sense of it all, their
raised voices are like symbols, which, she thinks, were
she only able to string them together, would allow
her to get "at the truth of things." For coupled with
the morning's strangeness is its unnerving incoherence: "The grey-green light on the wall opposite. The
empty places. Such were some of the parts, but how
bring them together?"

When I first read *To the Lighthouse*, Lily Briscoe
bored and perhaps even repelled me slightly. "Poor Lily,"

Mrs. Ramsay calls her privately, thinking of how Mr. Ramsay finds her "skimpy," and the phrase stuck with me for reasons that no doubt betray a latent sexism— because she is a spinster, because Paul shuns her at dinner, because her "puckered-up" face is less appealing than Mrs. Ramsay's incomparable beauty or Minta's golden haze. She seemed an uninspiring substitute for the extraordinary woman we had lost. But there is a fire in Lily, that extraordinary woman tells us, "a thread of something; a flare of something." And today—fifteen years have passed—I can at last perceive that fire for myself. Lily is roughly the age that I am now when we first meet her, and it has become curiously easy to see myself in her story—in her conflicted feelings about marriage, in her determination to investigate the vicissitudes of loss. Her fears are those of the thirteen-year-old girl who stands beside her mother's corpse, worried at her inability to feel; her frustrations are those of the grown writer who must confront grief's fogginess, its unreliability. "Why repeat this over and over again?" she thinks angrily of her attempts to register the fact of Mrs. Ramsay's passing. "Why be always trying to bring up some feeling she had not got?" But it's Lily's response to these fears and frustrations, her proposed solution to the question of how to bring together the morning's inconsonant parts, that makes me like her best of all. Rather than performing her anguish for her hosts, or going through the motions of prayer, or even just heading back to bed, she decides to gather her paints and return to her picture of a decade earlier—to embark upon a true portrait of Mrs. Ramsay, a true portrait of Mrs. Ramsay's *absence*.

In her original notes for the novel, Woolf envisioned "Two blocks joined by a corridor," and drew a shape that looked a bit like a dumbbell:

The form would allow her to convey the devastating effects of the Great War, and to communicate the horrific rupture that had put an end to her childhood. It was also how she expressed the similarities between her own project and that of Lily, who wrestles throughout with the aesthetic dilemma of "how to connect this mass on the right hand with that on the left," and ultimately embraces the central corridor in the book's final sentences: "With a sudden intensity, as if she saw it clear for a second, she drew a line there, in the centre. It was done; it was finished." Lily's grief is a mirror of Virginia's own, and her painting a surrogate for the novel; both are an attempt to make sense of the death that set their authors' lives adrift. "Until I was in the forties," Virginia recalled, "the presence of my mother obsessed me. I could hear her voice, see her, imagine what she would do or say as I went about my day's doings."

The incoherence that so plagues Lily in the Hebrides has its forebear, surely, in the sense of unreality that swallowed up the Stephens as they mourned. But I expect that anyone who has lost anyone is well acquainted with that terrible abstraction—certainly it was the defining feature of my own bereavement. And it felt oddly revelatory when I realized that my favorite book was also contending with that issue; that while the novel offers a clear rejection of the Victoriana that so confined Virginia as a child, it embodies, too, her desire to find a workable replacement for that tradition, her understanding that we *all* need some structure by which to contain and grapple with our dead. Thus why *To the Lighthouse* is a novel full of shapes, why Lily struggles to compose her painting, why Woolf poured her family's story into such a strict, unusual mold. The book's radical form—not just a pioneering literary innovation—is also an endeavor to speak to and rectify grief's essential formlessness.

Is it any wonder that in writing my own family's story, I would choose that structure for myself? Use it to bind the disparate parts, to lay a path toward some sense of resolution? Virginia considered the writing of *To the Lighthouse* an exorcism: "I wrote the book very quickly; and when it was written, I ceased to be obsessed," she remembered. "I expressed some very long felt and deeply felt emotion. And in expressing it I explained it and then laid it to rest."

3

And yet.

Visiting my father's friends one weekend, far from Boston, far from New York, suddenly seared by the understanding he was dead, I had to run from the room before anyone could see me cry. ("It had seemed so safe, thinking of her," Lily muses indignantly when Mrs. Ramsay's absence at last gives rise to a terrible hollowness. "Ghost, air, nothingness, a thing you could play with easily and safely at any time of day or night, she had been that, and then suddenly she put her hand out and wrung the heart thus.") Appallingly capricious, unfathomably acute—that is grief too. For weeks and weeks it can lie low, not nearly as bad as you expect, or as you plead with it to be, until, without warning, it springs.

I climbed down to the beach beneath the house; I walked for several miles, settling eventually on a stranger's white plastic picnic table. I wept and wept; I felt I could have cried for twenty-four hours straight. "I love you so much," I howled at the space around me.

Empty, exhausted, I stayed until it grew dark. Then, looking out at the ocean, barely blue, glowing in the paling light, I saw the moon: a small sliver, an upside-down crescent. Just yesterday I'd written under its enormous light. I wondered if I had possibly gotten my facts wrong—maybe the moon did not wane gradually, but rather leapt from sphere to crescent overnight?

But no, of course not. It was an eclipse.

4

"You will find us much changed."

One of the more disturbing effects of Julia Stephen's death was the way in which the vibrant whirl of Virginia's childhood was replaced, immediately and completely, by a hushed, austere existence. "There it always was," she recalls, "the common life of the family, very merry, very stirring, crowded with people," and her mother "was the centre; it was herself. This was proved on May 5th 1895. For after that day there was nothing left of it." She remembers looking out the window that morning—the doctor was walking away from the house, his hands held behind his back—and having the sense that it was all over. Already she intuited how a "shrouded, cautious, dulled life" would supplant those merry, stirring crowds, how there would be no more of those thrilling moments—when her mother praised one of her stories, for instance, or took her arm while walking down to dinner. (Before my father died, I tried to convey my horror of the boredom that awaited, as if by confiding in him now he might be able to reach back from oblivion to save me. "I just have so much fun with you," I said. "I'm glad you think I'm fun," he said. "I was always dreading your coming home and being bored.")

This same perversion of the family characterizes the first few chapters of "The Lighthouse." Cam and James, teenagers now, have grown serious and sullen; Nancy—that wild creature whom we last saw scrabbling over the rocks—has been forced into the role of matriarch, despairing over what she should send to the lighthouse. Lily feels as if she has been thrust into "a house full of unrelated passions," and when, in the midst of this confusion, Mr. Ramsay presses her hand and says that she will find them altered, his words are a caution to Woolf's readers as much as to his houseguest. Indeed, Lily's later reflection that "life has changed completely" is in part a comment on the postwar world, but it also underscores the unrecognizability of existence without the woman who had set it all aglow.

Even a voyage to the lighthouse has had the fun sucked out of it. Furious with their father for conceiving and inflicting upon them a sentimentality they do not share, Cam and James forge a "great compact"—an unspoken agreement to oppose him, to deny him any semblance of affection or excitement. Their anger springs from separate sources; though no one compels her more than her father, though she is capable of thinking him brave and lovable and wise, Cam—like Virginia with her own father—cannot overlook the cruelty of his demands. James's hostility is more visceral; imagining the inevitable moment at which his father will criticize his helming of the sailboat, he thinks how he will "take a knife and strike him to the heart," much like that enraged, impotent six-year-old who once longed to gash his father's breast.

Mr. Ramsay's behavior has always been tyrannical, of course, but Mrs. Ramsay's death has robbed his children of the one person who could protect them from it. And that's what the third section of *To the Lighthouse* evokes so well for me—not just the pain of losing a parent but also the loneliness of the diminished family life that we must lead in the wake of that loss. I see in James and Cam's great compact the insult and indignity of being abandoned to the lesser parent—the parent who never understood or said the right thing, the parent against whom one has always raged. I see the ferocious privacy that a child in mourning erects around her grief, her refusal to expose even a fraction of the misery that roils her; and her contempt for the conventionality of the lesser parent's sorrow, her unwillingness to condone or share in that sorrow, though they both mourn the same death. And yet I see, too, the impossible position of the parent, who has also been abandoned, who could never hope to replicate the fun gone missing, and whose efforts to do so only serve to drive the wedge still deeper.

IN THE EARLY days of our bereavement, when my mother and I faced together the unfamiliar emptiness of the house, navigated together the new behaviors required of a grieving wife and daughter, I felt with her a comforting solidarity. At the memorial party I was proud of her; at other times I was protective. But it was not long before our experiences diverged.

In the weeks before his death, my mother had concentrated on my father—or rather, on all that was peripheral to him—with blinkered intensity. Her life revolved around visits to the hospital, trying to track down certain doctors, and supervision of his meals and medication. She was obsessed with planning for a future that must have seemed hypothetical until the very moment it arrived; she still carries in her wallet her notes from the evenings on which they outlined all there was to do when he was gone. Then he died. It felt, she said, as if she had been fired from her job. For months she wandered in a fog. One morning she forgot how to drive out of Charlestown, where we had lived for twenty-five years; another time she neglected to empty the car of trash bags and returned one week later to find maggots writhing on the backseat and a nauseating odor so bad she had to sell the vehicle.

She also grew increasingly reclusive—which my father's friends made easy. I thought she expected an unrealistic degree of solicitude, but I, too, was surprised by the number of people who, having sent a card or flowers, simply disappeared. Some fell away with an alarming swiftness. One weekend she drove to Rhode Island and spent three days cleaning out the boat, asking a sailing friend—a man who'd spoken at my father's party the week before—if he would help her carry home the contents. They agreed that she would call him on Sunday; when she called, he didn't answer. She made three trips between the marina and the house. She never heard from him again.

Nor did it help that my father's death coincided with an almost comically relentless streak of bad luck. Some things would have been unremarkable had they not been coupled with my mother's general misery—a failed freezer, a failed boiler; a dispute over an encroaching maple tree; a minor car accident. But other incidents were more core-shaking. She fought with our next-door neighbors, for instance, worried that the two-story garage they were building without permission would foil her plans to sell our house and move back to Sydney. She had already sent a battery of angry letters to the city council when the garage burned to the ground one night, and might have even borne the brunt of the suspicion had not the fire also taken with it our fence, garden shed, and garden, including the dogwood my parents had planted to mark their ten-year anniversary.

My mother is shy, and she is not a businesswoman; had my father been alive, all this would have been within his purview. When I imagine now the helplessness she must have felt during those months, I'm overcome with pity. At the time, however, I was back in New York, and my distance from Boston shielded me from the force of these events. Sympathy, boredom, irritation at her martyred tone—that was my reaction to the catalogue of suffering that met me daily on the phone. I was frustrated by her resentment toward most people, as well as by her self-preoccupation.

I remember one phone conversation in which I finally bridled at her descriptions of the countless trials that she faced: she had not once asked how I was doing. "It's hard for me too," I said. "I lost someone too." She started to sob, so hysterically that she could hardly breathe. "It's *not* as hard for you, Katharine!" she screamed. "It's *not* as hard for you! You may be sad, you may be upset, Dad might have even loved you more than he loved me. But your life isn't different the way that mine is different. It just isn't."

She was right, of course. Her day-to-day had been utterly transformed, while on the surface mine looked more or less the same. But I was incapable of mining my recognition of that fact for the compassion that she sought from me; I was incapable of even meeting her halfway. Disconcerted by his daughter's distance on the sailboat, Mr. Ramsay resolves that he will make Cam smile at him and begins to pepper her with questions about their new puppy. Who was looking after it? What would they name it? He himself had had a childhood dog, he adds, whom they had called Frisk. James looks on angrily, anticipating his sister's surrender, but in the end she surprises him by saying nothing, and Mr. Ramsay picks up his book: it's he who will surrender. Within Cam, though, is a jumble of conflicting emotions, her allegiance to the great compact bumping up against the paternal adoration that she also feels. Despite appearing impassive, she wishes, "passionately, to move some obstacle that lay upon her tongue."

I felt similarly paralyzed that whole year. Driving through Connecticut one morning, I saw my mother's eyes fill with tears. "It's just that we sailed here," she said and then, "If only Dad were here." I looked out the window at a sailboat passing beneath one of those anonymous Connecticut bridges—I too remembered that sailing trip. I had driven alone from Boston to Old Saybrook and met my parents at the marina; we left for Long Island the next day, and to my father's embarrassment ran aground at the entrance to Sag Harbor. For an instant the memory brought tears to my own eyes, and with it that strange, uncertain revelation: it didn't have to be this way. But it *is* this way, I reminded myself, angered anew by my mother's feeble fantasies, by her need to share them, by the performative nature of her grief. And rather than confiding the deep emotion her recollection had aroused in me—we might have laughed at the thought of my father's mortification; we might even have acknowledged the hatchet that had been taken to our family—I was silent, stone-faced, and she, tears still running down her face, was none the wiser. Frankly, I must have seemed a little monstrous.

MY FATHER WAS cavalier about what would happen to him after his death. He did not want a funeral. Of his ashes, he said, "Just put me in a plastic baggie." He later considered more seriously. "Perhaps you can sprinkle some in Rhode Island, and some near my mother's house, and some in Sydney Harbour. You can have little parties in each place."

Three months after he died, my mother and I met at Heathrow Airport; she had flown from Boston, and when the woman at the check-in counter asked the purpose of her visit, she said, "I'm delivering my husband's ashes," and started weeping. They bumped her up to first class. We shared a car to my aunt and uncle's house, and as we passed Marylebone Town Hall, she cried again: "We were married there," she said. Andrew and Corinne served us a late dinner. I remember studying Andrew's face, searching for something of my father. He was rounder, larger, but they had the same coloring—the same reddish complexion and yellow-gray hair. Eyes that same blue. If I looked just at the place where his jaw met his neck, the skin slack and smooth, I could pretend it was my father's face.

A few days later we drove to Seafield, my grandmother's house, arriving to a spring day unseasonably warm and fair. It was the first time I had seen my grandmother since her visit to the Boston hospital; we ate lunch in the conservatory and listened to her muse, not for the first time, about the fox living in her garden.

"I had a man come to look at the dishwasher," she said, "and when I asked him what was wrong with it, he said, 'You have a fox on your lawn.' "

"We're not on the bloody fox again!" Andrew exclaimed.

"I said, 'I know I have a fox on my lawn' "—my grandmother ignored him—" 'but what about the dishwasher?' " She paused. "He's rather a nice fox. He comes in the morning and curls up for a few hours in the shrubbery."

"Are you sure you're not thinking of Robert?" Andrew interrupted, and Corinne snorted. We could see my other uncle through the glass. Halfway through the meal he had excused himself and was now lying recumbent on a woolen blanket in the garden. There was nothing unusual about his abrupt departure, but this habit of sleeping on the grass was new.

"Les thinks my fox is ill," my grandmother said, still ignoring Andrew, and Corinne laughed. "How can he tell?" she asked.

"He says he looks thin," my grandmother said.

"Christ almighty," said Andrew.

After we had finished eating, my grandmother led us without speaking to the edge of the garden, where she bent to pick a flower, pink. Her face was expressionless, and if at lunch she had seemed foolish, now she was formidable. We were leaving to scatter the ashes soon, and I realized I was scared to watch her, scared of what her sorrow in particular might look like. It was as much for her as for my father that we all picked flowers too.

The harbor that day was sleek and green. There were windsurfers tacking back and forth, and dinghies, some with orange sails and others white. Andrew led us to an empty pontoon; at our back was the millpond, full of swans, and farther down the promenade, the sailing club. "Go on, darling," my mother said, and I took the box of ashes from my bag. My father's name was stamped across the top, and beneath it, the name of the crematorium. Inside was a clear plastic pouch with a red tie. The ashes looked like ground oyster shells. They were heavy as stones. I kneeled down—the water beneath my shadow darkened—and shook the ashes free. They carried with the shaking, and once beneath the surface, spread and swirled like smoke. My grandmother threw in her flower, we all threw in our flowers (mine a yellow tulip streaked with red); there was silence. At dinner, Mrs. Ramsay imagines her husband's words of poetry to be like flowers floating on the ocean, unfurled, autonomous, "as if no one had said them, but they had come into existence of themselves." Held up to our sacrifice, that dreamlike image at last clicked into place. Then my grandmother said she hoped the sea was not too cold for him. "Oh no," my mother said. "Geoffrey swam in Maine."

The flowers sank. Andrew took my grandmother's arm and led her up the ramp, and Corinne and Robert followed, leaving my mother and me behind. With the others, my mother had been polite, had busied herself taking pictures of the garden in the sea. Now she sat down next to me and rolled up her trousers, baring her dry, white legs to the sun. All day her self-possession had surprised me. She squeezed my hand and smiled; she was lost, but also strong, and also girlish, as if the years between us no longer added up. She did not cry. We sat there a while, saying little, then walked home along the millpond. At the stone jetty we passed some swans asleep, their beaks tucked as if for warmth into the feathers of their backs. My mother told the story of how, before I was born, she and my father had arrived at one of my grandmother's garden parties in galoshes and by boat, bringing the inflatable dinghy up the millpond as far as it could go. At the main road they had pulled the boat from the water, carried it fifty yards down the street, and dropped it on the lawn among the guests. I could put them, the young couple, into the distance, carrying the boat between them.

The others were not at home. "I expect they're having a drink at the sailing club," my mother said, unfolding Robert's blanket and lying down on the grass like Robert and the fox before her. Half an hour later, their car pulled into the driveway. "Mother needed a drink," Andrew confirmed, "and come to think of it, I did too."

That evening, after dinner, I had a very specific vision of my father. He was a small, energetic ghost, bound first for the Solent and next the Atlantic. He floated above the waves on something that looked like a log, but leaned forward as if he were galloping a horse; he was determined and cheerful, and all was blue and black and echoing—the sea and sky made an enormous half globe through which he passed—and his translucent form and pieces of the ocean glittered white beneath the stars.

5

During that same England trip, Andrew and Corinne threw a party in my father's memory. It was a buffet dinner at the Agra, the Indian restaurant where he had been a regular in his twenties; they'd invited forty people, mainly his friends from architecture school, and I knew almost no one. The pink room was hot and crowded, and I watched as the guests, many of whom hadn't seen one another in years, hugged and laughed, exclaiming over the pictures of my father we had tacked to the wall. Then there were murmurs: a famous architect had arrived, wearing a black-and-white houndstooth coat, clear plastic glasses, and a white cashmere scarf. We stared, we ate and drank. One woman called out that she had been having a curry at the Agra when she went into labor; another that she remembered the days when my father had lived on New Cavendish Street and Andrew on Warren. She herself had lived on Little Titchfield.

These were the young, glamorous people from my father's pictures. That thin, bearded man was John, with whom my father had painted huge Coca-Cola bottles onto stage flats in the sixth form. That short, plump woman was Caroline, creator of those silver ties and the girl my father dated at nineteen. "Darling," my mother called, beckoning me to her. "Have you met Vivien?" Vivien! The striking girl from the photograph (tight green T-shirt, white-blond hair smooth and sleek like a helmet). *My old girlfriend*, my father had said. *She's pretty, Dad*, I said, and he had shrugged. She was still striking—her long honey-blond hair hung past her shoulders, but it was rougher now, and her tanned face lined and severe. She smiled at me, not unkindly but not warmly either, and her eyes were deep brown and intimidating. With her was Tom, the man (I'd heard) for whom she left my father.

Vivien had slept with my father. So had Caroline. Who else? All the lives that hadn't been, I thought. Caroline tapped me on the shoulder. "I'd heard that Geoffrey was a father," she said, "and I never could picture it. But now, looking at that photograph"—one of him and me in the cockpit when I was two years old, he adjusting my life jacket—"I understand what a wonderful one he would have been." There was something I didn't like about Caroline. I felt traitorous for opening up to her. Still: "He was an extraordinary father," I said, and my voice cracked. "No one here knows it, but he was an extraordinary father."

"Peter's going to give a speech," my uncle called above the voices and the heat, and we quieted, making room for my father's old friend. Peter said some things about *Clip-Kit*; some things too about how my father was a good writer. "He passed that on to his daughter, Katharine," he said, recalling the summer when I'd worked for him in London. Everyone turned to look at me—Oh, so *that's* who that is. When Peter finished, he asked if anyone else would like to speak. A few people did, and then with small commotion and much encouragement, the famous architect stepped forward. He brushed a lock of long white hair from his forehead and smiled at the room. "Geoffrey was our first employee," he began, "when we were just a four-person firm. And—" he said. He paused, suddenly puzzled. "Why did he leave?" he asked. "I can't remember—I think he went off to New York."

"No!" everyone yelled. "He went to start his own practice!"

"Oh, did he?" said the architect.

"It was Andrew who went to New York," my mother muttered.

There was silence, then Caroline cried out: "I will never be able to eat a tuna mayo sandwich without thinking of Geoffrey!"

But my father hadn't liked tuna fish.

"I'll never eat a Peppermint Pattie without thinking of Geoffrey!" someone else cried to loud laughter. Things were growing absurd.

I was hot and drunk, irritated and wistful. Angry with the famous architect for thinking he was doing my father a favor by speaking at his party; angry with my aunt for saying later, saying twice, how good it was of him to attend ("He must be *very* busy"). Angry with myself for caring that he *had* attended. Angry, most of all, that this is what comes of a life. (Peppermint Patties, tuna mayo sandwiches!) Sad too. And yet my father would have loved this party at the Agra. He would have had a fantastic time. He would have mingled and reminisced and laughed and had too much to drink, and later he would have called it a great bash.

And even if he hadn't been able to make it, if I were somehow able to tell him about it, even then he would be pleased. He would understand my indignation, he would think it sweet. "Oh, Katharine," he would say, laughing. "What do you expect? People are snobs." But they are also old friends, and they hold memories dear—perhaps he did like tuna mayo sandwiches, at one point—and they came together on a London night because long ago they knew and maybe loved my father, and long ago he knew and maybe loved them too, and if I can accept that people die, then I will admit that the party at the Agra was, indeed, a great bash.

In pairs and groups, the guests began to leave. They said good-bye and promised to keep in touch; on that evening, I thought we might. By midnight, only my family remained. We pushed the chairs back into place and unstuck pictures from the wall—one of my father wearing a denim jumpsuit and leaning against a motorcycle; one of him and me on the roof of the Rhode Island studio. Then we left as well, and with our departure, as with the departure of each last guest before us, my father died a little more fully, belonged more firmly to the past.

6

"Who knows what we are, what we feel? Who knows
even at the moment of intimacy, This is knowledge?"

The last time I saw Zette, my father's friend, she asked
if I had been in touch with his Harvard girlfriend. "The
beautiful one," she said, "the glamorous one. What was
her name?" I must have looked puzzled—I wasn't aware
of any Harvard girlfriend.

"I know she existed," she said. "He brought her down
to Westport once. This must have been '78 or '79. We
had a Memorial Day softball game on this big beautiful
field, and I remember them being there. Ahh, what was
her name?"

I was doing frantic calculations—by Memorial Day
of '78 my parents would have been engaged.

"I *really* liked her," Zette said. "Black hair, very
pretty. It seemed intense; I remember thinking that
she was a little too much for him, that he was somehow
out of his depth." She paused. "Denise? I keep thinking
Denise."

At home I turned to the Internet, and within minutes I had found a possible match. A dark, attractive
older woman who lived in Paris, this Denise was a

graduate of Smith and Harvard Business School and had recently been awarded the Legion of Honour. I took a screenshot and sent it to Zette. "It's certainly possible that she is the one I remember, and liked," she wrote. "I suppose the only thing to do is ask her!"

In the months after my father's death, I couldn't rid my mind of Vanessa Bell's response to *To the Lighthouse*—Vanessa wrote that her sister, in inventing the character of Mrs. Ramsay, had "given a portrait of mother which is more like her to me than anything I could ever have conceived of as possible. It is almost painful to have her so raised from the dead. You have made one feel the extraordinary beauty of her character, which must be the most difficult thing in the world to do." For years it was this goal that governed my writing—to paint a perfect portrait of my father, to maybe even raise him from the dead. But I didn't pay close enough attention to Vanessa's words. I didn't grasp that perfection, no less than resurrection, would be the most difficult thing in the world to do.

"WHAT CAN ONE know even of the people one lives with every day?" asks Sally Seton in the final pages of *Mrs. Dalloway*. For Virginia Woolf fans, the question is indelibly familiar—some version of it is always haunting her life and work. "I sometimes feel that no one ever has or ever can share something," she wrote in that remarkable letter to Leonard about their courtship. "Its the thing that makes you call me like a hill, or a rock." Years later, while writing *To the Lighthouse*, she expressed something similar to Vita: "I'm so orderly am I? I wish you could live in my brain for a week. It is washed with the most violent waves of emotion. . . . Do we then know nobody?—only our own versions of them, which, as likely as not, are emanations from ourselves." In *To the Lighthouse*, it's Lily who wrestles most vigorously with these questions, offering up dozens of tentative, often clashing reflections upon the experience of knowing (and appraising) our fellow human beings. "How then did it work out, all this?" she wonders, weighing the abominations and delights of Mr. Ramsay's character. "How did one judge people, think of them? How did one add up this and that and conclude that it was liking one felt, or disliking?" Of Charles Tansley—a man she would almost certainly dislike, were it not "impossible to dislike any one if one looked at them"—she concludes, "She would never know him. He would never know her. Human relations were all like that." But when she later considers the shallowness of her interactions with the enigmatic Mr. Carmichael, she concedes that knowledge, far from a fixed entity, wears innumerable guises. "This was one way of knowing people, she thought: to know the outline, not the detail. . . . She knew him in that way."

Nowhere are Lily's struggles with the limitations of intimacy more pronounced than in her study of Mrs. Ramsay; in one sense, the whole book is about her relentless efforts to pin the older woman down—to get inside her, to *become* her, even—and in so doing, to know her absolutely. "How did she differ?" she asks herself again and again of her friend's fascination for her. "What was the spirit in her, the essential thing?" When she returns to her picture years later, concentrating on the empty steps where Mrs. Ramsay used to sit, her painterly journey parallels that quest to capture her friend's character. "She must try to get hold of something that evaded her. It evaded her when she thought of Mrs. Ramsay; it evaded her now when she thought of her picture." Try as she might to summon her, though—to revive her in her thoughts as on her canvas—Mrs. Ramsay's ghost is as elusive as the flesh and blood had been: "Fifty pairs of eyes were not enough to get round that one woman with."

Virginia might have said something similar of Julia Stephen. "I'm in a terrible state of pleasure that you should think Mrs Ramsay so like mother," she wrote in response to her sister's letter, even as she went on to enumerate the challenges she faced with the portrait, among them the temptations of hagiography ("one would have suspected that one had made up a sham—an ideal"). So too in "A Sketch of the Past," in which—gathering all the different memories, juggling all the disparate facts—she seeks to piece together a likeness of the woman who has forever slipped from her grasp. Though in imagining a garden party in 1860, she can easily conjure up a plate of strawberries or picture her uncle Thoby as he recites the Persian poets, her mother, then fourteen, remains opaque. "How difficult it is to single her out as she really was," Virginia writes, "to imagine what she was thinking, to put a single sentence into her mouth!" It's no accident that we never learn Mrs. Ramsay's first name.

I HAD FOUND the right Denise. She was twenty-four when she arrived at Harvard, hardworking, straight-edge, a bit naive: not the hardheaded siren Zette remembers. She met my father in the early fall—he was already wearing his eye patch—and they started dating almost immediately. She thought him intuitive, enjoyable, empathetic; she felt he could learn anything, that he had a way of cutting into the thick of any question. He was also fidgety and nervous, always fiddling with his collar or looking around him in a restaurant. If a fly landed on the next table, he would get up and shoo it.

They went rowing and played squash; sometimes he cooked for them at his place. They spent a winter weekend at her friend's parents' house, and they visited Zette on the coast—sitting on lobster traps, eating sandwiches out of brown paper bags, visiting the Breakers in Newport. In the spring he taught her how to drive a stick shift, in preparation for her summer in Europe, and though they didn't talk about the future, it was her understanding that they would be together, that one day they might even wed. The following fall, when they returned to Cambridge, he told her he had gotten married. She never spoke to him again.

I learned all this over the phone, in one of the strangest conversations of my life. To my surprise, Denise herself had answered when I dialed the number of her company in Paris; after some flustered explaining on my end, we agreed to talk later that day. She seemed wary when we reconnected, but also energized, a woman hungry to tunnel deep into the past. "Your call was extremely positive for me," she said at once.

For weeks I had doubted Zette's version of events, chalking it up to the pitfalls of middle-aged memory. It wasn't that I believed my father, or any man, incapable of cheating—though there *was* an asexual quality I'd sensed in him that made the prospect feel unlikely to me. Nor did my resistance spring from some morality or principle, some yearning to preserve my father's virtue. The question of whether his deeds were "right" or "wrong" seemed very much beside the point. No, my skepticism lay rather in the fact that to lead two such different lives—to bring one woman away for the weekend even as you are engaged to another—requires a deceitfulness, and perhaps also a callowness and capacity for casuistry, that I simply couldn't reconcile with my father's character. The tape he sent my mother in January 1978, a good four months into his liaison, is full of seemingly casual asides about his failure to take advantage of what appears to have been an open relationship. "I haven't made a habit of going out with any girls while I've been here," he says, "and haven't had the opportunity or the time." And again, "It's been so long since I've gone out with anyone but you." I wouldn't have thought my father interested in such fluid, brazen lies. The recklessness with which he treated Denise was even harder for me to resolve.

Which is why I continued to distrust in their relationship even as I was on the phone with her, as if she had called me and not the other way around. My first inkling of their closeness was when, describing the appeal of dating a thirty-year-old, she said, "I think the most common age at business school was twenty-four, and he was born in '47, right?" Yes, I said, startled by her effortless recollection of his birth year. Later she started going through old photographs, sometimes getting lost within them—"It's hard to imagine," she said, "that this was real, that we were there." Eventually she e-mailed me some and we looked at them together as we talked. One was of a group of students picnicking on a quad; my father wore shorts and no shirt, his hands clasped around his knees, and next to him, in much the same pose, a petite, dark-haired woman in a black tank top. She looked like my mother at that age. Another was of my father alone, submerged in a glossy, tree-lined lake, hanging from the prow of a rowboat and wearing an expression of such astonishing happiness that I felt cold inside.

Denise had known my father was dead—she'd read it in the alumni magazine—but she didn't know any of the details, and the disclosure he had been an alcoholic appeared to give her some satisfaction, as if she'd dodged a bullet. The same was true of my allusion to turbulence within my parents' marriage; it seemed to play into a story she had told herself about that year, one that managed to preserve the integrity both of their relationship and of my father himself. In her rendition, his decision to marry my mother was not a romantic vow but an ethical choice, a resolution to honor the promises he'd made to the woman who had gotten there first.

I liked Denise a lot—her thoughtfulness, her honesty. I found myself wishing that he had chosen her instead, wondering what that life might have looked like. I also had the spooky sense that I was talking to my real mother, the woman who *should* have been my mother, as if this were a homecoming. Was Denise right about my father's motives? Probably not. As Lily remarks in *To the Lighthouse*, "Half one's notions of other people were, after all, grotesque. They served private purposes of one's own." But Denise was also wise enough to understand that hers was just a theory, after all. "Everybody is a mystery," she said before we hung up. "We are all a bunch of contradictions. He seemed to have such a good time, he seemed to really enjoy us, and yet he did something else."

IT'S BEEN NEARLY four years since I first tracked her down. In that time, we've forged an odd kind of friendship, exchanging photographs and occasional e-mails. We met in person for the first time when she flew to New York to visit family. I still like her very much, but time has eroded her flawlessness; she has become more human. I no longer think, as I did when we first spoke, that my father made the wrong decision.

On the day he died, I believed I knew my father, believed that I saw clearly to his core; today, after over a decade of trying to explain him to the world and exposure to secrets like this one, he is more of a stranger to me than he has ever been. The more I learn about him, the more distant he becomes. You might think there'd be reward in this—that even dead he has the chance to grow, the power to astound and challenge— and yet I find his certain silence painful in the face of such discovery; it's yet another testament to the finality of death. And to realize, moreover, that the stories I grew up with were fabrications, or incomplete at best; that even sober he was capable of such unkindness; that there must be so much more about him I don't know— these revelations cause the entire edifice of his character to crumble, as if there were *nothing* that I could hold up to the light and say with confidence: This was him. This was my father.

Such is the cost of striving to see one's parent through the eyes of an adult, the same task that Virginia set for herself in her memoir, putting aside the rage and love her father aroused and instead looking to capture him "as I think he must have been, not to me, but to the world at large." How did it not occur to me that these two men were not one and the same, that in seeking to raise my father from the dead, seeking to raise *all* of him, the minor god whom I knew would only continue to recede?

I think often of that photograph of the rowboat—of how happy my father looked, how totally *himself.* It still unmoors me to see him so contented in a life I didn't know existed. And like Virginia, trying and failing to imagine her mother on a summer afternoon, I struggle to picture such a day beyond the frame. What was he thinking? When Denise put down her camera, what did they say and do? The gaps give rise to fantasies about what might have been, and to fantasies, too, about the costs of relinquishing that future—was the loss of Denise the reason why my father was the way he was? Love stories hold a power all their own, and they encourage all kinds of received ideas; that's why Lily, speculating about Mrs. Ramsay's depths, can't help but wonder whether the key to understanding her lies in some past love affair: "What was there behind it—her beauty and splendour? Had he blown his brains out . . . some other, earlier lover, of whom rumours reached one? Or was there nothing?" I have since seen other pictures of my father and Denise—Zette unearthed some of that Memorial Day weekend. They sit on lawn chairs beside a bowl of apples; they stand abreast before the Breakers' great façade. In almost all of them, my father is unsmiling and inscrutable. Pictures tell us nothing.

He will remain unknowable to me, of course, as we all remain unknowable to others. (Perhaps even to ourselves: it "explains why people say the things they do," Virginia complained of Henry James's *The Golden Bowl*, "which is always a mystery even to the speaker.") But I don't regret the pursuit, and the truth is that returning to it day after day, wrestling with my father's portrait as Lily wrestles with her painting, *is* a kind of resurrection—or at least a standing appointment with his memory. *To the Lighthouse* is a ghost story; consider that queer moment toward the end at which, just for an instant, Lily does succeed at grabbing hold of what evades her and raising her idol from the dead. "Mrs. Ramsay—it was part of her perfect goodness—sat there quite simply, in the chair, flicked her needles to and fro, knitted her reddish-brown stocking, cast her shadow on the step. There she sat."

My father was my father; I knew him in that way.

7

"What does it mean then, what can it all mean?"

I traveled incessantly in the months following my father's death. I went to Florida, to California, to an empty fishing village in Mexico, where hot-pink bougainvillea dripped from the trees, and leathery, blinking iguanas ran across the terra-cotta rooftops. For months I led a wholly unserious life, drifting from experience to experience, skimming the surface of each one; while the old, familiar refrain continued to sound—*my father is dead*—it was not very often that I dove down, that I was *able* to dive down, into the roiling waters beneath.

"What does it mean then, what can it all mean?" asks Lily in the opening lines of "The Lighthouse." Hers is a hollow, ineffectual question, we are supposed to understand—a byword that fits "her thought loosely," a phrase intended to "cover the blankness of her mind." Death confounds language, brings to light its limitations; there are no words to properly convey the brain's frustrated, confused, hopeless, determined scrambling to comprehend what it means that its favorite person has simply *vanished*; nor to convey its little, concomitant bursts of understanding, for it sometimes feels as if we could have all the answers if only we knew how to *say* them. "I had a notion that I could describe the tremendous feeling at R.'s funeral," Virginia wrote of the death of Roger Fry—the painter to whom she would have dedicated *To the Lighthouse* had she not thought it "so bad"—"but of course I cant. I mean the universal feeling: how we all fought with our brains loves & so on; & *must* be vanquished. Then the vanquisher, this outer force became so clear; the indifferent. & we so small fine delicate." Lily endures a similar maelstrom of syntax and emotion, striving and failing to communicate her own universal feeling to Mr. Carmichael—she wants "to say not one thing, but everything . . . 'About life, about death; about Mrs. Ramsay,'" but at once finds herself thwarted and her discovery fleeting: "Words fluttered sideways and struck the object inches too low. Then one gave it up; then the idea sunk back again."

But one of the things I love about Lily is her willingness to utter such meaningless questions, her hope that splashing around the edges of the unfathomable depths they represent may one day yield a truth that will persist. She seeks nothing less than the meaning of life itself, she admits at one point, with an earnestness that is almost embarrassing. And I sometimes feel that *To the Lighthouse*, with all of its thrashing and mumbling, all of its false starts and pedestrian insights, all of its saying things poorly and waving in the general direction of truth, has actually nailed it. To grieve is to be floored, again and again, by a series of epiphanies that, put to paper, sound painfully banal. To grieve is likewise to be plagued by questions that can only gesture toward the clarity we seek and occasionally even find—these are the shorthand by which we must stumble through an experience too vast and too disorienting to express in its totality.

IN MEXICO I slept in a state of half lucidity. The louvered bungalow let in moonlight and the howling of dogs; I felt outraged every time their snarling woke me from a dream. I had dreams to spare, though—a dozen befell me each night, nearly all of them about my father. Sometimes he was sick and soon to perish; sometimes he had been granted a reprieve. It came to feel as though he had returned then, as though he were actually with me, concrete, corporeal, not just some shimmer I'd created. Virginia also marveled at the realism of dreams about the dead; the nighttime appearance of Katherine Mansfield evoked "so much more emotion, than thinking," she wrote, that it was "almost as if she came back in person & was outside one, actively making one feel." I screamed in my dreams; my whole body convulsed with the agony of understanding. Then, gradually, I woke to that porous room in Mexico, to the bars of light falling across the bed and the low hum of the fan, to birdcalls, and to the realization, Oh, my father is dead. I felt so punctured then, and so jealous of the dream self, who had not yet awoken to the hard, unpleasant day-fact: what's left is this.

Sometimes I called my mother from a pay phone installed in the dirt at the foot of the hill. It was a hundred degrees and very humid. Dogs like wolves loped down the street. I wanted a mother, but found instead a woman angry with a friend in Australia who had e-mailed only three times since my father's death. "People just don't get it," she said, and wondered aloud if she should send the friend a chapter from her current favorite book, a self-help guide for grieving widows. She had already mailed a photocopy to my father's business partner and me. I agreed that the friend's behavior was callous, but thought nervously of the growing number of people whom my mother had dismissed since January, for not responding well or not responding at all. We argued a little, then I apologized and tried to clarify: the reason I did not like her widow book, I said, was that it seemed to suggest that widows were the only ones who suffered. Children, hardly at all.

One day I walked several miles to Zipolite, a beach that according to the guidebook drowned several swimmers a year. I lay sweating on the sand; I started *Blood Meridian*, wondering whether to abandon it in favor of a friendlier book. A little ways down shore I saw an object being buffeted about the heaving, sucking waves. I went to investigate—it was a turtle. The animal, dead, was about four feet in diameter; his head, legs, and arms flopped on the waterline, and his salted, mauve intestines spilled through a crack in his stomach armor. I would have coveted the shell, in spite of myself, but it was broken. Later I saw a man burying him in the sand, and for that I was grateful: the creature's limp somersaults had wrecked me.

8

"She watched a procession go, drawn on by some
stress of common feeling which made it, faltering and
flagging as it was, a little company bound together."

As the Ramsays' boat draws nearer the lighthouse,
Cam—sitting alone in the bow, trailing her fingers
through the water—feels a change come over her. No
longer tormented by her father's despotism or her brother's judgment, she experiences a rush of happiness that
calls to mind her late mother's ecstasy; she can hardly
believe "that she should be alive, that she should be
there." It's alongside this joy that the version of her father she despises begins to recede, giving way instead
to an endearing old man who sits in his study, and,
catching sight of her as she borrows a book, inquires
gently—so gently!—if there is anything she needs. In
case this is wrong, in case hers is a fantasy, she turns to
Mr. Ramsay in the cockpit, where he is reading a slim
volume with yellowed pages and a mottled cover like a
bird's egg. "No; it was right," she thinks, relieved. "Look
at him now, she wanted to say aloud to James."

James is more stubborn. Despite a growing understanding that he and his father "alone knew each

other"—that they are bound by a loneliness that they both see as the truth about life—it's not until Mr. Ramsay compliments his son on his steering that the siblings' great compact is finally dissolved. The unexpected praise fills the boy with quiet euphoria; you can practically *feel* him trying not to smile. "He was so pleased that he would not look at her or at his father or at any one. . . . He was so pleased that he was not going to let anybody share a grain of his pleasure." Sometimes I think it's Woolf's mastery of moments like these—moments that hold up a mirror to our private tumult while also revealing how much we as humans share—that most draws me to her. I have been that sulky teenager, feigning indifference at my father frothing up the jellyfish; I have felt the disproportionate pride that followed from his praise ("Gosh, you're good, Katharine," he told me in the hospital, and I thought that I would burst). Haven't we *all* felt those things? And is not the sight of ourselves laid bare on the page—endlessly complex, and yet not singular at all—one of reading's humblest, most delightful rewards?

Moved by their father's dignity and stoicism, Cam and James now wish more than anything that they could give him what he needs. "What do you want? they both wanted to ask. They both wanted to say, Ask us anything and we will give it you." But Mr. Ramsay, who has for years besieged them with his emotional demands, is silent: "He sat and looked at the island and he might be thinking, We perished, each alone, or he might be thinking, I have reached it. I have found it, but he said nothing." As Lily realized earlier that morning, her own anger at his histrionics transformed into a flood of sympathy, "There was no helping Mr. Ramsay on the journey he was going."

I SPENT MOST of that first summer in Rhode Island. Six months had passed since my father's death, and in those six months I had lived a largely peripatetic life. My sadness had not been especially extreme, and I had the feeling I had been moving from one diversion to the next. Enough, I thought. It's time to get down to the business of mourning.

During those weeks my mother and I rarely argued; at nightly meals we were cautious and polite. I was unaccustomed to the lightness of living in a house where there was neither violence nor the threat of violence, and where the specter of imminent death had already come and gone. This was the flip side of the unbelievable boredom my father's death had spawned—I had the sense of having been allowed to exhale after years of holding my breath. My mother had avoided alcohol when he was alive, but she now developed a taste for gin and tonics, which I fixed with lemon peel and which we drank on the deck together as the sun set. I think we enjoyed the mildness of each other's company. Women are so often the ones left behind, and the feminine space they afterward inhabit—which reminds me of the drained, oddly calm feeling one has after sobbing—was a useful place for my mother and me, and, by definition, not one to which we'd had access while my father was still living.

I remember one evening in particular. I was heading down to the end of the dock for a swim when I thought to ask if she would join me. I knew she would say no—she never swam—and was unsurprised when she looked up apologetically: "Maybe in a little while?" But a few minutes later she emerged onto the lawn wearing a bathing suit and T-shirt.

I watched her walk down the dock; every so often she paused to inspect some detail—the frayed rope handrail, the bronze sundial nailed to the top of a piling—as if to suggest that *they* were the subject of her thoughts. How much she loves me, I thought, and how uneventful it is to be loved by her, a person whose very existence was so dependable that I rarely, if ever, considered it. It was such a different experience from loving and being loved by my father, the thrills and devastations of which I could not help remembering now with a hint of exhaustion.

"How's the water?" she asked when she reached the float.

"I don't know," I said, putting down my book. "I haven't felt it yet." She approached the wooden ladder my father had built years before and examined its top rung. One end had come loose. "I know," I said. "It's falling apart."

"No, that'll be easy to fix," she said. "Just remind me."

She climbed down the ladder, and I dove from the float. It was one of those late summer evenings when a big low sun turns the surface white and blinding, flimsy somehow. We swam a few strokes and floated, looking back at the house. The wooden shingles and walls of windows, the concrete seawall and green-white porcelain vine; the deck, the hammock, and the trellis, sagging beneath the weight of the wisteria—all was vivid in the evening light. It was a sight so familiar to me, but one my mother rarely saw. "It really is lovely here, isn't it?" she said.

MY MOTHER IS nothing like Mr. Ramsay, our relationship nothing like his relationship with his children. We do not share a common truth, like he and James; I often think that we don't know each other very well. And if at his best he gives Cam a feeling of security—"I shan't fall over a precipice or be drowned, for there he is, keeping his eye on me," she thinks—it sometimes feels, to me at least, as though my father's death transformed me, my mother's only child, from her daughter to her parent overnight. There is no one more capable of arousing my fury; there is no one more capable of summoning my pity and protectiveness. "I never did enough for him all those years," Virginia wrote to Violet Dickinson a few days after Leslie's death, putting to words the kind of guilt and remorse that our parents alone can elicit. "He was so lonely often, and I never helped him as I might have done." I feel something similar about my mother nearly every time she leaves the room.

But for all the differences between their story and our own, the pathos of Mr. Ramsay's clumsy relationship with Cam and James after his wife's passing has helped me to see our bond more warmly, while also giving me a better sense of her experience, and of the unexpected depth of her reserves. Of course my father's disappearance from our tiny family would wholly alter our relations—his death stripped us of our central source of worry, joy, and competition, which, coupled with her move to Sydney, has made our lives much simpler. But what I wasn't expecting was for my quest to better understand my father to also challenge and enlarge my vision of *her.* All the while I was growing up, I saw my mother as instantly and inherently graspable; in contrast to my father's multiplicity and brilliance, I thought, were the transparency of her emotions, the predictability of her ideas. That's why it wasn't until well after his death that I finally took the time to ask for her memories, to listen to her own account of grief. She surprised me—with her candor and deliberation, her self-awareness and humor, her willingness to acknowledge the most base and human of impulses. "There were times I almost wished that Dad would die," she admitted, reflecting on the darkest moments in their marriage and weirdly charming me. "This was before he was so sick again—I thought, This is all just unbearable. He probably wished I would as well, I don't know." The longer she talked, the more tangled and compelling her past appeared, the more whole she began to seem.

I feel closer to my mother today than at any other time in our lives. I find myself *liking* the woman who set off alone for the Venice fish market so as to present her lover with a living squid; *liking* the woman who on her honeymoon stood beside a vase of hyacinths in the tower room of a crumbling castle, looking out over the fields and fairly thrumming with happiness. And as I've watched her reconstruct her life of late—renovating a house in Australia, taking up aqua aerobics, reuniting with old friends from architecture school (though never, ever dating)—I have come to believe that, for all her apparent fragility, she is nevertheless possessed of a certain self-sufficiency and toughness; that she draws deep from that well of privacy I've mentioned; and that she has ultimately borne the unique miseries of widowhood, a condition to which I probably still haven't given adequate consideration, with estimable resilience.

In our final image of Mr. Ramsay, he continues to refuse his children's tenderness and pity, instead vaulting toward the lighthouse on his own. "He rose and stood in the bow of the boat, very straight and tall, for all the world, James thought, as if he were saying, 'There is no God,' and Cam thought, as if he were leaping into space, and they both rose to follow him as he sprang, lightly like a young man, holding his parcel, on to the rock." This revision of the moment when Mrs. Ramsay decided to marry him—when, stretching out his hand, he "raised her from a boat" and "she stepped slowly, quietly on shore"—communicates all that Mr. Ramsay has lost; as Lily must finish her painting without the inspiration of her muse, so must he complete his journey without his wife's protection (which, paradoxically, is always earned by his protecting her). But it's a testament to his courage that he does not also stretch out a hand to his children, who would so gladly allow him to help; like Mrs. Ramsay before him, he has come to accept that it's a lonely, godless world we live in, and one that we must navigate alone. But it's also one deserving of our heroism, and though the book concludes before he can reach the lighthouse—it closes "as" he springs onto the island—we may trust that in our absence, as in his wife's absence, he will always continue that voyage to the light.

9

Some months after my father's death, feeling a twinge of
regret at the prospect of bidding good-bye to my childhood home, I made my mother nervous by asking her
why, again, we were selling the house in Charlestown.
But at the end of the summer, returned to Boston for
the removal of my wisdom teeth, I spent a groggy evening after the surgery walking around the place where
I had grown up. I passed the Bunker Hill Monument,
silhouetted against an orange-purple sky; the USS *Con-
stitution* and the fountain in the Navy Yard where I had
played as a girl.

And on that night—one of the last that I would
spend in Boston—I was amazed at how insubstantial
was my connection to the city and even the home in
which I had been raised. Thirty years before, as a student at Harvard, my father had taken the first steps toward putting down roots here; when I was a child, and
even a teenager, it was impossible to tell that these had
not taken. But they had not and they did not, and it
is still stunning to me how easily expunged was the

metaphysical framework that held the three of us for all that time. The house was sold nearly ten years ago, to a couple with young children who made a line of cocktail mixers and planned on filming infomercials in the kitchen; I have not been to Boston since. It is almost as if this framework never existed—certainly the world would be no different had it not.

10

"To want and not to have—to want and want—how
that wrung the heart, and wrung it again and again!"

In April 1924, when Virginia's niece Angelica was
struck down by a motor car, she accompanied her sister to Middlesex Hospital, where the child lay motionless behind a screen; for a short while, Vanessa believed
that her daughter was dead. Virginia saw then on her
sister's face an "extraordinary look of anguish, dumb,
not complaining," notable not only for its visceral power
but also for its contrast to her own lack of emotion, her
sense of being separate from events. "My feeling was 'a
pane of glass shelters me,' " she wrote in her diary afterward. " 'I'm only allowed to look on at this.' at which
I was half envious, half grieved. . . . What I felt was, not
sorrow or pity for Angelica." As it turned out, Angelica would emerge unscathed—"it was only a joke this
time"—and yet the episode remained another iteration
of Virginia's anxiety at "not feeling enough," another
iteration of the capriciousness of grief.

By the time I sequestered myself in Rhode Island
that summer, courting the kind of pain that had felled
that well-dressed woman on the street—my own version

of Vanessa's look of anguish—I had become obsessed by the idea I was not grieving properly. Where was my abyss of sorrow, I wondered, where were my hysteria and tears? It wasn't that I felt guilty, exactly; perhaps confused would be a better word. Hysteria and tears seemed the only response commensurate with what I'd lost; the only response, too, in keeping with the emotional collapse that our culture of grief worship had led me to expect. Instead my days were vague and muffled; instead I just felt tired. I longed for moments of breakdown, of which there were only a handful; I coveted their intensity, their sheer, deranged despair. Virginia describes a similar appreciation of pain in "Reminiscences," a letter-essay of sorts to her nephew Julian. "We were quite naturally unhappy," she writes, reflecting on the family's period of mourning his grandmother, "feeling a definite need, unbearably keen at moments, which was never to be satisfied." And yet the appearance of such acute sadness was preferable to the cloudiness of daily experience: "that was recognizable pain, and the sharp pang grew to be almost welcome in the midst of the sultry and opaque life which was not felt, had nothing real in it, and yet swam about us, and choked us and blinded us." Still in Rhode Island, still in thrall to my own opaque and sultry life, I chalked up my muted feelings to shock or denial, confident that in a week or two or six I would finally unravel.

I have called ours a culture of grief worship; I have blamed it for deceiving me. And it's true, I think, that we have become invested in the idea that grief has on us an unconditional impact, that it alters us, that it *explains* us, at the same time as it brings us to our knees. How many contemporary books and films purposefully allude to the earlier death of the protagonist's mother—or brother or fiancée or son—as if that fact alone proves the existence of a deep, irrecoverable wound, and not mere laziness on the part of the writer or director? How many adopt for this allusion a tone of oblique, quiet stoicism, as if to convey what can *only* have been a crushing experience of loss? And how many, should the protagonist maintain he is intact in the wake of his bereavement, insist that he is rather in a state of deep denial that must be exploded later on? I have lost count. Of course there are works that, taking loss as their subject or backstory, treat it with the necessary thoughtfulness; of course our grief can wound us, leaving scars that never heal. But I rebel against the notion that the death of a loved one is *necessarily* disfiguring, and that, as such, it may be used as a substitute for character development. There is no more validity to grief than to boredom; grief need not be more transformative than joy.

Virginia offered her own critique of society's untenable expectations around mourning, one that clarified for me the great cost of these narratives. Starting with the nurse who sobbed beside her mother's deathbed— "She's pretending, I said"—she often turned to the metaphor of theater to describe the kinds of behaviors that, in her view, concealed a more authentic response to loss. Her mother's death forced her and her siblings "to act parts that we did not feel," she wrote; it gave rise to countless "foolish and sentimental ideas." The same is true of Mrs. Ramsay's death in *To the Lighthouse*, in which Mr. Ramsay enrages Lily and his children by enacting a version of Leslie Stephen's own appalling scenes: "Sitting in the boat, he bowed, he crouched himself, acting instantly his part—the part of a desolate man, widowed, bereft." It's this kind of playacting that alienates the searchers among us, those of us who bridle at its false prescriptions and its melodrama; but it's this kind of performance, too, that leads—through fraudulent example—to the bewilderment and shame we share with Lily at not feeling more. "All these tears and groans," Virginia recalled, "reproaches and protestations of affection . . . were doubtless what we should feel if we felt properly, and yet we had but a dull sense of gloom which could not honestly be referred to the dead." The adult writer's tone may be tongue-in-cheek, skewering the notion of a "proper" way to grieve, but the child who lived it still felt herself a failure.

But for all this—all we absorb about grief making—my own innate assumptions about the toll that loss must take were most deceptive. I couldn't conceive of a world in which my father could die and leave me whole; I couldn't conceive of that world even after I had made my home in it. Those clichés about grief endure precisely because they play well with our expectations.

Over a decade has passed since I called my mother from that university hallway to learn that my father was dead. Not once in that time have I taken leave of my senses or even managed to escape my own self-consciousness; I doubt I ever will. At some point, I stopped waiting for shock or denial to pass, confident that I had not been prey to either one. I had longed for a steep, rocky terrain upon which to stagger and fall, Colorado perhaps, but if my experience had been a landscape, it would have looked like Iowa, with its hills and vales and fields that sometimes flatten in the breeze. Today I think the flatness *was* the grief, the way that grief expressed itself for me; that grief is above all a malaise, awful *because* of its monotony and not in spite of it.

It's writers like Woolf, their refusal to give in to popular ideas about bereavement, who have helped me to accept the nature of this misery. For all her anger at the "unpardonable mischief" wrought by the conventions of sorrow, and at those play-actors who force upon us insincere performances, she is equally attuned to the disquiet that arises when it feels as if our capacity for grief has malfunctioned; she knows the utter loneliness of this sensation. "It was a miserable machine," Lily thinks of the human apparatus for feeling; "it always broke down at the critical moment." There may be readers who find this unrelatable—certainly my mother, who had more regrets than I did about the life she lived with my father, struggled more than I did with his death. Yet there are other readers for whom Woolf's nuanced portrayal of loss—which acknowledges the frustration, inconstancy, and even tedium of grief in addition to its horror—provides not just a welcome challenge to the prevailing wisdom but also a vital consolation. From my father's death, I learned that grief is personal and unpredictable, that it will confound our expectations as often as fulfill them, that the disappearance of a loved one, even the *most* loved one, is not necessarily the insurmountable setback we foresee. But it remains at once comforting and validating to find these lessons mirrored on the page; it makes one feel that one is not alone. And I know that even my mother would recognize something of herself in *To the Lighthouse*—in Mr. Ramsay's underlying strength, perhaps. For even she recovered, even she rebuilt her life. As I think my father realized all along—"You'll be just fine," he always said—human beings are resilient things.

IT WAS NEARLY fall when, still alone in Rhode Island, I woke from a bad dream about my father. I was used to bad dreams about him, of course, and used as well to the jarring juxtaposition between them and consciousness. On that morning, though, I had the sense that the dream had crossed over into real life. I felt it as soon as I opened my eyes: here was a raw new world, clear and hard as a diamond, in which everything that normally pleased was dripping with death, in which everything that had all summer seemed the same had suddenly revealed itself to be sinister. Am I overstating it? Perhaps, but then again, neither before nor since have I brooked such a strong sense of what Virginia, her evening shot through with the sight of a woman pinned beneath a motor car, once described as "the brutality & wildness of the world."

I made the bed, I went downstairs, I put on the kettle, I opened the blinds; for hours I quivered, half-present (drinking tea, reading the paper) and half-behind a scrim of memory, or rather a sort of demi-memory, for I felt that I was nearly flogging myself in an effort to recall him. I began with an August just two years earlier, when my mother was in Australia—I remembered that we had carried in the rolled-up sisal rug from the studio for the cats to climb, had propped it against the window in the living room, and that my father was so delighted by their scampering that we turned off the movie and watched them instead. I remembered that he helped me to make a denim skirt from an old pair of jeans, that he asked our neighbor Pam to come round and show me how to use the sewing machine. I begged him not to bother her, embarrassed, and he chided me as he often did for being so shy.

But I could summon nothing else from those weeks, and so turned to the house itself, moving from room to room, scouring each one for the habitual. From the living room I retrieved the image of him next to the CD player—he had just put in Mozart and was standing with his eyes closed, swaying slightly, humming happily in time to the rich, smooth opening sounds—*Bom, bom, ba-bom.* (He often closed his eyes in anticipation of a glorious movement, smiling faintly and holding up a finger while he listened.) On the deck I saw him sitting in the far chair, feet planted on the wooden planks, and later sitting along the railing, looking out across the water: the now-spent vision of the way he grasped the roof with one hand and reached for a glass of wine with the other. Then I tried to imagine him lighting the coal stove in winter, but could not picture how he must have kneeled or squatted—I have no image of him crouching. Every memory is like that, even now. Certain details are clear—the arm holding the roof; the finger raised to halt the drift of life—but the whole is shadowy, and the more fiercely I try to seize the center, the more quickly it eludes me, and grows not like him at all.

So having failed I went down to the dock and spread out my towel; returned to *War and Peace* (the death of Prince Andrei loomed); and then saw out of the corner of my eye something white floating in the water. It looked like a feather, but it was fleshy, like a tiny squid—I never did learn what it was—and the little green minnows, the same green as the sea when the sun shines through it, were pulling at it with their dumb, round mouths, flicking it away, then drawing it near, playing tug of war, until a larger minnow snatched it decisively in his mouth. He swam in tight circles, chased by the others as he was, until eventually the feather-like thing, which was growing smaller all the while, disappeared completely. It was in the minnow's belly, shining palely and grotesquely through his translucent skin. But then, *splah*, and the white thing was expelled and returned to its original shape, and the game of tug of war recommenced, stopping only when a school of bigger fish— who are the size of salad plates and swim nearer the sea floor, making it seem when they pass beneath the minnows as if the ocean is made up of shelves of glass— rose suddenly to the surface and frightened the minnows away.

And then Prince Andrei died, and the day grew harder and clearer and even more diamond-like, and I remembered, as I sometimes remember, that I was not the only one who was mourning, who had mourned— that there was death after death after death, and that it was not my sorrow alone on the waterfront, but mine and many others; that John's wife, Barbara, sunning herself the next dock over, might have lost her mother a few years back; that the doctor two doors down might think daily of his younger brother's memory. And suddenly the thought of all that sadness—both incompatible with the brittle beauty of the day and somehow equal to it—was terrifying to me, and terrible, and I saw it expanding, a filmy, diaphanous fabric settling over everything and at the same time rising up into the bright blue vibrating sky, and I wondered where

it all went, and how it all fit, and how we as human
beings continue. I had thought it before, of course—
remembered how, in the months when my father was
dying, being human and alive suddenly struck me as a
larger, greater task than it had ever seemed before, and
how the dimensions of the world abruptly changed as
what we face crept in. And how was it, I wondered on
the dock, that I had not noticed this fabric before? How
was it that just yesterday I had laughed on the phone
with friends and thought the blue sky big and ordinary?
This was not grieving, surely, but yet more biding of
time.

Toward the end of *To the Lighthouse*, the anguish
that Lily has been trying to summon all morning
reaches a dreadful climax—a caution, perhaps, to those
like me who would court suffering, who cannot conceive
the misery of the very misery they seek. And yet coupled with Lily's pain is her conviction that it must hold
great power, even the power to raise Mrs. Ramsay. I get
it: How could something so consuming, so gigantic, so
utterly undoing, contain no force at all? How could the
despair I'd felt that night of the eclipse not power whole
cities; how could the heartache that consumed me on
the dock not call back not just my own father but Barbara's mother and the doctor's brother as well? That, I
think, is the final point to be made about grief: that it
recalls to us our impotence, reminds us that our longing
counts for nothing. Lily's "heart leapt at her and seized
her and tortured her. 'Mrs. Ramsay! Mrs. Ramsay!'
she cried, feeling the old horror come back—to want
and want and not to have. Could she inflict that still?"
To want and want and not to have—my god, the pri-
mal, powerful injustice of that phrase! and the terrible

simplicity of the problem, insoluble, that death presents us with.

Lily's agony will pass, of course—it's just moments after she cries out for her friend that her yearning begins to recede. And so too on the dock in Rhode Island, where even as I was trying to figure them out, the fabric was lifting and the feeling passing on. The sun beat down on my face; I wanted a swim, and the minnows kissing the otherwise smooth surface of the water seemed no longer sinister, murderous, but like small stupid fish that would leave me in peace when I broke the surface myself. And the basin was beautiful again, only beautiful, and the sound of a neighbor repairing his roof, the metallic blows ringing out across the water, was no longer merciless, but a call for good, hard work, the kind that gets the blood flowing, and yes, I longed to dive in. But I missed him. That's always what it comes down to, after all. I miss him, and sometimes it is bearable, and sometimes it is not.

11

Eventually it came time to tackle his ephemera. I sat at the family room table, sorting through résumés, letters, the articles he had published in architecture school; I flipped through his wine label collection, thirteen years' worth of crinkled insignia paired with prices, dates, and comments ("Another excellent Barolo. I do like them, but seldom get the time to let them romp around in the atmosphere before finishing them off"). The onslaught was exhausting: I was about to go to bed when I saw my name, rendered in his blocky scrawl, on a sheet upon a pile of sheets. "Katharine," I read, "who entertained us on a drive to Amalfi with stories of the sirens, who reputedly hung around the Li Galli islands just off Positano, was fascinated at a whirlpool which we saw from Ravello, some thousands of feet below in the sea off Minori. We concurred that it was probably some monstrous phenomenon of time immemorial, despite suspicions to the contrary." My father's Italian diary! I thought it had gone missing years before.

I sucked down the words, some thirty pages of them; I heard his voice as clearly as if he were speaking from across the table:

> Did I write about tourism with a cricked (how do you spell it?) neck? I don't know whether it was a papal curse, or simply the pillow of our Rome pensione. Anyway I can assure you that some 50% of the delights of a tourist in Italy are denied you if you have this complaint. At St. Peter's Katharine was kind enough to invite me to relax, supine, to admire the interior of the cupola. The crack and groan as I resurrected would not have been acceptable when we were younger and the Church more uptight.

This was a kind of alchemy, I thought, wide awake now and rejoicing at the life within the lines; as Lily declares, imagining Mr. Carmichael's reaction to her searching questions, "That would have been his answer, presumably—how 'you' and 'I' and 'she' pass and vanish; nothing stays; all changes; but not words, not paint." Yes.

~

> We drove down the coast toward the airport, and as a last destination arrived at the Etruscan burial mounds at Cevetri, is it? More buses, more kids, but well worth the trip. [. . .] Boy the Romans did a good job of wiping out Etruscan culture. If they can have had such pretty and interesting burial chambers, they must have had neat real

settlements. While most of the chambers are empty and plain—though atmospheric—one was completely as found, sans skeletons, with delightful murals and all the bits and bobs of daily living, hanging from the walls or embedded in the friezes. Remarkable. All too much.

It was a very successful holiday, particularly we hope from Katharine's point of view. I remember how trying it was to travel as a 10 yr old, especially if you can't even go swimming. Though, as we discovered, the Med in March is about the same temperature as the Gulf of Maine in August. In Fiumincino, Fiumicini (I have not a map, but know that it ends in a vowel), we spent our last night as the sole occupants of a pensione overlooking the port, vieux or nouvelle, whichever. It was good to be back by the sea again, and I was envious of a small yacht which had just sailed in from Malta. Its occupants were off to visit Rome. Maybe I'll be able to return some day in the same style.

12

"Of such moments, she thought,
the thing is made that endures."

In November I flew to England to visit my grand-mother—nearly a year had passed since my father's death. I landed at Heathrow in the evening, and later went wandering through the West End of London look-ing for something to eat. The city shone from recent rain, the street lamps reflected wetly on the pavement, and somehow I lost my way, ending up at Tottenham Court Road, and had to turn back, bearing left and left again. That was when I saw the Agra, its red-and-white sign the only attraction in an otherwise empty street. I was startled and disoriented—on the night of my fa-ther's memorial party, we had approached it from the other direction—and the entire city seemed to flip as I realized where I was.

As I waited for the meal to come, I thought how good it was to be once more in London. There was a time when I had known the city well, and when knowing it well had seemed to matter—how important I had deemed it to recognize the streets; to get from A to B without a map. Even tonight, driving from the airport,

I had forced myself to name each new landmark before it appeared: here was the V&A and here Hyde Park; here the Serpentine and next Marble Arch. It shocked me, remembering that I had gotten lost this evening, to think how much I had known and how little I knew now.

Then the food arrived—tandoori lamb, still hissing in a cast-iron pan—and I took out my diary and a pen. I had asked my father, when he was dying, if he had written at all—I could imagine not keeping a diary, but I could not imagine dying and not keeping one. Perhaps, too, it was my roundabout way of asking him what I was too scared to ask him: What does a dying person think about? How does he bear it? "No," he said. "I was never a writer."

"But you wrote in Italy," I said.

"That's right," he said. "I think I was just emulating you." He paused, smiling. "I remember sitting at cafés with you," he said. "In the Piazza Navona." I remembered it too—the pigeons and the morning light.

Before going to sleep that night, he asked if I would help him make a to-do list. He wanted to (1) write a boat prospectus for the broker and (2) figure out how to say good-bye to his mother.

"That's not too much," I said.

"No," he said. "But I want to leave quietly. I'm trying to leave behind a very small space." He was silent for a moment. "I occupied a small space in this world, and I intend to leave only a small, empty void in my place."

When the waiter came for the bill, I said that the Agra had been one of my father's favorite restaurants, and that we had held a service for him here last spring. The waiter looked puzzled, but then said, "Yes, of course—I know your uncle. He comes here a lot."

I nodded. "He likes it too," I said, feeling foolish. Of course Andrew would be a bigger presence for this waiter than my father's memory. But it was always shocking to be reminded of how quickly and completely my father's effect had been diminished on his death—I expect most people leave behind a small space, whether they intend to or not. Then the waiter returned to the kitchen, and I was left only with the vague dissatisfaction that arises when I mention something that is meaningful to me to a stranger or even a friend to whom it is not meaningful at all. (The same thing happened when I visited the exhibition on little magazines in New York. "My father started *Clip-Kit* with Peter Murray," I made myself say to the girl working behind the front desk. "Oh, yeah?" she said. "Cool.")

I was still glad to have come. I looked at the door and imagined my father walking in when he was a student at the Architectural Association, then imagined us both walking in during the winter when I was seventeen—we had sat at the table near the window. I thought of the middle-aged men and women who had filled the room during the party a few months earlier. I did not think of Virginia Woolf, who for years had lived just blocks away, who had haunted these same streets, who had almost certainly set foot upon the pavement right outside. The layers that accumulate, the memories we graft upon a place—these are a source of solace.

"TO FRESHEN MY memory of the war," Virginia wrote in 1933, "I read some old diaries. How close the tears come, again & again; as I read of L. & me at the Green. . . . The sense of all that floating away for ever down the stream, unknown for ever; queer sense of the past swallowing so much of oneself." This idea—the power of the past to erase us, to steal from us every last moment of which our lives are composed—is omnipresent in *To the Lighthouse*. The sound of the waves on the beach seems to Mrs. Ramsay like a warning to "her whose day had slipped past in one quick doing after another that it was all ephemeral as a rainbow," and she will later seek to stop such slippage, pausing on the threshold of the dining room to take stock of an evening that is already beginning to vanish. I did the same upon tucking my father into bed that night, that night so long ago when we stayed up talking and crafting his to-do list; I stayed up even later in the living room, recording every word I could remember, pretending we were in that conversation still, knowing full well that it had fled forever.

But what if there were some way of retrieving the moment, *really* retrieving it, so that we need never pause on the threshold, need never agonize over saying good-bye? Virginia was captive to the way in which the past "can still be more real than the present," by how the Cornwall nursery held more reality for her than the present-day sight of the gardener outside. "At times I can go back to St Ives more completely than I can this morning," she declares and then, taking this truth to its logical conclusion, envisions a futuristic contraption that we could plug into the wall to access *all* our missing moments (August 1890, say); a contraption by which we may "live our lives through from the start."

I can imagine Mrs. Ramsay's girlish delight at the prospect of such an invention—Mrs. Ramsay who at dinner, reminded of a weekend when she stayed with old friends, cannot wait to escape the Hebridean table for that drawing room of decades past. She still remembers all the details—how cold she was as they went up the river, how Herbert pinned a wasp beneath a spoon—and stands in awe of how that day has continued to exist, of how she is even able to return to it, albeit only as a phantom: "And it was still going on, Mrs. Ramsay mused, gliding like a ghost among the chairs and tables . . . it fascinated her, as if, while she had changed, that particular day, now become very still and beautiful, had remained there, all these years." Her recognition that such a weekend endures—that it is untouched—holds a strange, consoling logic: If a moment must pass, it must remain the same. What has happened, happens always. "However long they lived," she supposes of her guests, they would "come back to this night; this moon; this wind; this house: and to her too."

On the morning after my Agra dinner, I took the train to my grandmother's village. She and I passed a quiet afternoon and evening, until my uncle Robert surprised us by showing up unannounced after dinner and taking us to see the Guy Fawkes fireworks. It was a cold, clear night; my grandmother had forgotten her cane, and she clung to my arm as we walked along the promenade separating the millpond from the harbor. Before long there were fireworks in the distance, faint sparks showering on Hayling, and then the sky itself seemed to erupt—the sailing club had set off its own rockets. Drops of light rained down toward the water, and in so doing illuminated the nearby pontoon where six months before we had scattered my father's remains. I thought of him, of course, of the water turning green beneath my shadow; and then I thought of another night long ago when I had left my uncle at the Blue

Bell, his pub, walking home alone to the harsh, sweet smell of a bonfire.

And then again the following day, when, after a visit to the Royal Oak, my father's pub, I headed back along the promenade. It was a bright, hot afternoon—I was too warm in my turtleneck sweater—and the tide was out, the mud verdant and shining. I sat down beside a swan asleep, marveled at how clean and white she was; there were dozens more swans floating in the pond, and as I sat there a pair prepared to take off, their wingtips sounding like a spray of bullets as they struck the water. And with their ascent I had a sudden vision, steadily expanding, of all the millpond moments existing simultaneously (set one atop the other like transparencies); a vision of a hundred selves, layering, going about their business—not just the ash scattering and Blue Bell walk but also my young parents dragging the dinghy from the water, and my childhood trips to the Royal Oak, and the previous evening when my grandmother had taken my arm and faced the blazing, burning sky, and even the existing moment (the sleeping swan beside me), which I knew would never, could never, be divorced from all the rest. And why does it have to be *now*, I wondered, as opposed to *then*, or *then*? Why can't I glide back and forth—so long as I am sitting here on the bank of the millpond?

At lunch, Robert had said, "Your uncle Andrew, last time he was here, remarked that it would be a pity to give this place up." He was referring to Seafield, my grandmother's house, and later I pressed him: Was Andrew thinking of buying it? Robert looked pained and waved my question away. But I felt a quiver of hope— why not? When my grandmother died, Andrew could buy Seafield, Robert could live here, and then we would never have to give anything up. For wasn't this house also a place that made it especially easy to dip into time? My grandmother was harder of hearing now, and Robert's limp was worse. There were more photographs of my father. But there had always been photographs, and there was little else to mark the passing years, and so it might have been my father and not my uncle sitting in that chair, or so it might have been that I was twenty and reading *To the Lighthouse* well into the night, or that my father and I were about to set off on foot, through thawing fields, for late-morning drinks at the Royal Oak. What had happened once was happening still; all those moments, all those selves, existing at once, existing forever—what a cluttered world!—and all one had to do was pick one to today inhabit; pick another to tomorrow inhabit.

In the same diary entry in which Virginia recounted her 1905 visit to Talland House, she described the wild fantasies that accompanied returning to the place that was for her synonymous with happiness. The Great Western train that carried her and her siblings toward Cornwall was a "wizard who was to transport us into another world, almost into another age," while Cornwall itself was a time capsule, hermetically sealed until now: "We would fain have believed that this little corner of England had slept under some enchanters spell since we last set eyes on it ten years ago, & that no breath of change had stirred its leaves." Her greatest wish of all, though, was that contact with St Ives would actually *return* her to the past, actually provide a conduit by which to relive all those marvelous days of childhood, their yellow light and breaking waves, and by which to relive, too, presumably, the brief stretch of years when she and her mother overlapped. In Cornwall, she imagined, "we should find our past preserved, as though through all this time it had been guarded & treasured for us to come back to one day. . . . Many were the summers we had spent in St Ives; was it not reasonable to believe that . . . here on the spot where we left them we should be able to recover something tangible of their substance?"

But Virginia's expedition to Talland House revealed the folly of this conceit—once there, it was impossible to escape the fact that the "lights were not our lights," that "the voices were the voices of strangers." And so too the folly of my own hope: Of course we would have to give up Seafield. As we had given up the boat, and the friends, and the living room with its marble fireplaces and silver mirrors, and even the hospital, so would we give up my grandmother's house. It was just as well, for when she was gone there would be nothing to draw us back. The memories were not enough; even poor Robert was not enough. And from my post by the millpond I suddenly saw him, roaming the shore with a strange cocker spaniel. I laughed out loud—whose dog was that? The spaniel was pulling at the leash, excited by the swans, and my uncle shuffling to keep up. Then the birds moved on, the dog calmed down, and together they paused at the water, panting slightly and looking out over the harbor.

Later, the sitting room quiet and the fire lit, the windows shuttered and the velvet curtains drawn, my grandmother asked me what I was writing about. I told her that more and more I was writing about my father. "I think about him all the time," she said and then, almost indignant, "He seemed so well when we saw him at the hospital!" She asked if I remembered the night during their visit when he and Andrew had stayed up late; I said that I did. "Andrew said he wanted to talk about all kinds of funny things—about the past."

She set down her whiskey and stood. "There's something I want you to have," she said. I waited while she climbed the stairs; she returned holding a small box. Inside was a ring, a topaz that her husband, Charles, had smuggled back from the Middle East in the handle of a hairbrush. A champagne-colored stone held fast by four golden claws, it was glowing and golden and weightless throughout; looking down into it was like looking into a pale, light-slanted pool. "You take it with you when you go," she said. "You'll have it soon enough." But there was something in the way she looked at the ring on my hand that made me say I would take it some other time. And I was glad that I did, for she seemed immediately grateful to hold on to it, this gift from her husband, for a little while longer.

"And all the lives we ever lived and all the lives to be
are full of trees and changing leaves."

On my first night back in New York, sometime around
dawn, I had another dream about my father. In it, the
Rhode Island house had been sold and this was to be our
final visit; the property, no longer wooden and worn,
was an apartment on the ninth floor, and new kitchen
cabinets and a washing machine blocked much of the
view. The walls looked flimsy enough to blow away in
the next strong wind. We wandered around, pausing at
the one window to reveal the sea far below. "It's such an
insensitive renovation," I said. "God, I'll say," my father
said.

"You'll need to find somewhere else to go."

"Every time I needed to leave I went to Rhode
Island."

"Couldn't you find another house in Rhode Island?"
I asked, but he demurred.

Then we were walking along the beach, longer now,
rockier, and strewn with green and purple seaweed.
It seemed to stretch forever—the ocean was simply a

suggestion—and seemed too to have all of life bound up in it, for there in the distance was a dovecote, now boarded up, that had once belonged to my uncle Andrew in France, and then the faraway figure of an old neighbor from Boston. But the farther we walked, the more desolate the beach became; water pooled and ran in rivulets between obsidian rocks, as if to say we might finally be reaching the shoreline, and then, suddenly, my father faltered and collapsed. I wasn't expecting it but knew at once that it was time, and I kneeled down next to him and touched his face. His eyes were closed, but he was still breathing. The feeling of impotence was far greater than it had ever been in real life. "You were the best father," I told him. And with that he opened his eyes—his head was flat and pale against the rounded stones—and somehow I understood that my use of the past tense, *were*, had succeeded in making his death real to him for the first time. And the expression on his face (he was looking not at me but past me) was one of terror; he saw something true and looming in this landscape, and whatever it was he saw caused him to wince and say, in a single, despairing breath: "Crikey."

He closed his eyes.

VIRGINIA WOOLF ONCE published a short story called "A Haunted House," about a man and woman, long dead, who return to the home they shared in search of something—"buried treasure," the narrator (and present occupant) calls the nameless thing they seek. The pair moves hand in hand between the rooms, draw-

ing back curtains, opening drawers, as all the while
the residence plays a soothing accompaniment: " 'Safe,
safe, safe,' the pulse of the house beat softly. . . . 'Safe,
safe, safe,' the pulse of the house beat gladly." Eventually, reaching the bedroom where the living owners lie
asleep, the ghosts reflect on their reunion: "Again you
found me," the man says. "Here," the woman replies,
"sleeping; in the garden reading; laughing, rolling apples in the loft. Here we left our treasure." As they bend
toward the slumbering couple, the narrator finally stirs,
realizing the true nature of their riches, and that they
lie within her: "Waking, I cry 'Oh, is this *your* buried
treasure? The light in the heart.' "

"A Haunted House" is a peculiar story, one whose
mystery is probably better left preserved, but it makes
me wonder about the blurred boundaries between a
house and its inhabitants, about the role our houses
play in protecting and sustaining us—it's the couple's
home that enables their reunion, their home that is in-
separable from the everyday doings (sleeping, reading,
laughing) that is the fiber of their lives. And I love that
"your" is italicized in the last line—"Oh, is this *your*
buried treasure?"—as if to say that the light we carry in
our hearts, and that our houses hold within their walls,
exists independently of us; belongs to the men and
women who precede us; spreads to the men and women
who come after. We *are* our houses, the story seems to
insist, as our forebears are our houses, and these shelters
will preserve us and our buried treasure long after we
are dead.

Perhaps it's unsurprising that Woolf, a writer unusually well versed in the loss of place and people both,

would forever return to these ideas. As Hermione Lee notes, each of the deaths she endured in youth "precipitated the loss of a home: Julia's, Talland House; Leslie's, Hyde Park Gate; Thoby's, Gordon Square." At times she affected a kind of nonchalance about rooting herself, expressing an urge to travel or set up shop in France or Italy; her niece Angelica recalled her contention "that one ought to have houses all about the country, and directly one has become imbued with the atmosphere of one's house, and indifferent to it, one ought to move to another." As Virginia and Leonard argued over the costs associated with their country home—including whether or not to hire a full-time gardener—she worried that further investment in it would limit their horizons: "we shall be tying ourselves to come here; shall never travel; & it will be assumed that Monks House is the hub of the world."

And yet she was deeply, perhaps inextricably, bound to certain places—Cornwall, London, Sussex—and deeply cognizant, too, of the bonds that form between people and their palaces. (The name she chose for her first Sussex cottage? Little Talland House.) "Half the beauty of a country or a house comes from knowing it," she wrote in 1928. "One remembers old lovelinesses: knows that it is now looking ugly; waits to see it light up; knows where to find its beauty; how to ignore the bad things. This one can't do the first time of seeing." The ghostly couple in "A Haunted House" has seen and seen and seen—they remember rising in the mornings and pottering in the garden; the advent of summer and snowfall in winter—and it's impossible to think of the home they pervade without also thinking of Monk's

House, which, Virginia declared in 1919, would "be our address for ever and ever; Indeed I've already marked out our graves in the yard which joins our meadow." Seen through this lens, Leonard and Virginia play both roles, not just that of the house's living couple but also the phantom pair who haunts its halls.

In *To the Lighthouse*, it's Mrs. Ramsay who holds the light in the heart, Mrs. Ramsay who, like the house in Woolf's story, promises her friends and family that she will keep them safe. And as she climbs toward the nursery, imagining herself forever wound in *their* hearts, and recalling her own parents as she sees their furniture on the landing, she glimpses an immortality like that of the ghosts—"that community of feeling with other people which emotion gives as if the walls of partition had become so thin that practically (the feeling was one of relief and happiness) it was all one stream, and chairs, tables, maps, were hers, were theirs, it did not matter whose, and Paul and Minta would carry it on when she was dead." How curious, how compelling, this vision of the dissolution of the boundaries between people, so that it all—our houses, our belongings, our selves—becomes communal, becomes eternal; passes from us to our friends, to their friends, to their friends; a single, steady river that will forever flow.

My father is dead. I say that not as I did in that first year (trying to make it real, trying to understand what it might signify), but as a fact, and one that sometimes makes me wonder whether all this—this reading, this remembering, this reflecting, this reckoning, this parsing, this clarifying, this hoping, this hypothesizing, this meaning making, this solace seeking, this *writing*—counts for anything all. Have I come up with anything, has Woolf come up with anything, that is more than merely circling a brutal truth? I mean that literally—does there exist *any* revelation that could lessen loss, that could help to make the fact of death okay? I doubt it; almost certainly not. *To want and want and not to have*: there is no escaping that lot. My father is dead. My father is dead. But I keep returning, still—I can't help it—to those invisible ties between people and places; to the force of a moment; to a world that sings the song of everyone who has ever been; to art, to love, to memory; and to that quixotic notion— the light in the heart.

"All the lives we ever lived and all the lives to be," says Mr. Ramsay at dinner, his voice at once melancholy and exultant, and Mrs. Ramsay will repeat the phrase as she sits knitting in the sitting room. The words are from a poem by Charles Elton that envisions the speaker and his subject as living over and over and over again, roaming primordial forests, and paying tribute to the world's great kings, and lying cold beneath a church-yard tree, and always, always rising; as if to say those lives were theirs, were ours, it does not matter whose, for nothing gets lost, everything gets carried forward. It's just another fantasy, of course—*my father is dead*— but I can't shake it: to think that Mrs. Ramsay's light is burning; to think my father's light is burning; that they survive in me, in you; that even in their absence they will guide us (for was it not just yesterday night I saw him last? running along a path so quickly that the gravel blurred beneath my feet and leaping at the wa-ter's edge into his boat, the wheel turning—Safe, safe, safe!—and laughing at his greeting, so right, so easy, and thinking as we sped away, Oh, of course, there is *no one* like him! . . .). A fantasy, yes, but its relief and happiness are real.

WHEN I ARRIVED in Rhode Island on our last weekend there—it was November, just weeks before my father went on hospice—he was dismantling the billiard table that had been his fortieth birthday present and giving instructions to the two men who were going to buy it. "Hello, lovey," he said when he saw me; his voice was weary, and before I could hug him hello, he made a terrible face, waved me away, and ran outside. I found him kneeling over the seawall, his hands spread against the concrete, vomiting pink onto the rocks below. He was still retching when the men walked by carrying the table's green felt top. They looked uncomfortable and averted their eyes. "He has cancer," I felt like saying, but instead I said nothing and stared out over the basin until they had gone. It was a blank day, the gray sky one shade lighter than the sea. I touched my father on the shoulder and asked if he wanted some water. "Go away," he said. "Go on, go away."

My parents had arrived that morning to find the house reeking of rotting meat—the electricity had gone out weeks before when a tree fell across a power line. They had placed most of the freezer contents in trash bags on the front porch, but my father wanted to get rid of the meat as soon as possible. "Pops, do me a favor," he said when he was feeling better, "and chuck it into the sea before the sun sets. I don't want the raccoons getting at it." I procrastinated until I saw stark low lines of orange light between the clouds, then put on an old coat and carried the plastic freezer drawer down to the end of the dock.

The hunks of meat had been sealed in clear plastic bags, but several weeks of putrefaction had turned these into taut, bloody balloons. When I punctured one, I heard a pop, and instantly the rancid smell I had carried with me down the dock was overpowering. I gagged and turned my head away; the air was cold enough to burn the back of my throat, but I was sure the smell would make me sick. I held the bag at arm's length and dropped its contents, a steak, into the water below. The meat fell with a plop and immediately sank. In this way, I dropped whitefish, scallops, duck; more steak, lamb shank, and several pounds of shrimp. Sometimes I botched the job of slicing open the bags, and when this happened sour liquid ran down my wrists and splashed onto the wooden planks. The chicken breasts didn't sink, but floated away like phantom ships; they caused a stir among the seagulls, who all at once rose screaming from their perches and swooped down to seize the easy prey. When I was done, I dunked the freezer drawer in the sea, and as I did this I had to fend off the circling gulls with my hand. The odor of decay had made them bold.

I returned to the house to find my father leaving for a pack of cigarettes. He was wearing pajamas, slippers, and a dressing gown. His hair was wild. "I'm off to terrify the poor clerks," he said. While he was gone, I showered and scrubbed my hands—the sweet, acidic meat smell would linger for days; I scrubbed so hard my mother took to calling me Lady Macbeth—and then I settled in the living room with a copy of the *Sakonnet Times*. The front-page story was about the old railway bridge at the basin's northern end: after more than a century, they were finally tearing it down. I thought of all the times that we had passed this bridge by boat—at the narrow channel the water churned and thickened, and the tiller leapt from my hands. I was still reading when my father returned.

"You lot have no sense of lighting!" he exclaimed, offended by the naked windows. He shuffled from spot to spot, turning on lamps and lowering blinds; he put on Vivaldi, a guitar concerto, and kneeled to rake the stove, sifting ashes into the pan below, unearthing liquid orange coals. As he worked, I read aloud another article, this one about a horse named Duncan who had been stuck in a swamp in the Weetamoo Woods— Duncan was sedated, lifted into the air in a giant sling, and carried back to his stables. "That's nothing compared to my goat," my father said, and retrieved from the recycling basket an earlier story about a goat who had fallen from the back of a truck and showed up three days later on a rock in Stafford Pond. "All the animals here are saved," I said. My father grunted, unwilling to engage in a conversation so ridiculous.

After dinner, though, he called me over to the nautical chart of Narragansett Bay that was mounted on the landing, and together we traced the tracks of the missing animals: the woods where the horse was drawn from a swamp; the pond where the goat found refuge on a rock. My attention wandered to a beige oval in the center of the bay. "Have we ever been to Conanicut Island?"

"Yes, that's where Jamestown is," my father said.

"What about Prudence?" I asked, looking at the island above it. "Do people live there?"

"Yes, unfortunately. It's ridden with Lyme disease, and there are two schools and terrible water." Then, smiling suddenly, he pointed toward Providence. "Do you remember taking *Mistral* up the river that time? You were only little—we ran aground, and had to plough backwards through the mud." I didn't, but no matter: he was still smiling, thinking of it. Finally he ran his finger along a squiggle of water above Fall River. "I've always wanted to take the dinghy up there as far as it could go," he said. "Let's do that next summer, shall we?"

EVERY FALL, I travel to Rhode Island to close up the house for winter. I empty the fridge and drain the pipes, turn off the heat and let the rooms freeze over; sometimes, in the depths of February, I imagine the bleakness of the place, its faraway gelidity, and I shiver, marveling at the notion of its parallel existence. The ritual is a recent one—after my mother moved to Australia—and it joins a host of other new behaviors: long days spent working in the studio, solitary walks along abandoned railroad tracks, gin and tonics on the deck at sunset. We have replaced the chain-link fence with picket and clad the seawall in teak; a gardener was hired, the rattling windows repaired, the rooms upstairs repainted peach and cream and blue. I could list a dozen other changes, too (the renovated kitchen; the library that supplanted the billiard table), but the truth is that, for all we have altered, for all we have lost, the house still floods with lemon heat, the water still reflects upon the ceiling; the light still bleaches spines of books, and the nautical chart of the bay—mounted on foam core, a little black

pushpin marking the location of our home—still deco-
rates the landing where my father screwed it to the wall
some thirty years ago.

The chart's scale is such that I can sketch and measure the various running routes I have devised over the
years: one up the hill to the library and down past Sin
and Flesh Brook, a stream named for a Quaker who was
murdered and thrown to its waters; another along the
basin, past Gould Island, to the banks of Nanaquaket
Pond; and yet another through an almost rural length
of land on which grow flaxen, papery crops of corn. But
the distance covered by this chart is large enough, too,
to include the destinations to which we used to sail, and
the towns to which we used to drive, and looking at it
closely, I can feel the years piling atop one another, the
encounters accruing, gathering in messy, lifelike heaps;
so that halted on the landing, studying the light brown
fingers of land and pale blue stretches of water, I am
returned to all that came before—not just to the night
I stood here with my father, so gladly wasting time, but
also to the weekends moored in Wickford Harbor and
the regattas off Block Island, to tumbling down fine-
as-flour dunes in Island Park and jumping from the
cliffs at Brenton Cove; to wandering the rocks at Fog-
land Beach, and sneaking off toward Sakonnet Light,
and passing by boat beneath the Mount Hope Bridge,
its soaring metal underbelly; and to hearing, as a
child, the voice of the man who phoned from Point
Judith to say he had found on the beach the letter in a
bottle I had flung into the bay some weeks before.

And I am returned, finally, to the last night in Rhode
Island that my father and I ever spent together—my
hair still drying from a bath, he determined not to

tire—to an evening that was cold and glowing and blue, to a short walk that took us north, past the houses, to the foot of the elevated green highway. There we stopped to rest, and watched as a crane loaded corroded pieces of metal onto a barge moored in the middle of the basin. With a shock I realized, looking at the now-empty sweep of water beneath the overpass, that they were the rusty remains of the old railway bridge. The crane was yellow, and as it clumsily pushed about the growing mound of steel, I was reminded of a timid animal searching and sniffing for food. But then the crane grasped a long, reddish-brown beam in its mouth, raised its head, magnificent, and let this beam drop from an immense height down upon the pile; there was a split second of silence, and next a great booming roar that roused the water and shook the street, and as we watched a haze of orange dust rose up from the barge, ascending higher and higher before floating away to nothing against the deep blue air. We stood there for a long time, hearing the thunder and watching rust speckle the sky; again, hearing the thunder and watching rust speckle the sky, and only when the power and beauty of this spectacle had diminished, did we return, our bodies flushed with winter, to the warmth of our waterfront home.

NOTES

When I first read *To the Lighthouse*, I had no idea how different was my battered 1955 Harcourt, Brace edition from the original British—that "laboriously correcting two sets of proofs," as Virginia wrote to Vita Sackville-West in February 1927, would give rise to a host of variant versions that diverge in sometimes significant ways. (For more on this subject, see Mark Hussey and Peter Shillingsburg's essay "The Composition, Revision, Printing and Publication of *To the Lighthouse*.") Since then, I have immersed myself in a handful of different copies, cobbling together an ideal novel that incorporates my favorite passages; though I'm drawn to the last lines of "The Window" as they appear in the American first edition, for instance, I'm partial to the wording and syntax of Mrs. Ramsay's death as it unfolds in the 1992 Penguin. Unless otherwise noted, I have drawn all quotations in this book from the 1981 Harcourt, Brace edition of *To the Lighthouse*—a difficult decision, but one that seemed to make sense given my initial introduction to the novel and its familiarity to American readers.

My engagement with Virginia Woolf and her work has been an occasionally haphazard process, one stretching nearly two decades. In college I threw myself into a great pool of criticism—books and essays by Erich Auerbach, John Batchelor, E. M. Forster, Mark Hussey, James Wood, and Alex Zwerdling in particular—but I have since focused my reading on biographies and memoirs, including Julia Briggs's *Virginia Woolf: An Inner Life*, Viviane Forrester's *Virginia Woolf: A Portrait*, and Amy Licence's *Living in Squares, Loving in Triangles: The Lives and Loves of Virginia Woolf and the Bloomsbury Group*. The literary scholar Arnold Weinstein, who oversaw a senior honors thesis that I wrote on Woolf in college, has also been a major influence and an unflagging source of inspiration.

I am indebted above all to the work of Hermione Lee, not just to her wise, empathetic biography but also to her incisive notes and criticism. Ever since I had the privilege of attending Lee's lectures as a student at Oxford, her mastery of Virginia Woolf has indelibly shaped my own understanding of my favorite author's life and writing. Many of the quotes that I incorporate from Woolf's diaries and letters I initially encountered in Lee, and so too many of the scenes from her life; these extracts have often led me down new paths, but it was Lee who showed me how and where to wander in the first place.

I have drawn the lion's share of Woolf's autobiographical writing from "A Sketch of the Past," her 1939 memoir; at times I have pulled from "Reminiscences" (1908) and "Hyde Park Gate" (1920) as well.

All three essays appear in *Moments of Being*, a collection edited by Jeanne Schulkind that was published posthumously in 1976 and revised in 1985; in all cases, I have relied on the 1985 edition. It's worth noting, too, that while I have occasionally altered verb tenses and capital or lowercase letters for clarity, I have otherwise maintained Woolf's original spelling and punctuation whenever I quote from her letters, diaries, books, and manuscripts.

Much the same is true of my father's Italian diary and his letters from Harvard: aside from cutting a few extraneous words and one or two commas for clarity, I have otherwise maintained his original spelling and punctuation. Finally, all character names are unchanged, with the exception of my grandmother's friend Claudette, whose real name, confusingly, is also Zette.

ABBREVIATIONS

> *D: The Diary of Virginia Woolf*
>
> *E: The Essays of Virginia Woolf*
>
> *L: The Letters of Virginia Woolf*
>
> *MB: Moments of Being*
>
> *PA: A Passionate Apprentice: The Early Journals of Virginia Woolf*

PREFACE

"**queasy undergraduate**" *D*, 2:188–89, 16 August 1922.

"**Never never have I**" *D*, 3:58, 8 February 1926.

"**close on 40,000 words**" Virginia Woolf to Vita Sackville-West, 16 March 1926, *L*, 3:249.

"**Against you I will fling**" *The Waves*, 297.

PART ONE, CHAPTER 1

In Chapter 1, I am grateful to Hermione Lee and her biography *Virginia Woolf* for drawing my attention to both the darkness of the Stephens' London home and Virginia's and Vanessa's later recollections of it.

"**If life has a base**" "A Sketch of the Past," in *MB*, 64–65.

"**the most important**" "A Sketch of the Past," in *MB*, 64.

"**busts shrined in crimson**" "Hyde Park Gate," in *MB*, 164.

"**faces loomed**" Vanessa Bell, "Life at Hyde Park Gate after 1897," in *Sketches in Pen and Ink*, 81.

"**to go sailing**" "A Sketch of the Past," in *MB*, 127–28.

"**is where she sites**" Lee, *Virginia Woolf*, 22.

"**Father instantly decided**" "A Sketch of the Past," in *MB*, 136.

"**An old creature**" Virginia Woolf to Vita Sackville-West, 13 May 1927, *L*, 3:374.

"**there are no rooks**" Virginia Woolf to Vanessa Bell, 22 May 1927, *L*, 3:379.

"**This time tomorrow**" *D*, 2:103, 22 March 1921.

"**old waves**" *D*, 2:103, 22 March 1921.

"**the sea is to be heard**" *D*, 3:34, 27 June 1925.

"**A square house**" "A Sketch of the Past," in *MB*, 128.

"**a garden of an acre**" Stephen, *Mausoleum Book*, 62.

"**onto her balcony**" "A Sketch of the Past," in *MB*, 66.

"**we linger in front**" "How Should One Read a Book?," in *The Second Common Reader*, 261.

PART ONE, CHAPTER 3

"obsessed . . . full of her" "A Sketch of the Past," in *MB*, 80–83.

"of red and purple flowers" "A Sketch of the Past," in *MB*, 64.

"I suspect the word" "A Sketch of the Past," in *MB*, 83.

a writer who couldn't "Can I remember ever being alone with her for more than a few minutes? Someone was always interrupting." "A Sketch of the Past," in *MB*, 83.

PART ONE, CHAPTER 4

In Chapter 4, the observation that Virginia switches from "I" to "we" while writing to Leonard belongs to Hermione Lee, who offers an insightful analysis of the letter in her biography. The account of Leonard and Virginia's wedding is drawn from Viviane Forrester's *Virginia Woolf: A Portrait.*

"How did father . . . admiration for his mind" "A Sketch of the Past," in *MB*, 91.

Gordon and Fitzroy Squares Virginia lived with Vanessa, Thoby, and Adrian Stephen at 46 Gordon Square from 1904 to 1907; following Thoby's death and Vanessa's marriage to Clive Bell, Virginia and Adrian moved to 29 Fitzroy Square, where they lived until 1911.

the birthplace of "Then one day walking round Tavistock Square I made up, as I sometimes make up my books, *To the Lighthouse*; in a great, apparently involuntary, rush." "A Sketch of the Past," in MB, 81.

"detestable" Virginia Woolf to Vanessa Bell, 25 April 1913, *L*, 2:24.

"exalted views" Stephen, *Mausoleum Book*, 77.

"God, I see the risk" Leonard Woolf to Virginia Woolf, 12 January 1912, *Letters of Leonard Woolf*, 169.

"the complete failure" Virginia Woolf to Vanessa Bell, 24 October 1938, *L*, 6:294.

"earth would open" Virginia Woolf to Lytton Strachey, 6 October 1909, *L*, 1:413.

"the man to whom" Virginia Woolf to Clive Bell, 4 September 1910, *L*, 1:434.

"As I did it" Lytton Strachey to Leonard Woolf, 19 February 1909, in Holroyd, *Lytton Strachey*, 201.

"I didn't mean" Virginia Woolf to Molly MacCarthy, March 1912, *L*, 1:492.

"When I am . . . how splendid!" Virginia Woolf to Leonard Woolf, 1 May 1912, *L*, 1:496–97.

"One thing at a time" Leonard Woolf, *Beginning Again*, 70.

"go on, as before" Virginia Woolf to Leonard Woolf, 1 May 1912, *L*, 1:496.

PART ONE, CHAPTER 7

In Chapter 7, much of the account of Julia Jackson's relationship with Herbert Duckworth is based upon Amy Licence's own exploration of that time in *Living in Squares, Loving in Triangles*. The assertion that Leslie Stephen's religious skepticism is what first attracted Julia to him is drawn from Peter Dally's *The Marriage of Heaven and Hell: Manic Depression and the Life of Virginia Woolf*.

"What my mother was" "A Sketch of the Past," in *MB*, 89.

"possibly rather dim" Lee, *Virginia Woolf*, 93.

"thorough gentleman" Stephen, *Mausoleum Book*, 35.

"aloof . . . for anyone to be" "A Sketch of the Past," in *MB*, 88–90.

"her sweet large blue eyes" Julia Margaret Cameron to Maria Jackson, 6 February 1878, in Lee, *Virginia Woolf*, 93.

"a superlative expression" "A Sketch of the Past," in *MB*, 90.

"solitary and independent" "A Sketch of the Past," in *MB*, 90.

"I was only 24" Stephen, *Mausoleum Book*, 40.

"looked very sad … dip into privately" "A Sketch of the Past," in *MB*, 82.

"I have been as unhappy" "A Sketch of the Past," in *MB*, 89.

"so tragic" *D*, 2:72, 25 October 1920.

"If there is any good" "A Sketch of the Past," in *MB*, 137.

PART ONE, CHAPTER 8

"I would see" "A Sketch of the Past," in *MB*, 137.

PART ONE, CHAPTER 9

"snatched" "A Sketch of the Past," in *MB*, 94.

"How did I first" "A Sketch of the Past," in *MB*, 82.

"We think back" *A Room of One's Own*, 76.

"never, *ever* fucking" "It is the lack of copulation—either actual or implied—that worries me," wrote Lytton Strachey of *To the Lighthouse,* a work he otherwise considered "a most extraordinary form of literature." Lytton Strachey to Roger Senhouse, 11 May 1927, in Holroyd, *Lytton Strachey*, 569.

PART ONE, CHAPTER 10

"The mind is full" "The Narrow Bridge of Art," in *Granite and Rainbow*, 12.

PART ONE, CHAPTER 14

In Chapter 14, I am obliged to John Batchelor and his book *Virginia Woolf: The Major Novels* for the suggestion that Woolf's alphabet analogy is grounded in Leslie Stephen's own efforts to complete the *Dictionary of National Biography*.

"human character" "Mr. Bennett and Mrs. Brown," in *The Captain's Death Bed*, 91.

"narrow preoccupations" Murray and Smyth, "Manifesto," in *Clip-Kit*, 1.

"Despite his obvious" Lee, *Virginia Woolf*, 73.

"you wont like it" Virginia Woolf to Violet Dickinson, 22 May 1912, *L*, 1:499.

"I have never suffered" *D*, 5:17, 16 March 1936.

"crept into the garden" Leonard Woolf, *Downhill All the Way*, 154.

"a week of intense" *D*, 5:24, 21 June 1936.

"easily the best" *D*, 3:117, 23 November 1926.

"rather thin" *D*, 3:106, 5 September 1926.

"sentimental" *D*, 3:106, 5 September 1926.

"it will be too like" *D*, 3:49, 7 December 1925.

"all my facts" Virginia Woolf to Angus Davidson, 25 December 1926, *L*, 3:310.

"After transferring" Sunwoo, "Clip-Kit, London," in Colomina and Buckley, *Clip/Stamp/Fold: The Radical Architecture of Little Magazines*, 98.

PART ONE, CHAPTER 15

"Any man's death" Donne, "Meditation XVII," in *Devotions upon Emergent Occasions*, 103.

PART ONE, CHAPTER 16

"L. & I were too" *D*, 3:8–9, 8 April 1925.

"I enjoy almost everything" *D*, 3:62, 27 February 1926.

"wastes and deserts . . . a ship far out at sea" *On Being Ill,* 3–12.

PART ONE, CHAPTER 17

In Chapter 17, I've drawn the accounts of St Ives's many shipwrecks from John Hobson Matthews's *A History of the Parishes of St Ives, Lelant, Towednack and Zennor in the County of Cornwall* and Marion Whybrow's *Virginia Woolf & Vanessa Bell: A Childhood in St Ives.* It's also Whybrow who first alerted me to the treachery of the Stones and the role that William Freeman, the Stephens' boatman, would later play in the wreck of the *John and Sarah Eliza Stych.*

"On Saturday morning" *Hyde Park Gate News* (British Library), in Lee, *Virginia Woolf,* 33–34.

PART ONE, CHAPTER 18

"I was overcome" *D*, 5:115, 22 October 1937.

PART TWO

In Part Two, I am indebted to Hermione Lee and her biography for enriching my understanding of the Stephen siblings' return to Cornwall in 1905.

"this impersonal thing" *D*, 3:36, 20 July 1925.

"withdrawing from . . . physical body is empty" Karnes, *Gone from My Sight,* 3–11.

"I could hardly bear" Stephen, *Mausoleum Book*, 62.

"Most fiction" "Sir Thomas Browne," in *E*, 3:369.

"Who am I" *D*, 3:62–63, 27 February 1926.

"It was dusk . . . footsteps we turned away" *PA*, 11 August 1905, 282.

PART THREE, CHAPTER 1

In Chapter 1, the observation that the common thread between Woolf's various accounts of losing her mother is her inability to feel belongs to Hermione Lee, who gathers these diary entries together in her biography's chapter on Virginia's adolescence.

"the greatest disaster" "Reminiscences," in *MB*, 40.

"laughed" *D*, 2:301, 5 May 1921.

"I remember turning" *D*, 4:242, 12 September 1934.

"immeasurably distant . . . kissing cold iron" "A Sketch of the Past," in *MB*, 92.

PART THREE, CHAPTER 2

"astonishing intensity . . . the hall table" "A Sketch of the Past," in *MB*, 92.

"It's nice that she" "A Sketch of the Past," in *MB*, 92.

"a luxurious dwelling" *D*, 3:264, 2 November 1929.

"muffled dulness . . . conventions of sorrow" "A Sketch of the Past," in *MB*, 93–95.

"Two blocks joined" *"To the Lighthouse:* Holograph Notes," in *Notes for Writing: Holograph Notebook*, 11.

"Until I was . . . laid it to rest" "A Sketch of the Past," in *MB*, 80–81.

PART THREE, CHAPTER 4

"There it always was" "A Sketch of the Past," in *MB*, 84.

"shrouded, cautious" "A Sketch of the Past," in *MB*, 94.

PART THREE, CHAPTER 6

In Chapter 6, the revelation that *To the Lighthouse* is a ghost story belongs to Arnold Weinstein, who was the first reader to draw my attention to Mrs. Ramsay's strange return.

"given a portrait" Vanessa Bell to Virginia Woolf, 11 May 1927, *L*, 3:572.

"What can one know" *Mrs. Dalloway*, 192.

"I sometimes feel" Virginia Woolf to Leonard Woolf, 1 May 1912, *L*, 1:496.

"I'm so orderly" Virginia Woolf to Vita Sackville-West, 2 March 1926, *L*, 3:245.

"I'm in a terrible state" Virginia Woolf to Vanessa Bell, 25 May 1927, *L*, 3:383.

"How difficult it is" "A Sketch of the Past," in *MB*, 87.

"as I think" "A Sketch of the Past," in *MB*, 108.

"explains why people" *E*, 1:382, Appendix III.

PART THREE, CHAPTER 7

"I had a notion . . . fine delicate" *D*, 4:244, 19 September 1934.

"so bad" Virginia Woolf to Roger Fry, 27 May 1927, *L*, 3:385.

"so much more emotion" *D*, 3:187, 7 July 1928.

PART THREE, CHAPTER 8

"I never did enough" Virginia Woolf to Violet Dickinson, 28 February 1904, *L*, 1:130.

PART THREE, CHAPTER 10

"extraordinary look . . . joke this time" *D*, 2:299, 5 April 1924.

"We were quite . . . blinded us" "Reminiscences," in *MB*, 45.

"to act parts . . . sentimental ideas" "A Sketch of the Past," in *MB*, 95.

"All these tears" "Reminiscences," in *MB*, 45.

"unpardonable mischief" "Reminiscences," in *MB*, 45.

"the brutality & wildness" *D*, 3:6, 8 April 1925.

PART THREE, CHAPTER 12

"To freshen my memory" *D*, 4:193, 17 December 1933.

"can still be more real . . . from the start" "A Sketch of the Past," in *MB*, 67.

"wizard who was . . . of their substance?" *PA*, 11 August 1905, 282.

PART THREE, CHAPTER 13

The connection I draw in Chapter 13 between Monk's House and the haunted house of Woolf's story is my own fantasy; according to Leonard Woolf, "A Haunted House" was based on Asheham, the eighteenth-century home that the Woolfs leased prior to their move to Rodmell. "It sounded as if two people were walking from room to room," Leonard recalled, "opening and shutting doors, sighing, whispering . . ."

"buried treasure . . . 'in the heart'" "A Haunted House," in *A Haunted House*, 10–11.

"precipitated the loss" Lee, *Virginia Woolf,* 232.

"that one ought" Angelica Bell to David Garnett, 17 April 1939, in Lee, *Virginia Woolf,* 714.

"we shall be tying" *D*, 3:112, 28 September 1926.

"Half the beauty" *D*, 3:192, 14 August 1928.

"be our address for ever" Virginia Woolf to Katherine Arnold-Forster, 12 August 1919, *L*, 2:382.

NOTES

"laboriously correcting" Virginia Woolf to Vita Sackville-West, 21 February 1927, *L*, 3:333.

"It sounded as if" Leonard Woolf, *Beginning Again,* 57.

SELECTED BIBLIOGRAPHY

WORKS BY VIRGINIA WOOLF

The Captain's Death Bed and Other Essays. London: Hogarth Press, 1950.

The Diary of Virginia Woolf. 5 vols. Edited by Anne Olivier Bell and Andrew McNeillie. San Diego: Harcourt, Brace & Company, 1977–84.

The Essays of Virginia Woolf. 6 vols. Edited by Andrew McNeillie. London: Hogarth Press, 1986.

Granite and Rainbow. Edited by Leonard Woolf. New York: Harcourt, Brace & Company, 1958.

A Haunted House and Other Stories. Harmondsworth: Penguin Books, 1973.

The Letters of Virginia Woolf. 6 vols. Edited by Nigel Nicolson and Joanne Trautmann. New York: Harcourt Brace Jovanovich, 1975–80.

Moments of Being. Edited by Jeanne Schulkind. San Diego: Harcourt Brace Jovanovich, 1985.

Mrs. Dalloway. San Diego: Harcourt, Inc., 1925.

Notes for Writing: Holograph Notebook. Virginia Woolf Collection of Papers. The Henry W. and Albert A. Berg Collection of English and American Literature, the New York Public Library.

On Being Ill. Ashfield, MA: Paris Press, 2002.

A Passionate Apprentice: The Early Journals of Virginia Woolf. Edited by Mitchell A. Leaska. London: Hogarth Press, 1990.

A Room of One's Own. San Diego: Harcourt, Brace & Company, 1929.

The Second Common Reader. Edited by Andrew McNeillie. San Diego: Harcourt, Inc., 1986.

To the Lighthouse. San Diego: Harcourt, Brace & Company, 1981.

The Waves. San Diego: Harcourt, Brace & Company, 1931.

OTHER WORKS CONSULTED

Alexander, Peter F. *Leonard and Virginia Woolf: A Literary Partnership*. New York: St. Martin's Press, 1992.

Auerbach, Erich. *Mimesis: The Representation of Reality in Western Literature*. Translated by Willard R. Trask. Princeton, NJ: Princeton University Press, 1953.

Batchelor, John. *Virginia Woolf: The Major Novels*. Cambridge: Cambridge University Press, 1991.

Bell, Quentin. *Virginia Woolf: A Biography*. 2 vols. London: Hogarth Press, 1972.

Bell, Vanessa. *Sketches in Pen and Ink: A Bloomsbury Memoir*. Edited by Lia Giachero. London: Pimlico, 1998.

Briggs, Julia. *Virginia Woolf: An Inner Life*. London: Penguin Books, 2005.

Dally, Peter. *The Marriage of Heaven and Hell: Manic Depression and the Life of Virginia Woolf.* New York: St. Martin's Press, 1999.

Donne, John. *Devotions upon Emergent Occasions and Death's Duel.* New York: Vintage Spiritual Classics, 1999.

Forrester, Viviane. *Virginia Woolf: A Portrait.* Translated by Jody Gladding. New York: Columbia University Press, 2015.

Forster, E. M. "Virginia Woolf." In *Virginia Woolf: A Collection of Critical Essays.* Edited by Claire Sprague. Englewood Cliffs, NJ: Prentice-Hall, Inc., 1971.

Guiguet, Jean. *Virginia Woolf and Her Works.* New York: Harcourt, Brace & World, Inc., 1962.

Holroyd, Michael. *Lytton Strachey: The New Biography.* New York: Farrar, Straus and Giroux, 1994.

Hussey, Mark. *The Singing of the Real World: The Philosophy of Virginia Woolf's Fiction.* Columbus: Ohio State University Press, 1986.

Hussey, Mark, and Peter Shillingsburg. "The Composition, Revision, Printing and Publication of *To the Lighthouse.*" *Woolf Online.* Edited by Pamela L. Caughie, Nick Hayward, Mark Hussey, Peter Shillingsburg, and George K. Thiruvathukal. Accessed on April 22, 2018. http://www.woolfonline.com/?node=content/contextual/transcriptions&project=1&parent=45&taxa=47&content=6955&pos=3.

Karnes, Barbara. *Gone from My Sight: The Dying Experience.* Depoe Bay, OR: Barbara Karnes Books, 2005.

Laing, Olivia. *To the River.* Edinburgh: Canongate, 2012.

Lee, Hermione. "Notes." In *To the Lighthouse.* Edited by Stella McNichol. London: Penguin Books, 1992.

———. *The Novels of Virginia Woolf.* New York: Holmes and Meier, 1977.

————. *Virginia Woolf.* London: Vintage, 1997.

Licence, Amy. *Living in Squares, Loving in Triangles: The Lives and Loves of Virginia Woolf and the Bloomsbury Group.* Stroud, UK: Amberley Publishing, 2016.

Matthews, John Hobson. *A History of the Parishes of Saint Ives, Lelant, Towednack and Zennor in the County of Cornwall.* London: Elliot Stock, 1892.

Murray, Peter, and Geoffrey Smyth. "Manifesto." In *Clip-Kit: Studies in Environmental Design.* Edited by Peter Murray and Geoffrey Smyth. London: Architectural Association, 1966.

Reid, Panthea. *Art and Affection: A Life of Virginia Woolf.* Oxford: Oxford University Press, 1996.

Stephen, Leslie. *Sir Leslie Stephen's Mausoleum Book.* Edited by Alan Bell. Oxford: Clarendon Press, 1977.

Sunwoo, Irene. "Clip-Kit, London." In *Clip/Stamp/Fold: The Radical Architecture of Little Magazines, 196X–197X.* Edited by Beatriz Colomina and Craig Buckley. Barcelona: Actar, 2010.

Weinstein, Arnold. *Recovering Your Story: Proust, Joyce, Woolf, Faulkner, Morrison.* New York: Random House, 2007.

Whybrow, Marion. *Virginia Woolf & Vanessa Bell: A Childhood in St Ives.* Wellington, UK: Halstar, 2014.

Wood, James. *The Broken Estate: Essays on Literature and Belief.* New York: Random House, 1999.

Woolf, Leonard. *Beginning Again: An Autobiography of the Years 1911–1918.* London: Hogarth Press, 1964.

————. *Downhill All the Way: An Autobiography of the Years 1919–1939.* London: Hogarth Press, 1967.

————. *Letters of Leonard Woolf.* Edited by Frederic Spotts. London: Weidenfeld & Nicolson, 1990.

Zwerdling, Alex. *Virginia Woolf and the Real World.* Berkeley: University of California Press, 1986.

ACKNOWLEDGMENTS

During the long years that I've been working on this project, I have relied upon the knowledge, expertise, and encouragement of a great many people, and I'm thrilled to have a chance to acknowledge them here.

First and foremost, I would like to thank my editor, Claire Potter, for her wisdom, thoughtfulness, boundless energy, and almost preternatural understanding of what I was hoping to achieve; I feel so lucky to have an editor who not only shares my vision but also enlarges it. This book is richer, smarter, and more luminous because of you.

I am equally indebted to my agent, Anna Stein, for her unbelievable advocacy and support. Thank you, Anna, for your unrelenting faith in the work, your compassion, and for always taking the long view.

Thank you, too, to terrific team at Crown, including Julia Bradshaw, Eliana Seochand, and Amelia Zaleman and to Lisa Dowdeswell at the Society of Authors, Ron Hussey at Houghton Mifflin Harcourt, and Alicia Ofori at Penguin Random House UK for helping me to navigate the labyrinthine world of Virginia Woolf permissions.

This portrait of my father would have been impossible without the recollections and insights of the friends and family members who knew him best. Whether they sat for interviews or sent long letters, their contributions have been vital to helping me see Geoffrey Smyth as he must have been—not to me but to the world at large. My deepest gratitude to Michael Ben-Eli, Grenville Byford, Zette Emmons, Michael Fletcher, Vivien Fowler, Adam Klein, Trevor Murch, Peter Murray, Denise Silber, Stephen Smith, and William de Winton; to my uncles, Andrew Smyth and Robert Smyth; and to my grandmother, Betty Smyth.

Over the course of this project I have also turned to countless friends for their assistance, editorial and otherwise. In particular, I would like to thank Jon Baskin, Damaris Colhoun, Sean Quinn, Sarah Ramey, Beth Raymer, and Jessa Sherman. I feel honored to think of the time and effort you have each dedicated to making this a better book; you are the most formidable of readers *and* friends.

Finally, I am grateful to my mother, Minty Smyth, for more than I can possibly enumerate here. Thank you for your limitless encouragement and acceptance, and for the tolerance and grace you have shown in sharing your past not only with your daughter but her readers.

CREDITS

garth Press. · Excerpt from *The Diary of Virginia Woolf: Volume III 1925–1930* by Virginia Woolf, copyright © 1980, published by The Hogarth Press. · Excerpt from *The Diary of Virginia Woolf: Volume IV 1931–1935* by Virginia Woolf, copyright © 1982, published by The Hogarth Press. · Excerpt from *The Diary of Virginia Woolf: Volume V 1936–1941* by Virginia Woolf, copyright © 1988, published by The Hogarth Press. · Excerpts from *The Essays of Virginia Woolf: Volume I 1904–1912* by Virginia Woolf, copyright © 1986, published by The Hogarth Press. · Excerpt from *The Essays of Virginia Woolf: Volume III 1919–1924* by Virginia Woolf, copyright © 1988, published by The Hogarth Press. · Excerpt from *The Flight of the Mind: The Letters of Virginia Woolf: Volume I 1888–1912* by Virginia Woolf, copyright © 1975, published by The Hogarth Press. · Excerpt from *Granite and Rainbow* by Virginia Woolf, copyright © 1958, published by The Hogarth Press Ltd. · Excerpt from *Moments of Being* by Virginia Woolf, copyright © 1976 and 1985, published by The Hogarth Press. · Excerpt from *A Passionate Apprentice: The Early Journals 1897–1909* by Virginia Woolf, copyright © 1990, published by The Hogarth Press. · Excerpt from *The Question of Things Happening: The Letters of Virginia Woolf: Volume II 1912-1922* by Virginia Woolf, copyright © 1976, published by Chatto & Windus Ltd. · Excerpt from *A Reflection of the Other Person: The Letters of Virginia Woolf: Volume IV 1929–1931* by Virginia Woolf, copyright © 1978, published by Chatto & Windus Ltd. Reprinted by permission of The Random House Group Limited.

I am grateful to the University of Sussex and the Society of Authors as the literary representative of the

Estate of Leonard Woolf for permission to quote from Leonard Woolf's letters and autobiographies.

I would also like to thank the Society of Authors as the literary representative of the Estate of Leslie Stephen for permission to quote from *Sir Leslie Stephen's Mausoleum Book*; and as the literary representative of the Estate of Lytton Strachey for permission to quote from Strachey's letters, many of which were published for the first time in Michael Holroyd's definitive biography.

I am grateful to Henrietta Garnett as the literary representative of the Estate of Vanessa Bell for permission to quote from Bell's letters and essays; and as the literary representative of the Estate of Angelica Garnett for permission to quote from Garnett's letters.

Finally, I am grateful to Barbara Karnes for permission to quote from her book *Gone from My Sight: The Dying Experience*.

A   NOTE   ABOUT   THE   AUTHOR

Katharine Smyth is a graduate of Brown University.
She has worked for *The Paris Review* and taught at
Columbia University, where she received her MFA
in nonfiction. She lives in Brooklyn, New York.